Whom God Wishes to Destroy

Whom God Wishes to Destroy . . .

Francis Coppola and the New Hollywood

Jon Lewis

Duke University Press   *Durham and London 1995*

©1995 Duke University Press

Printed in the United States of America on acid-free paper ∞

Typeset in Minion by Keystone Typesetting, Inc.

Library of Congress Cataloging-in-Publication Data appear
on the last printed page of this book.

for Martha, Adam, and Guy

Contents

Acknowledgments

Big thanks to: Richard deCordova, Michael Oriard, Dana Polan, and Eric Smoodin for helping me write this book; Ken Wissoker, my editor at Duke, and everyone else at the press for being so supportive and honest; photographer Michel Haddi and his agent Franco Marsala, photographer Patricia Williams, and Teri Bond Michael at UCLA for the terrific cover and frontispiece photos; Justin Wyatt for the last minute stuff; the Center for the Humanities at Oregon State University for the release time; my parents and sister for their encouragement, etc.; and finally, most of all, on the home front, Copy, Q, and the boys for the love, understanding, and quiet mornings downstairs.

Introduction

This is a town of supporters and detractors. Basically, Hollywood is like high school with money.—Joel Silver, movie producer[1]

On March 25, 1980, Francis Coppola purchased a 10.5-acre movie production lot on the corner of Santa Monica Boulevard and Las Palmas Avenue in the heart of Hollywood. At the time, it was difficult to know just how significant the deal would become. *Variety,* the industry's principal trade publication, for example, dutifully tracked Coppola's purchase of the former Hollywood General Studios from the first rumor of his interest in the property, through the acrimonious dispute between studio lien holder James Nasser and the studio's nominal owner, Glen Speidel, to the deal that finally transferred ownership of the property to Coppola. But when money finally changed hands and it was revealed that Coppola had acquired the property for (in Hollywood terms) a *mere* $6.7 million, *Variety* announced the deal in just two column inches.[2]

Though the purchase of the studio was, for him, a stretch financially, Coppola immediately announced plans to extensively renovate the facility (renamed Zoetrope Studios), to research and develop new distribution and exhibition technologies (utilizing satellites and high-resolution video), and, by 1982, to release a full slate of feature films to compete with the major studios.[3] He announced his intention to reinvest the profits from the studios' first films back into the company in order to finance his plans.

By leveraging the purchase of the studio and the various renovations against future box office revenues, Coppola was, from the very start, "playing" with his own money. At risk was his personal fortune, his professional reputation, and, ultimately, the fate of a generation of university film school–educated directors, most of whom got their first big break after the box office success of Coppola's *The Godfather.*

The larger significance of Coppola's purchase of Hollywood General and his attempt to create an alternative studio in the very heart of Hollywood was that it carried with it the promise of an American *auteur* cinema in which the director might someday control *the product* from development to release. It was, though it might not have seemed so at the time, one of the boldest moves in the history of the movie business.

After the release of *The Godfather,* the studios' embrace of the *auteur* theory—the academic-historical notion that a film director should be viewed as the sole author in creative control of a motion picture—seemed to signal a shift in power away from studio producers and executives. But the shift was both brief and superficial. The studios' participation in and financial support of the 1970s American *auteur* renaissance evinced little if any erosion of their power base, which, fairly speaking, has nothing to do with the creative process and everything to do with money.

To a large extent, the studio executives' ready acceptance of an American *auteur* cinema in the 1970s was the result of a characteristic industrywide cautiousness. By allowing the *auteurs* to take more responsibility for *their* movies, studio executives were able to shift the blame for box office failure away from themselves.

As a result, at the start of the 1980s, when *auteur* films began to lose money, the studio executives were in a position to blame not only individual directors but also the very system the studios had formerly exploited. By supporting an American *auteur* cinema in the 1970s, studio executives maintained a position in which they could avoid culpability no matter when or how the *auteur* period fizzled out.

Francis Coppola and the New Hollywood

Hollywood can't do anything but do what Hollywood does, which is hope that everybody who is doing well gets caught in some secret nightmare. . . . [Hollywood] is a town that doesn't just want you to fail, it wants you to die.—David Geffen, movie and record producer[4]

Coppola's ability to unsettle the studio establishment with his purchase of a rundown $6.7 million studio and his unlikely threats to revolutionize the industry reveals both his prestige and *perceived* power in 1980 and the industry establishment's penchant for hysteria and panic at any sign of a challenge. Practically speaking, the studios had nothing to fear from Coppola's Zoetrope Studios, but they set about making sure he didn't succeed anyway.

The capital required to maintain a studio—even the amount of money required just to make movies—had, by 1980, grown well beyond the reach of even such a wealthy cine-entrepreneur as Francis Coppola. With short-term interest rates reaching 20 percent and the cost of production increasing far faster than the cost of living, even the well-capitalized major studios set about diversifying their assets within the growing entertainment marketplace. More often than not, they sought conglomerate, outside ownership in order to maintain sufficient capital reserves and gain access to more extensive lines of credit at the banks. Smaller studios, like American International Pictures, Filmways, Weintraub, Cannon, Lorimar, Vista, New Century, and the Atlantic Releasing Corporation failed to keep pace and simply went out of the business of making and distributing movies altogether.

That Coppola picked 1980 to make his move was particularly unlucky and unfortunate. Of course, that was when he had both the money and the opportunity to buy Hollywood General, but he could not have picked a worse moment in the history of Hollywood to try to use his prestige as a motion picture director to take on the studio establishment, who themselves were in the process of adapting to a changing economy and thus were even more anxious than usual about any challenge posed to their authority over the industry.

Zoetrope Studios was in business for less than four years, and the lot was up for auction in less than two. By the time the first round of bids on the property were submitted, the studio had released just one feature, Coppola's much misunderstood *One from the Heart*. The commonly held perception about Zoetrope is that Coppola bankrupted the studio by making an overly expensive and terrible movie that nobody went to see and the critics all hated. Such is the perception, but it is largely an inaccurate one; indeed, it misses altogether the larger story: how the business of making and distributing movies was, in the early 1980s, in the process of significant change, and how Coppola's *One from the Heart* got caught up in this larger corporate drama.

It is the aim of this book to challenge these faulty perceptions of Coppola, *One from the Heart*, and Zoetrope Studios, and in doing so to develop a larger argument regarding the ways in which movies get or don't get made, and directors succeed or don't succeed, in the new Hollywood.[5]

Francis Coppola, Tragic Hero

If I had one wish, I guess it would be some Faustian thing. You know, total knowledge or something.—Francis Coppola, 1981[6]

The authorship of major studio films evolves over a period of years. The actual production of a motion picture begins only after a series of industrial concerns—the acquisition of adequate financing, the optioning of a screenplay, casting, and so on—are finally settled. And even then, film production involves far more than just creative concerns. Even a director with as much of a stake in controlling the product as Coppola is forced to develop each picture through a series of negotiations, and what ends up on the screen is not only a miracle of persistence and inspiration but also the result of certain practical concessions to the limitations of the studio system.

I am, as the title of this book suggests, primarily interested in Francis Coppola's work as a director, producer, and cine-entrepreneur during his tenure as artistic director of Zoetrope Studios. But a project such as this one inevitably leads to larger issues regarding the industry as a whole and the process of developing, producing, and releasing motion pictures. Much of what follows, then, depends on my assumption that what happened to Coppola in the early 1980s, a time when he was the industry's best known *auteur,* is more than just a simple drama involving one man and an industry that rather easily dismissed him when it seemed necessary or expedient to do so.

Thus, though my main concern is to examine four years in the professional life of one director—a director, I should confess, whose work I greatly admire—I hope also to provide at least an introduction to the ways that movies these days are products of a complex and often irrational system. What follows, then, is something of an alternative Hollywood history, one based not on so-called important movies and specific readings of these important movies, but instead on trade information, rumor, and gossip. In other words, this is a history of the new American cinema and its most famous director based largely on the very discourse with which the industry historicizes itself.

The narrative of Coppola's ill-fated battle with the studio establishment in the first half of the 1980s unfolds as something of a cautionary fable about power and independence, the privilege of ownership, and the inevitable isolation of the individual artist. There is a lesson to be learned from the brief history of Zoetrope Studios, and though it is to some extent an unsurprising lesson, Coppola's story nevertheless offers a useful introduction to the larger narrative regarding the nature of making movies and doing business in Hollywood today.

One Hollywood General

I have a letter [Francis] wrote me at 9. . . . "Dear Mommy, I want to be rich and famous. I'm so discouraged. I don't think it will come true."—Italia Coppola[1]

Though facts are seldom what they seem in Hollywood, rumors—especially if they appear in the trades—are more often true than not. But truth, even in the best of circumstances, is relative. And as filmmaker Joel Schumacher reminds us, in Hollywood, "the truth changes from moment to moment."[2]

The rumor mill plays an essential part in the free flow of information within the Hollywood subculture. Savvy industry players view unsubstantiated stories repeated in trade papers like *Variety* and the *Hollywood Reporter* as a kind of informal (and highly codified) press release; the rumor introduces "the story," and the industry's reaction to the story governs how events eventually take shape.

As such, the industry rumor is information in its most volatile state. At the same time, however, the rumor is accessible only to those who can fathom its codes and context. Those who wait for the official story lose any opportunity to change the course of the rumor. As a result, Hollywood players pay close attention to the rumor mill and often attempt to redirect one rumor with another of their own.

On May 16, 1979, *Variety* introduced a story: "Francis Coppola is understood to be in negotiations to assume control of a Hollywood production lot. Specific locale being bandied about in trade circles is the Hollywood General Studios lot, formerly General Service, and predating back to Nassour Studios." Tom Sternberg, then Coppola's "right-hand man," and Douglas Ferguson, his attorney, refused to confirm or deny the story and in doing so seemed to suggest that it was all true.

In the meantime, Hollywood General Studios's vice president, Bill Speidel, told *Variety* that as far as he knew, no one, Coppola included, had officially made a "good faith offer" for the studio.³ But to those used to reading between the lines, the mere mention of "Coppola" and "good faith offer" in the same sentence coupled with Speidel's qualified denial suggested that negotiations between the two parties were indeed under way.

Two months later, the story reemerged in a more substantial and substantiated form. In the July 18 issue of *Variety*, Hollywood General Studios president Glen Speidel confirmed the rumor regarding an imminent sale to Coppola, hoping by doing so to affirm his control over the property.⁴ By dealing with Hollywood General as if it was his to sell, Speidel hoped to counter industry speculation that he had run out of money and planned to file for Chapter 11 bankruptcy protection. Unfortunately for Speidel, the announcement instead confirmed the desperate nature of his finances. His effort to sell out to Coppola, it seemed safe to assume, was merely an attempt to avoid bankruptcy.

Before negotiations between Speidel and Coppola could get very far, Hollywood General lien holder James Nasser called a press conference and introduced an alternative scenario: foreclosure. Nasser's move had two immediate effects: it placed the legality of Speidel's proposed sale of the studio in doubt, and it considerably weakened Speidel's and Coppola's respective bargaining positions.

Nasser's insistence on defending his rights as the ostensible owner of the property so complicated matters that all three parties ended up in court. This too seemed to Nasser's advantage, as time (if not the law as well) was on his side. Speidel, as the rumor mill had alleged, was out of cash. Nasser no doubt appreciated that fact and thus realized that while the three parties were waiting for the courts to sort things out, Speidel would default on the Hollywood General mortgage and thus lose control over the property even if the courts eventually found in his favor.

Speidel covered his position by ignoring the pending court case and formalizing a sale of the property to Coppola, who then began to make interim payments to Nasser on Speidel's behalf. Nasser objected to what amounted to Coppola's assumption of Speidel's mortgage. Then, in response to Nasser's complaints, Speidel gave the story another new spin by announcing in the trades his intention to pay back the loan himself, in full, thus rendering the foreclosure suit moot.⁵

While awaiting their day in court, Speidel, Coppola, and Nasser continued to use the trades to better define their positions vis-à-vis Hollywood General. Whether or not their stories had any basis in law or fact was not necessarily relevant. Speidel, for example, maintained that he could pay back the loan if he had to. Though Coppola realized that Speidel did not have enough money to keep up with the monthly payments let alone purchase the property outright, he nevertheless continued to support Speidel's story in press releases in the trades. Through his attorney, Douglas Ferguson, Coppola dubbed Nasser's foreclosure filing "ridiculous" and then reminded everyone concerned that not only was his deal with Speidel secure in principle, but that American Zoetrope employees were already in place, as if Coppola already owned the studio.[6] Nasser countered by talking about auctioning the property himself for a price Coppola would not be able to afford.[7]

Unfortunately for Coppola and Speidel, when the suit went to trial, the court ruled in Nasser's favor. Coppola filed an appeal, but just as the California Supreme Court was about to hear the case, Coppola and Nasser announced a settlement agreement. The sale of the studio to Coppola was finalized on March 25, 1980. Robert Spiotta, the former president of Mobil Oil and the newly appointed president of Coppola's new Zoetrope Studios, announced that Coppola had agreed to pay Nasser $6.7 million for the property and (with profits largely earned from his work as a director) had already made a sizable down payment.[8] Two balloon payments loomed in the near future, but these Coppola planned to cover with the profits earned from the studio's first films.

When Coppola took possession of the 10.5-acre lot, it consisted of nine sound stages, thirty-four editing suites, an operational special effects facility, a number of projection rooms, executive offices, actors' bungalows, and various on-site technical services, all of them outdated. But despite the run-down condition of the property, industry wisdom at the time was that Nasser, especially in light of his court victory, had sold the lot far too cheaply.

The Studio Dream/The Studio Dreamed

You know, this is a town, and maybe other towns are like it, but this is a town and this is an industry where information is perceived as being a great power, and if you have information—well, information in the hands of a certain type of personality is a very—You know, it's a very powerful thing. Makes you feel you're a big man.—Sidney Sheinberg, president of MCA[9]

When Hollywood General was first built in 1919 by John Jasper, it was a revolutionary facility, the only site in Hollywood that could accommodate twenty-four hour production (thanks to Jasper's unique sliding roof shutter design). The first important film shot on the lot was Harold Lloyd's *Grandma's Boy* in 1922. And though the studio never emerged as a major site in the sound era, it nevertheless housed the production of some very interesting movies, including Howard Hughes's *Hell's Angels* and the Mae West vehicle *Go West Young Man*, directed by Henry Hathaway. In the early 1950s, as film production declined on the lot, Hollywood General became the exclusive site for the production of the *I Love Lucy* television show.

Coppola was, no doubt, attracted by the studio's rich history, which seemed to afford him the opportunity to share in a tradition that included the likes of Lloyd and Hathaway and Hughes and Desilu. But of equal interest was the challenge of updating the facility. Not only had the studio's poor condition brought the price down to his level, it offered Coppola the opportunity to reshape things to suit his own specific needs and plans for the future. Coppola's first press release as artistic director (i.e., chief executive officer) at Zoetrope elaborated his plan to invest $5 million in renovations before a single foot of film was shot.

While the renovations were under way, Coppola proposed a positively nostalgic production structure for Zoetrope, one that recalled the halcyon days of studio Hollywood when moguls ran things on instinct and actors and directors were tied to the studio by contract. The advantages of the old studio system, Coppola argued, included a greater consistency of product—a uniform and recognizable "studio look"—and a greater control over the cost of filmmaking (an important factor for Coppola, who was significantly undercapitalized after the purchase of the studio).

"In the old days," Coppola mused, "you could have said that MGM films were this and the Warner Brothers films were that. I believe the time has come for the new technology to give rise to a studio based on the repertory principle—a place where you have writers and actors and art designers and special effects people and photographers, all of whom agree to come to work under the highest possible standards with real discipline."[10]

Though it seemed rather oxymoronic for Hollywood's reigning *auteur* to identify so readily with the moguls of the past, Coppola seemed positively entranced by the chance to relive the good old days. "There is no one like Zanuck around anymore," Coppola quipped before the release of *One from the Heart*, "and there are no studios like there used to be. I can envision Zoetrope being that way . . . with a great restaurant where we can all sit around . . . with a lot of cute girls . . . the way it was, what I missed out on."[11]

Though Zoetrope was, even by 1980 standards, a very small operation, the prospect that Hollywood's principal *auteur* might challenge or maybe even join the studio establishment was big news at the time—so much so that in February 1981, *Newsweek* ran a feature story on Zoetrope in which movie reviewer Jack Kroll predicted that Coppola would "recreate the Golden Age of Hollywood, with himself as the studio mogul and resident artist—Zanuck and Welles rolled into one."

While most in the moviegoing public at the time found the comparison with Welles far more appropriate—each, after all, was the dominant *auteur* of his era in reputation if not in fact—Coppola's willingness to take on a management role in the industry seemed at the very least out of character. But Kroll ably depicted Coppola's less publicized Zanuck-like side by canvassing (mostly unhappy) former co-workers, many of whom proved anxious to qualify Coppola's reputation as an *auteur* who, like Welles, preferred to remain aloof from the corporate side of the industry.

For example, one former employee complained that "[Coppola is] more intrusive in the creative process than Zanuck or Thalberg ever dreamed of being." Another anonymous source added: "He's a true visionary . . . but no director with any clout will work [for him]; who'd put up with all the interference." Yet another unnamed co-worker labeled Coppola "a brat" and concluded, "It's his club and he gets to be the boss. When you work with him, your art is his art."

Carroll Ballard, who directed the Coppola-produced *The Black Stallion*, was more accommodating about Coppola's penchant for interfering with other directors' work. "Most of the people who run the studios today don't know their ass from a hot rock about who is capable of making a good film," Ballard remarked to Kroll. "Sure I can gripe. I got paid peanuts. But without Francis I would have had no chance to make a picture in Hollywood."[12]

What Ballard and the various unnamed sources Kroll cited all bore out was that Coppola was very much a new Hollywood *auteur*. Though he was attracted to the notion of creative autonomy and endeavored to establish a modicum of control over his work, Coppola realized that the only way to secure such power was to establish a position as a major player inside the industry. Such a strategy was at the very least a practical one. But it no doubt struck many other would-be *auteur*-directors that Coppola was all too willing to abandon the romantic notion that the business and the art of making motion pictures could somehow be separate. They're not, of course. And by the end of the 1970s Coppola seemed quite willing to appreciate that fact.

When Coppola took over at Hollywood General, he gave research and development a high priority, a practice that seemed in line with contemporary light industry and completely out of synch with both old and new Hollywood. In doing so, Coppola seemed to display a sophisticated under-standing of the relationship between his art (as a product)—after all, he was financing the studio with profits from his past and future films—and larger industrial concerns regarding the future of the motion picture industry and his own and Zoetrope's place in that future.

Immediately after taking over at Hollywood General, Coppola told the trades that a large percentage of Zoetrope's film revenues would be used to finance the studio's research and development projects, which would focus on new distribution and exhibition technologies. By focusing on distribu-tion and exhibition, Coppola revealed his larger corporate mission. Not only did he want to control his films from development to exhibition, he wanted to secure the "first money" position for himself and his studio.[13]

On the very day the studio deal was finalized, Coppola told *Variety* that "the day is sooner than we think when films will be distributed electronically by satellite."[14] Less than a year later, Coppola further contextualized the studio's research and development goals when he told *Newsweek:* "It's going to be survival of the fittest and the long established studios will be brought down."[15]

Certainly Coppola's remarks were taken to be hype, and in the scheme of things in Hollywood, hype, like rumor, is a code that must be contextualized in order to be understood. At the time Coppola made these pronounce-ments, Zoetrope was a very small studio without a single film in release. Coppola was a major *auteur* and most likely (along with his old friend George Lucas) one of the two wealthiest directors in Hollywood. But Ameri-can Zoetrope's credit line, which governed how much debt the studio could accumulate at one time, was insufficient to fund even one big-budget movie from development to release. Moreover, with interest rates topping out at 20 percent, it was unlikely that Coppola could carry a loan long enough to get a picture made even if he could somehow borrow the money from a bank.

Given Coppola's relatively weak cash position in 1980, the only way he could fund research and development in satellite technology was with his share of the profits of an as yet unreleased film. And since he could not afford to produce and distribute a film himself, the only way he could achieve his goal was with a major studio's financial help. In other words, if the other studios were bothered or worried about Coppola's future research and development, they could virtually shut him down by refusing to finance his next picture.

Nevertheless, Coppola pressed ahead undaunted, unheedful, and maybe even unaware. Though he understood that his (and his studio's) future still depended on industry financing, throughout the early 1980s Coppola continued to tweak the studios with more and more hype on his soon-to-be-patented "electronic cinema" process—a complex production process involving cutting-edge video technology Coppola had developed with then industry nemesis Sony[16]—and his intention to transmit his "films," mostly shot on high-resolution one-inch videotape, via satellite into homes equipped with high-density television receivers. Rather than downplay the technology's significance to his own particular place within the industry, Coppola continually emphasized the competitive nature of his project.

"What I'm trying to do now in Hollywood," Coppola told novelist Gay Talese in a 1981 interview published in *Esquire*, "is create a film studio that really makes sense—not a place where lawyers and businessmen make deals."[17] As for the corporate heads of the other studios, Coppola added: "I feel that the people who are deciding what to give the public are giving the lowest common level to keep their economic thing going."

The electronic cinema method and its accompanying distribution apparatus, Coppola argued, promised an alternative that both served the consumer better and was in its very nature egalitarian and inclusive in the very ways the present system was elitist and exclusionary. "I think electronic cinema is going to make art less expensive to make," Coppola concluded, "and available to more people. I think in two years there won't be any more film shot."[18]

There's No Such Thing as an Independent Filmmaker

Hollywood is like Egypt, with all of its crumbling pyramids, whose irreversible degradation will continue until the day when the wind will finally disintegrate the foundations of the last studio into the sand.—David O. Selznick, legendary studio mogul[19]

"The *auteur* theory is fine," Coppola remarked to William Murray in a 1975 *Playboy* interview, "but you have to exercise it in order to qualify, and the only way to qualify is by having earned the right to have control by turning out a series of incredibly good films. Some men have it and some men don't."[20]

From the very start of his career, Coppola attempted to balance his desire for creative autonomy with an ambition to make big, important movies. In order to understand the various paradoxes evinced in Coppola's anti-Hollywood Hollywood studio project, it must be viewed in the context of a decade-long series of confrontations and conciliations with the major studios regarding authorship, control, and cash.

1. Francis Coppola: godfather, *auteur,* visionary (Tri-Star Pictures, 1986).

Coppola's film career began rather conventionally. His first "big" break came while he was working for B movie mogul Roger Corman and he made the transition into "A" Hollywood by writing scripts for major studio projects like *Patton* and *The Great Gatsby.* But while he seemed willing to work his way up through the ranks, as he might have had to in the "good old days," Coppola never saw his future within the industry in conventional terms. And though he seemed altogether willing to play the studios' game in order to get a chance to direct, from the very beginning he saw himself as at once an outsider wanting in and an insider wanting out.

In what seems in retrospect an embrace of the *auteurist* catechism that imbued the late 1960s film school curriculum, Coppola looked forward and ahead to an American *auteur* cinema that might approximate the European method and style. In such a cinema, Coppola felt, there would have to be a shift in power away from studio executives and into the hands of powerful directors. In 1968, four years before the release of *The Godfather,* Coppola remarked: "I don't think there'll be a Hollywood as we know it when this generation of film students gets out of college."[21] Seven years later, by then a studio film veteran, Coppola added: "The authority these days is almost always shared with people who have no business being producers and studio executives. With one or two exceptions, there is no one running the studios who's qualified . . . so you have a vacuum, and the director has to fill it."[22]

In November 1969, with four relatively undistinguished films to his credit, Coppola made his first significant attempt to put just such an *auteur* theory into effect by somehow talking Warner Brothers into staking him (and a cast of creative characters that included George Lucas, Jim McBride, Carroll Ballard, Walter Murch, Gloria Katz, Willard Huyck, John Korty, Robert Dalva, Matt Robbins, and Hal Barwood) to form an alternative movie studio in San Francisco. Coppola dubbed the new studio American Zoetrope, a corporate title that has persisted, more or less unchanged, to 1994.[23]

The deal with Warner Brothers was relatively simple. The studio fronted Coppola $600,000 to develop movies for the youth market; in exchange, Warners acquired the right of first refusal to any and all American Zoetrope projects. Warners's show of confidence in Coppola seemed at the time somewhat mysterious; after all, he had yet to direct a successful movie. But in reality the studio's gamble on American Zoetrope had little to do with admiration for Coppola or his work. Instead, the investment was the result of an industrywide panic to re-create the surprise hit of the previous year, *Easy Rider,* which successfully exploited the youth audience for the first time in a decade. The studio executives felt that Coppola and his entourage of young cineastes up in San Francisco (the very capital of youth territory) might have a better shot at hitting the target audience than more established, and establishment, directors and producers in Hollywood.

But if Warners wanted cheap, B movie sequels to *Easy Rider,* Coppola had far loftier things in mind. Instead of using the $600,000 to develop youth audience pictures, Coppola dumped $500,000 of it into state-of-the-art equipment, including several KEM editing tables (before any of the major studios had them), a custom-built Keller sound-mixing console,[24] and a 35-mm screening room (which was used primarily to show the "important" foreign films and classics favored by the mostly film school–educated American Zoetrope crew). American Zoetrope rather quickly took shape as a film student's concept of what a studio should be like: all the best equipment, smart people sharing ideas and expertise, and lots of screenings of classic old and important contemporary movies.

Though it was precisely not what Warner Brothers wanted to hear, Coppola proclaimed to the press that American Zoetrope was a radically new, alternative studio concept. "I feel like someone starting the first air-mail run from Kansas to Omaha," Coppola told San Francisco's *Show* magazine in 1970. "In ten years, the giants of the film industry are going to be companies that are so small now no one's ever heard of them, or major studios totally recreated."[25] As to his own role in such a history, Coppola offered the following romantic notion: "Just say Francis Coppola is up in San Francisco in an old warehouse making films."[26]

Approximately a year after taking Warners's money, Coppola had three projects to bring to the studio executives: the virtually complete *THX-1138* and scripts for *The Conversation* and *Apocalypse Now*.[27] Coppola pitched all three. The studio executives were so unimpressed they demanded their money back. Since most of the money was already spent, Coppola and his well-educated and very ambitious co-workers put their state-of-the-art equipment to use producing television commercials and state-funded documentaries in order to pay Warners back.

For Coppola, the down side of Warners's decision to withdraw its support from American Zoetrope seemed rather dramatically evident in the ignominy of having to prostitute himself for clients like Rice-a-Roni. But the up side, which was far less apparent at the time, was that Coppola retained control over the three projects, and he managed to maintain control of the three films-in-development until after the release of *The Godfather*. By then, he was Hollywood's most influential and powerful director, and the American Zoetrope projects gained prestige and value accordingly.

At first, Warners considered itself well rid of Coppola and American Zoetrope. But after the release of *The Godfather*, it was clear that the executives should have shown more patience. Had Warner Brothers continued to support American Zoetrope (which at $600,000 was hardly a significant investment), it would have been in the first-money position for three of the most important films of the 1970s. Both *The Conversation* and *Apocalypse Now* won the Grand Prix at Cannes, and, more importantly, for the studio at least, both *Apocalypse Now* and American Zoetrope's fourth feature in development, *American Graffiti*, were box office blockbusters.

In a 1971 interview, shortly after the demise of American Zoetrope, Coppola reflected on his willingness—indeed his anxiousness—even as a relatively idealistic film student to work within the system. "I was still at UCLA,"

Coppola recalled, "and I was seriously critiqued by a lot of people my own age for deciding to go into exploitation films. I was called a cop-out because I was willing to compromise—and I still am."[28]

But to be fair, Coppola's relationship to studio Hollywood has always been deeply ambivalent. At the core of his penchant for compromise resides not only an understanding of the complex relationship between creation and commerce but an almost megalomaniacal ambition—an ambition he has hardly disguised over the years. For example, in 1968 Coppola told the press: "The way to come to power is not always to merely challenge the establishment, but first to make a place in it and then challenge and double cross the establishment."[29] Or, as he put it a few years later, "You are never going to take over the industry with your back turned to it."[30]

Early in his career, Coppola seemed quite willing to accept the facts of life in the movie industry: "You don't make films on anything but money," he remarked in 1972. "You've got to make your alliance with the establishment."[31] But this penchant for conciliation merely complicated and concealed Coppola's larger plans: "Businessmen like predictability. When they put their money into a film, they want to know how much is going into the package and how much is coming out of it. None of this has anything to do with actual filmmaking, but the money has to come from someplace. You can't just shake your fist at the establishment and put them down for not giving you the chance. You have to beat them down and take that money from them. . . . You have to set your sights and be unscrupulous."[32]

In 1972, when Paramount offered *The Godfather* to Coppola, he was inclined to refuse. Organized protest against the film's depiction of an Italian-American Mafia had prompted significant objections from the Italian-American community, and as a result, two much better known directors, Constantin Costa-Gavras and Peter Yates, had already turned down studio offers to make the picture. Coppola, who came to Paramount's attention because he was an Italian American and because he could be hired cheaply, was no more anxious than Costa-Gavras or Yates to enter the fray. Moreover, *The Godfather* was a mainstream genre project, one he would have to leave San Francisco to make.

Legend has it that it was George Lucas who finally convinced Coppola to accept Paramount's offer. Lucas contended that *The Godfather* would be such a big film that Coppola would never have to make another studio genre picture again. Coppola took his friend's advice, directed the picture, and for the following ten years was able to use *The Godfather* to maintain a modicum of creative autonomy.

On the heels of the commercial success of *The Godfather*, Coppola joined

William Friedkin (the director of *The French Connection,* which won the Academy Award for Best Picture in 1971) and Peter Bogdanovich (who directed the critically acclaimed *The Last Picture Show*) to form the Directors Company. Ostensibly a production unit within the larger structure of a major studio, the company was the brainchild of Paramount chief executive Frank Yablans and was financed by the studio for $31.5 million.

The directors' contract with Paramount elaborated the following arrangement: each of the directors would make three movies during the following six years (a second version of the contract stipulated four films in twelve years) and act as executive producer on at least one film directed by one of the other company members. In consideration for Paramount's assurance of creative autonomy within its production and distribution superstructure, the guarantee of production funding (without the hassle of pitching ideas to the various studios), and a 50 percent profit participation on their films, the directors were obliged to work exclusively at and for Paramount for the duration of the contract.

For Yablans, the Directors Company was little more than a new spin on the old Hollywood practice of contracting talent. But that was not how he chose to tout the deal in the media. "This is a familial relationship," Yablans boasted. "What made this deal possible was the degree of simpático between the directors and the studio: we're all in our early thirties and we don't have a great hierarchy."[33]

As Yablans saw it, the Directors Company only *seemed* to perpetuate a growing acceptance of the *auteur* theory in Hollywood. What he and Paramount actually had in mind was a recontextualization of *auteurism* within the studio superstructure. Thus, for Yablans, the Directors Company conceded a modicum of autonomy and power over the product to three bankable directors, but it did so in exchange for what amounted to the directors' capitulation, their seeming unwillingness to make mainstream movies. "They've gone through their growth period," Yablans mused, "indulging their esoteric tastes. Coppola isn't interested in filming a pomegranate growing in the desert. They're all very commercial now."[34]

But Yablans's optimism was short-lived. First, he battled the Paramount board in his effort to transfer control over Coppola's still incomplete *The Godfather, Part II* from the studio proper to the Directors Company unit. The board blocked Yablans's plan by simply pointing out that the picture had been developed before the Directors Company was formed. In blocking the move, the board revealed its members' unwillingness to support what had become one of Yablans's pet projects at the studio. His failure to transfer control over the picture to the Directors Company soon proved to be the least of Yablans's problems with the picture, however. By the time it was finished, *The Godfather, Part II* was precisely what Yablans claimed that Coppola was no longer interested in doing, and, moreover, it was *not* what he or the studio wanted as a sequel to *The Godfather.*

What eventually made matters worse was that despite what Yablans viewed as the picture's "experimental structure" (and the hour or so of Italian subtitled in English!), *The Godfather, Part II* became a blockbuster success and won both Best Picture and Best Director Oscars at the 1974 Academy Awards. Further, the film was a great success with the critics, many of whom identified it as a landmark work. For example, Pauline Kael of the *New Yorker* wrote: "[*The Godfather, Part II*] is the work of a major artist, who else, when he got the chance and power, would have proceeded with the absolute conviction that he'd make the film the way it should be made? In movies, that's the inner voice of an authentic hero."[35]

What Kael seemed to be acknowledging was the historical significance of the picture in terms of a growing American *auteur* tradition. But for Yablans, *The Godfather, Part II* was historically significant only because it evinced just how unreliable his instincts had become and how much better Coppola seemed to understand the audience than he did. Though the film made the studio a lot of money and the Academy Awards brought a great deal of prestige to Yablans and Paramount, Yablans could not help but resent and to a certain extent fear Coppola's success. So far as Yablans was concerned, the box office success of *The Godfather, Part II* was a bad omen.

Yablans certainly realized that the success of *The Godfather, Part II* diminished his control over Coppola, and by extension the other Directors Company members as well. What had originally made the arrangement so attractive to Yablans and Paramount was the opportunity to secure and hype the studio's association with three famous directors. With its modest operating budget and the studio's 50 percent equity share after expenses, the Directors Company seemed certain to pay for itself within a year or two. Even if only one film brought in as much as the first *Godfather* picture, the rest of the projects could bomb and it wouldn't much matter. Financially speaking, the Directors Company seemed a sound business investment even if Coppola continued to move away from the commercial mainstream.

But after the release and blockbuster success of *The Godfather, Part II,* Yablans began to worry that Coppola might not need the Directors Company as much as it needed him. Yablans was well aware that Coppola had enjoyed a significant windfall from the profits of both *Godfather* films.

Coppola had 6 profit points on the first and, via an absurdly complicated formula, stood to gain somewhere between 10 and 15 percent on the profits of the sequel. Yablans still had Coppola under contract, of course, but after the success of *The Godfather, Part II,* he realized that he could no longer effectively control any films Coppola might make in the future.

Yablans's worst fears were realized when Coppola's first Directors Company project, *The Conversation,* was screened for executives at Paramount. At once Coppola's most original and personal work—only *Rumble Fish* comes close in that regard, and both are routinely cited by the director as his two favorites—*The Conversation* became a festival film (it won at Cannes), which in 1974 was a kiss of death commercially. For Yablans, the screening of *The Conversation* indicated that Coppola was no longer even interested in making commercial movies.

Within a year of the release of *The Conversation,* Yablans announced Paramount's decision to withdraw from the Directors Company deal. In its brief duration, the unit produced three films: *The Conversation* and Peter Bogdanovich's *Paper Moon* (which was a critical and commercial success) and *Daisy Miller* (a bomb on both counts). What Yablans and the rest of studio Hollywood learned from the experience was that however seductive it might be to contract directorial talent, studios could not afford to surrender control over the product in the bargain.

However seductive the *auteur* theory appeared at first, then, the studios soon came to realize how dangerous its implementation could be. After the release of *The Conversation,* Yablans had reason to fear the prospect of more big directors making little, personal films with the studio's money. And though it hadn't happened yet, an even more perilous scenario loomed: the possibility that a big director might make a big, personal film.

Cinema 5

I've done so much for [the studios], and yet they resent even putting me in a position where I don't have to go to one of them with my hat in my hand and have them tell me what movies I can or cannot make. . . . Perhaps the wisest thing to do is to use all my energies to make a film that grosses some stupendous amount, then go out and buy a major company and change it from the top.—Francis Coppola, 1975[36]

In 1974, Coppola purchased Cinema 5, a New York–based distribution house. Though he pledged to maintain Cinema 5 as "just a small, classy operation," he couldn't resist casting the deal in terms of his own struggle for control with studio Hollywood. As he put it at the time: "My motive [for purchasing Cinema 5] has been to bypass the kinds of deals filmmakers have to make . . . deals in which the filmmaker has to totally surrender owner-ship, final cut, any say in how a film is released, in order to get the dollars up front to make a movie."[37]

But Cinema 5 was woefully inadequate for the scale and scope of Cop-pola's plans. In 1975, on Lucas's advice, instead of following up *The Conversa-tion* with another European *auteur*–style project, Coppola began developing *Apocalypse Now.* The film eventually became a legendary American *auteur* picture, but it was hardly the sort of movie Coppola could release through Cinema 5. Ironically, *The Conversation,* which was released in 1974, would have been the perfect film to distribute through the Cinema 5 network. But that film was tied by contract to Paramount. And though the studio hated the picture and gave it a very limited distribution, Paramount was hardly willing to relinquish its distribution rights to Coppola's new company.

Coppola spent the next four years making *Apocalypse Now* and the follow-ing four trying to make Zoetrope Studios a success. As a result, he never distributed a single film of his own through Cinema 5.

Although he proved unwilling to accept downward mobility in exchange for creative autonomy, it would be unfair to argue that Coppola was insincere about trying to circumvent the studio establishment and about his desire to distribute his films his way—or, more likely, that his ego was too big to resist the high-stakes challenge of a big studio film. The reality of the situation was far more complex and ironic.

Auteurism, which emerged in the field of film studies in the late 1950s as a historical argument and then evolved into a utopian production principle embraced by a generation of film school–educated directors, was by the mid-1970s a term Hollywood was only just getting used to. While Coppola embraced the privileges of authorship, the studios' view on the subject was typified by Yablans, who saw the *auteur* theory in terms of the old Hol-lywood practice of contracting talent. *Auteurism,* in the view of the studio establishment, was just another way to market the product.

Coppola, on the other hand, understood that he had to promote himself as an *auteur,* much as an actor might promote him- or herself as a star, in order to maintain a strong position within the Hollywood subculture. It was a marketing strategy. Coppola consistently used the media to hype his battle with the studios over authorship and control because, after all, the role he had chosen to play in the industry required him to reinforce the view that he was an artist too smart for the studio executives to understand but too successful for them to dismiss.

But to support such a reputation, Coppola had to maintain a high profile in the mass media. And in order to do that, he had to continue making big-budget studio movies. Ironically, then, the scale and the scope of his own stardom—his own celebrity as an *auteur*—became the principal obstacle to any real independence from the Hollywood studio establishment. For Coppola, the only alternative was to control a major studio himself.

With the purchase of Hollywood General in 1980, Coppola took a logical first step toward just such a goal, and in doing so, he took American Zoetrope, the Directors Company, Cinema 5, and *auteurism* in general to another level. But as I mentioned earlier, his timing could not have been worse. The average cost of producing the only kind of film he was interested in making (and the only kind of film that could make enough money to support his ambitious research and development plans) was well over $20 million. His new studio was leveraged against profits from a film he had yet to make and could not afford to finance himself.

In retrospect, it is easy to see how unlikely Coppola's Hollywood General–Zoetrope project was. He had too little money and too many enemies; and while his enemies may not have had to collude to make sure that he failed, it certainly was to their advantage that he did. What seems particularly unhappy and unfortunate about Coppola's inability to succeed at American Zoetrope, the Directors Company, Cinema 5, or Zoetrope Studios was that each failure seems more or less symbolic of the absurdity of *auteurism* in Hollywood, the absurdity of the cult of the individual artist in an industry committed to product and profit.

Two The New Hollywood

Two guys in a bar . . . one turns to the other and says: "I got my IQ results back—194."
The other guy says: "I got 189. Let's talk about Einstein's theory of relativity." Someone says, "They're talking IQ down there. I just got mine: 123." His friend says, "I'm so
close—121. Have you seen the recent Richard Berger architectural drawings?" At the
very end of the bar, one guy says: "I just got my IQ—73." The other guy says: "Mine is
74—have you read any good scripts lately?"—Larry Thurman, producer of *The Graduate*[1]

It is easy enough today to look back on 1980 and see just how ill-timed,
how unlucky, and perhaps how foolish Francis Coppola was to mortgage
the purchase of Hollywood General against future film revenues and to
challenge the increasingly complex studio establishment. But exactly what
he saw, what he should have seen, and what he should have known at the
time are all difficult to appreciate.

As far back as 1968, four years before *The Godfather* made him the best
known director in America, Coppola predicted that his generation of film
school–educated *auteurs* would someday trigger significant change in the
movie business. His vision of an industry dominated by powerful, innovative *auteurs*—a dream surely shared by many first-generation film school–
educated directors—was from the start based on the naive notion that if a
director made a series of popular movies, he or she could somehow gain
more direct access to financing. Just how popular these movies would have
to be was uncertain; no filmmaker had ever made enough money to finance
his or her own pictures without the assistance of a third party—a production
company and/or a major studio—to help shoulder the risk that even the
most routine film production and distribution entail. Coppola's plan to
renovate Zoetrope Studios, release a full slate of films, and develop futuristic
distribution and exhibition technologies with bank loans secured against his
own future film revenues was at the very least an extraordinary bit of self-

confidence because it so defied the parameters of film financing in Hollywood.

Coppola's 1968 prediction that there wouldn't be "a Hollywood as we know it when this generation of film students gets out of college" has proven to be partly right.[2] The industry has changed, although certainly not in the ways Coppola had once hoped it would—and he, along with fellow *auteurs* George Lucas and Steven Spielberg, are partly to blame.

The dazzling box office success of expensive *auteurist* movies like *The Godfather, Jaws,* and *Star Wars*—the very sort of movies Coppola had once believed would foster a new American *auteur* industry—led to an industrywide focus on blockbuster box office revenues. The success of *auteur* films in the 1970s did not, as Coppola had hoped it would, give *auteur* directors increased access to film financing. Instead, directors became increasingly dependent on studio financing to produce and distribute such "big" films.

With the possibility of enormous revenues to be derived from a single product (a single motion picture), the studios began to focus their efforts on a search for the next *Godfather, Jaws,* or *Star Wars* at the expense of anything and everything else. At the far end of *auteurism,* then, was not increased independence for *auteur* directors (as epitomized and symbolized at Coppola's Zoetrope Studios) or an increase in choice for the consumer. Instead, by 1980, Hollywood seemed to be shrinking, and the role of the middlemen who could put production and distribution financing together grew more important than ever before.

The Multinationalization of Hollywood

How do films get made? . . . There's no rational answer. . . . Do you realize how many people in the film business don't even go to the movies?—David Picker, former president of United Artists[3]

In 1979, a federal task force in charge of investigating antitrust violations in the film industry glibly concluded that "the industry is clearly oligopolistic . . . major studios appear to be controlling the market to restrict competition and lessen output so as to maintain tight control over employees and an exceedingly low exhibitor [buyer] profit."[4] As the 1970s came to a close, the six major studios' dominance in the marketplace seemed only to be getting stronger.

By 1981, all six of the major film studios were either owned by or were themselves conglomerates. Gulf and Western, which owned Paramount, also owned Madison Square Garden, Roosevelt Raceway, Desilu, Paramount Pictures Television, and Simon and Schuster (and its subsidiaries, Pocket Books and Monarch Books), as well as Schrafft's Candies, Supp-Hose Stockings and Socks, the New Jersey Zinc Company, Bostonian Shoes, and some three hundred other, smaller companies. Only 4 percent of Gulf and Western's revenues came directly from Paramount Pictures, and only 11 percent of its total revenues derived from its various holdings in the entertainment field.[5]

Correspondingly, United Artists's film and television divisions accounted for only 12 percent of its parent company, Transamerica Insurance's, total revenues. MCA, Columbia Pictures Industries, and Warner Communications (of which Universal, Columbia Pictures, and Warner Brothers accounted for 22 percent, 39 percent, and 24 percent, respectively) were themselves entertainment industry multinationals. These entertainment business conglomerates modeled themselves after the larger multinationals and diversified their holdings in order to insulate themselves (with predictable revenues from various subsidiaries) against the inevitable lean years at the box office.

By 1979, only the Twentieth Century Fox Film Corporation, with almost two-thirds of its total revenues derived from its film division and 96 percent of its total revenues coming from its various entertainment industry subsidiaries, seemed much like the studios of past decades. But despite its success at the box office—Fox was the number two studio in 1975, number three in 1976, and number one (posting an astonishing 19.5 percent market share with the release of *Star Wars*) in 1977—its corporate mission was largely anachronistic. By 1981, the studio was unable on its own to maintain adequate capital reserves or extend its line of credit with the banks. As a result, the studio was sold to Denver oil tycoon Marvin Davis.

Davis's purchase of Fox marked the end of an era in Hollywood. The entrepreneurial style of doing business that characterized the old studios was finally, completely, a thing of the past. In its place was a far less personal and far more complex multinational industry. Fox's failure to maintain adequate capital reserves to survive in even the good times in the new Hollywood seemed, for cine-entrepreneurs like Coppola, a particularly daunting sign. If Fox, with all its real estate and all the box office and ancillary revenues from *Star Wars* to support it, could not maintain the old style of doing business, then what hope did an independent like Coppola have in the new Hollywood?

The reasons for the conglomeratization of Hollywood were relatively simple. Interest rates, especially on the kind of short-term debt routinely incurred by the studios when funding a production, had soared to 20 percent. The average production cost of a film had reached $13 million, and a growing number of pictures were being budgeted at twice that amount. As the stakes rose, the cash reserves and credit lines of the multinationals proved to be a useful hedge against the vagaries of the film marketplace. With pay television and videocassettes on the horizon, it no longer made any sense for the studios to remain autonomous if it meant that they would also be undercapitalized.

What was in it for the multinationals is only a slightly more difficult question. Both Paramount and United Artists, for example, are high-profile companies. But given the scale and scope at which Gulf and Western and Transamerica operate, both film companies were relatively cheaply bought and operated, and they accounted for a fraction of the larger companies' gross revenues.

The multinationals soon discovered that news from the film studios proved a useful distraction at annual stockholders' meetings from the more boring and the more controversial corporate practices and decisions. Gulf and Western, for example, had only to screen a new Paramount movie or trot out a major star to wave and pose to keep its stockholders happy.

Greater diversification allowed the new studios to better market their product lines. By the mid-1980s, all of the major studios routinely released their pictures on film, videocassette, and pay television. Additional markets were available through novelizations and comic books and through a variety of licensing arrangements with fast food chains and toy manufacturers. Such diversification (often accomplished by simply recycling films through the parent company's various subsidiaries) required a significant amount of capital but afforded those companies with access to sufficient credit the opportunity to exploit a growing and extremely lucrative entertainment marketplace.

Such high and good times for the major studios came at a cost to the consumer. Even a cursory look back at Hollywood at the end of the 1970s reveals the effect of conglomeratization. The early 1980s saw a dramatic decline in film starts at all six of the major studios and a pigeonholing of product to a degree never before seen in an industry already renowned for its primarily generic product lines.[6] The box office leaders at the time exemplify the impact of Hollywood's corporate overhaul. The top films from 1979 to 1983—roughly the years spanned from the release of *Apocalypse Now* to *The Cotton Club*—were *Superman, The Empire Strikes Back, Raiders of the Lost Ark, ET: The Extra-Terrestrial,* and *Return of the Jedi,* high-concept films that share common elements, narratives, and styles.[7]

In 1979, film historian James Monaco pointed out that the total market share attained by just the top ten films in release had increased threefold from the previous year. The trend continued through the first few years of the 1980s, effectively placing greater emphasis on the blockbuster package. In turn, the film audience—whose place in the supply and demand equation is never as simple as studio executives like to believe—witnessed a dramatic desaturation of the marketplace and an accompanying dramatic diminishment of choice. As Monaco aptly put it, "increasingly we are all going to see the same ten movies."[8]

As Hollywood moved into the 1980s and Coppola made his move at Hollywood General, four significant stories emerged in the trades: (1) an acrimonious and ultimately pivotal antitrust suit involving Kirk Kerkorian and Columbia Pictures Industries, (2) an actor's strike, (3) a lawsuit filed by Disney and Universal Studios against Sony, and (4) the demise of the legendary B movie company American International Pictures. All four stories, in retrospect, at least, offer an introduction to the new Hollywood and help establish the parameters of a place where Coppola's Zoetrope was doomed from the start.

On Trust and Antitrust in the New Hollywood

The same three things drive everyone. The fun of the business. Pride. And the fear of failure.—Herbert Allen, former CEO of Columbia Pictures[9]

The Kerkorian story broke on April 25, 1979, when the Las Vegas real estate entrepreneur and MGM CEO filed a notice with the Securities and Exchange Commission confirming the sale of 297,000 shares of his MGM stock. With the proceeds of the sale, Kerkorian secured a $38 million loan to finance the purchase of 1.75 million shares of Columbia Pictures Industries (CPI). The two related moves netted Kerkorian an additional 19 percent of CPI's stock, upping his total to 24 percent and making him the largest shareholder at both MGM and Columbia at the same time.[10]

Kerkorian had purchased MGM from Time, Inc., and Seagrams's Edgar Bronfman in 1969. Because studio management at the time opposed the deal, Kerkorian had to purchase 40 percent of the stock on the open market in order to force the sale. As a result, by the time he gained control of the company, he had no money left to run it. Kerkorian's liquid assets after the purchase of MGM were depleted from $553 million to $89 million. Moreover, he had an outstanding short-term debt of $72 million in 13 percent European bank loans.

In an effort to meet his various debt obligations, Kerkorian cut the MGM workforce from 6,200 to 1,200 between late 1969 and the beginning of 1971. By the end of the 1970s, things had gotten so bad at MGM that Kerkorian auctioned off valuable props and wardrobe articles from the studio's better days. And then, in a move that seemed to signal the end of MGM as a major player in the business, Kerkorian sold off the studio's domestic distribution rights to United Artists and its foreign rights to Cinema International (which was jointly owned by MCA-Universal and Gulf and Western–Paramount).[11]

The two deals significantly reduced Kerkorian's asset base at MGM but at the same time enabled him to vertically integrate the studio's interests with three of its competitors. Kerkorian seemed inclined to believe that his and the studio's luck might improve in a more cooperative, even collusive environment.

When Kerkorian first purchased a 5 percent stock interest in CPI in December 1978, nobody in the industry paid much attention. But then, when he upped his stake to 24 percent four months later, executives at both MGM and CPI and attorneys in the antitrust division of the U.S. Justice Department took notice.

Kerkorian's apparent interest in taking over Columbia seemed to suggest that he had abandoned any hope of turning MGM back into a major player in the industry. At the time, there were rumors that Kerkorian planned to shut down the studio altogether or merge it with CPI, or that he planned to maintain control over both studios and in doing so prevent MGM from competing with the far stronger CPI for the best film projects. The latter made good sense in view of the fact that Kerkorian's profit stake at CPI—which, unlike MGM, distributed its own films—was significantly greater than at MGM.

In order to force Kerkorian to divest interest in one of the two companies, the Justice Department filed an antitrust suit in federal court. But as early as August 7, 1979, the opening day of the trial, Judge Andrew Hauk questioned the validity of the government's suit. Since Kerkorian had signed a "standstill agreement"—in effect agreeing not to purchase any more CPI stock for three years—Hauk opined that there could be no antitrust implications unless the government could prove "actual Kerkorian intent to meddle in Columbia's affairs."[12]

The Justice Department opened its case by calling a series of major exhibitors, all of whom expressed concern about Kerkorian's dual interest in both MGM and CPI and its potential effect on "product supply." But when pressed by Judge Hauk, none of the exhibitors could cite evidence (in the four months since Kerkorian purchased the cpi stock) that there had been any effect at all.

By the time Herbert Allen, the New York investment banker who ran cpi, took the stand, the government's case was lost. Allen told the court that while he would have preferred that the standstill agreement held for ten instead of three years, he felt confident that Kerkorian had no "current anti-competitive scheme." Allen then pointed out that in his opinion, the problem with the Kerkorian-cpi connection was primarily perceptual; that independent producers doing business with cpi or mgm might be concerned that the two companies would someday merge or perhaps somehow work in collusion. These producers' fears were unfounded, Allen said, but he expressed concern because "in the motion picture business, perception is often more important than reality."

The oddest and most interesting moment in the case came when Judge Hauk called in two neutral University of California economics professors, Robert Clower and Fred Weston, to assess the situation. Both professors concluded that they saw no monopoly threat in Kerkorian's dual ownership, nor could they see any evidence that Kerkorian had purchased the stock for any reason other than investment.

Clower's testimony proved particularly damaging to the government's case. He argued that even an outright merger of mgm and cpi "would not significantly lessen competition in any line of commerce," adding that even if two of the more successful studios merged, "you still would have five or six distributors," and thus a reasonably competitive environment.[13]

On August 22, after a little more than a month of testimony, Judge Hauk concluded that the government had "failed completely to prove that Kerkorian's holdings violate the Clayton [antitrust] Act." He then admonished the government attorneys for pursuing the case in the first place. Hauk concluded, unironically: "How on earth the government can arrive at the thought that there will be a diminution of non-existent competition is beyond me."[14]

The court's decision to turn a blind eye to the antitrust implications of Kerkorian's dual ownership seemed to set in motion a significant loosening of federal regulations with regard to corporate interests in the movie business, regulations that continue to be unenforced—or unenforceable—in contemporary Hollywood. The decision in Kerkorian's favor also foregrounded a more cooperative (as opposed to competitive) and potentially collusive corporate environment. After this landmark court case, only studios able to diversify and vertically integrate their products within the deregulated entertainment marketplace—in other words, only studios with enough capital to establish such a network—seemed to have much of a future. It is well worth noting here that Coppola's Zoetrope was hardly such a place.

As far as Kerkorian was concerned, Judge Hauk's ruling placed him one step closer to taking over Columbia Pictures. On September 29, 1980, approximately a year after the court decided in his favor, Kerkorian made a tender offer to purchase an additional one million shares of CPI stock (via call options to be exercised on the date the standstill agreement was set to expire).

The proposed stock purchase promised to give Kerkorian control of 35 percent of the company. The CPI board, in a *Variety* piece titled "Kerkorian Plans to Control Columbia Pictures Come 1982," termed the offer "an outrageous assault" and, though they should have known better, "a blatant violation of anti-trust laws" and countered by announcing a bold stock move, a "convertible debenture" which, if successful, promised to reduce the percentage (but not the cash value) of Kerkorian's CPI holdings.[15] In response, Kerkorian formally announced his intention to take over the company.

Kerkorian filed suit to circumvent the standstill agreement that interfered with his plans to mount a takeover. In the suit Kerkorian alleged the following: (1) that, because the standstill agreement included a provision that compelled CPI to consult him in all major business decisions, the board's move to offer a convertible debenture without first contacting him amounted to a breach in CPI's fiduciary duty; (2) that CPI's recent issue of 300,000 new shares of stock (as part of the convertible debenture) was set up in order to put the additional shares in the "friendly hands" of in-house "independent" producer, Ray Stark; (3) that CPI had deliberately obstructed Kerkorian's attempts to sell his interest in the company; (4) that even though various stockholder publications indicated otherwise, CPI was presently being run by just two people, Herbert Allen on the operations side, and Ray Stark on the creative side; and (5) that CPI's most recent proxy statement failed to disclose certain payments to CPI officers (most important, a $1 million payment to one of Ray Stark's attorneys and several million dollars worth of underwriting costs paid to Herbert Allen's brokerage firm, Allen and Company).

But just as Kerkorian seemed ready to mount a proxy fight—a fight he seemed well positioned to win—a disastrous fire at the MGM Grand Hotel in Las Vegas compromised his cash position, and on February 11, 1981, just as

CPI's legal bills in the battle with Kerkorian topped $1 million, Allen announced an agreement in principle with Kerkorian to resolve their differences. Columbia promised to "repurchase" Kerkorian's 2.5 million shares and both parties agreed to terminate all pending litigation. Additionally Kerkorian pledged not to buy any CPI stock for ten years.[16]

Kerkorian's decision to settle netted him $137.5 million. With the massive project of rebuilding the MGM Grand in Las Vegas at hand, it seemed safe to assume that he would finally take his money out of Hollywood and invest it in Las Vegas. But within a very short time, rumors began to circulate regarding an offer made by Kerkorian to purchase Chris-Craft Industries' 22 percent holdings in Twentieth Century Fox.

The Fox deal unfolded quickly and strangely. On February 20, 1981, Marvin Davis tendered an offer of $720 million for the studio. Then, the following day, Davis mysteriously withdrew the offer. Three days later, news of Kerkorian's offer to buy Chris-Craft Industries' Fox stock appeared in the trades. In a panic to keep Kerkorian away, the Fox studio brass reopened negotiations with Davis, and a deal was swiftly closed.

It soon became apparent to Fox management that Davis had leveraged the purchase against the assets of the film company, exactly what Fox executives had feared Kerkorian would do if he bought the company. Within days of closing the deal, Davis began to sell off key Fox subsidiaries. It is ironic that Kerkorian, with the cash he had netted from his CPI stock sale, might not have had to liquidate any of Fox's assets at all if he had been allowed to purchase the company.

In 1984, Kerkorian reemerged as a principal in Saul Steinberg's attempted hostile takeover of Disney. Steinberg's proposed leveraged buyout was primarily engineered to upset Disney management and there is considerable doubt as to Steinberg's sincere interest in the company,[17] but Kerkorian was earnest in his cash offer for the Disney film studio. Ultimately, as most Wall Street experts expected he would, Steinberg settled for a greenmail payoff.[18]

Through the course of the 1980s, Kerkorian held significant stock in MGM, Columbia, and United Artists; negotiated distribution deals and thus vertically integrated MGM Filmco with United Artists, Paramount, and Universal; and made tender offers for Columbia, Fox, Disney, and United Artists. Though he professed little interest in movies, Kerkorian emerged as the most interesting and active, if not the most powerful, man in the film industry in the 1980s. The fluidity with which Kerkorian moved within the entertainment marketplace set the stage for greater consolidation, vertical integration, and dual ownership. Despite his quixotic, seemingly irrational business sense, it is Kerkorian—and not an *auteur* like Coppola—who now serves as the model new Hollywood player.

The Fight over the Ancillary Market

If you make a good movie, the American people will go see it. The emotional drive to want to go and see a movie has not been eliminated from the American psyche at all. Because [in 1986], irrespective of all this videotape stuff, still what—four billion bucks were spent at the box office. And ninety percent of those box offices were in shitholes somewhere in Cleveland.[19]—Paul Gurian, producer of *Peggy Sue Got Married*[19]

In 1980, just as production was set to begin on the fall television season, the Screen Actors Guild (SAG) went out on strike. Given past history, it seemed the perfect time for the union to make its move. But the union's leaders failed to appreciate how successfully the studios had insulated themselves against film box office and television revenue losses through diversification, vertical integration, and outside ownership, and thus failed to realize how little television revenues mattered in the larger scheme of things in the new Hollywood.

In the September 10, 1980, issue of *Variety,* two unrelated stories seemed to highlight the studios' strength. The first, under the headline "Columbia's Record Fiscal Year; Gross up 27%, Net Climbs 15%," revealed that even though Columbia had been embroiled in ongoing litigation with Kerkorian and had not had a particularly terrific year at the box office, due in large part to its diversified holdings it was still able to show a considerable profit for the year.[20] The second article was more directly related to the strike. Under the headline "Universal Suspends All Projects," the studio used the trade magazine to send the following message to the striking actors: "Universal has decided today [September 9, 1980] to invoke the *force majeure* clause in its contracts with filmmakers as of September 15, thus putting all of its projects on suspension. . . . Invoking the clause, which other studios are known to be considering as well, means that U[niversal] is cutting off payments to writers, directors and producers developing projects. Move is sure to put further pressure on the Screen Actors Guild to reach terms in strike negotiations."[21]

Universal's strategy was at once simple and effective. By shutting things down completely, it placed significant pressure on the actors not only to negotiate but also to settle in a timely fashion. While the Directors' and Writers' Guilds would have most likely gone out on strike eventually in sympathy, Universal cut off such a strategy by putting "everyone" out of work before any signs of solidarity could develop. In doing so, the studio not only stole the public relations advantage, it effectively pitted one guild against the other with SAG as the industry's apparent scapegoat. On a deeper and frankly more important level, Universal's willingness to invoke the force majeure clause also revealed the studio's position: it no longer needed to make movies or television shows to make money.

The studios' apparent invincibility was deeply problematic for the screen actors because the strike was extremely important with regard to their future income. Their beef with the studios concerned their stake in future revenues garnered from pay television and prerecorded videocassettes, two markets which at that time were unproven but seemed promising. What SAG wanted to establish were at least provisional guidelines for the number of days or hours of screenings on pay television before residuals were triggered, the percentage of gross profits earmarked for residuals once they were triggered, and the percentage of gross revenues from prerecorded videocassettes to be shared with "talent."

The studios countered with the argument that the union's discussion of "home box office revenues" was, though important, premature. Negotiators for the studios maintained that there should be a grace period of a year or two (during which no residuals would be paid) in order to let the market establish itself, after which an amicable agreement could be reached.

The SAG leadership at the time was a strange bunch: arch-conservative Charlton Heston and Hollywood liberals Ed Asner, Marlo Thomas, and Alan Alda. Frustrated by the studios' refusal to negotiate, the Screen Actors Guild leadership engineered a boycott of the annual Emmy Awards show and staged various benefits in the Hollywood area. At one such benefit at the Hollywood Bowl, Heston elaborated the inequity of management's argument: "The producers keep telling us the home box office we're striking over is ten years away. That may be so. I called Mike Medavoy [then the production chief at Orion Pictures] today, and all I can tell you is he wasn't available because they were busy transferring 10 to videocassettes."[22]

SAG's strike over future home box office revenues had an ironic and unanticipated effect. The strike, organized to call attention to a potential inequity in profit distribution, forced the studios to move more quickly than they had planned to establish control over pay television and prerecorded videocassettes. The studios swiftly solidified their power base and used the strike to establish a significant distance between themselves and the various guilds.

An October 1, 1980, *Variety* headline seemed to put the entire conflict into perspective: "Actors Walkout Hurts TV, Helps BO [Box Office] Boom."[23] With no power base, no public support, and growing fragmentation within the larger guild structure, the actors eventually backed down and the studios moved into the brave new world of home box office in complete control over what evolved into a large and very lucrative entertainment marketplace.

Disney and Universal Studios Versus Sony

Studios have different personalities. There are very hysterical, truly out-there studios and very paranoid studios. Disney is a very obsessive-compulsive studio. And you know obsessive-compulsives: when they have a problem, they will be very compulsive about how they deal with their problem.—Robert Cort, film producer[24]

The studios' growing concern over the prerecorded videocassette market was accompanied by anxiety about the home videotaping of copyrighted films aired on network and pay television. In what became for the industry a very important civil suit, Disney and Universal took on Sony, claiming that available technology did not enable the studios to effectively separate out or scramble programs they did not want duplicated. The Betamax machines produced by Sony, the studios argued, posed a fundamental copyright problem for the industry as a whole. In order to delay or perhaps even prevent the retail sale of the machines, Disney and Universal studio attorneys filed suit.

Sony seemed to have a compelling argument in the case. Back in the early 1960s the electronics conglomerate had offered Universal the opportunity to become a software supplier for Betamax and to participate in the development of the new technology. But Universal turned Sony down. In 1980, then, Sony seemed to be on firm ground when it argued that Universal had had its chance and blown it.

Universal's attorneys argued that Sony's videocassette equipment back in the 1960s was so expensive and cumbersome that it seemed to have little or no future retail market value. The machines Sony had developed for retail sale in the United States in 1980 were so significantly different from the machines Universal executives saw and decided not to invest in twenty years earlier that they constituted an entirely new and different technology.

Though many in the industry feared that Sony would prevail, Judge Warren J. Ferguson came to the conclusion that Sony would have gone ahead with research and development on Betamax whether or not Universal had ever expressed interest.[25] In his view, the new machines were indeed radically different from the 1960s prototypes, and their sale did pose a considerable copyright problem and further complicated a complex marketplace.

Sony appealed the decision, and the case was eventually settled out of court. But many of the issues raised by Sony's attorneys continue to complicate things in Hollywood. For example, throughout the disagreement with Universal and Disney, Sony held that the most important property at stake was not its product (Betamax), nor studio copyrights per se, but the airwaves and the individual citizen's right of access to the airwaves. It was Sony's contention throughout that when a broadcast signal is put into the air, "it becomes very close to public property," and whoever owns the means to receive such a signal has the right to change it to a form he or she can use and enjoy.[26] Such a point of view frees the video manufacturer and retailer from culpability in terms of potential user copyright violation, but it is fair to say that today, control over or free access to the airwaves is hardly in the hands of the average citizen.

Things have never been quite the same since the studios established a position in the home box office market. At this writing, in 1994, on the average, nearly 50 percent of the studios' revenues are derived from video rentals and sales, totaling more than $4 billion a year.[27] Additionally, Viacom, a cable television conglomerate, and its principal partner, Blockbuster Video, a prerecorded videocassette retailer, having fattened up on home box office revenues, recently purchased Paramount in a deal that has not met with a single successful antitrust challenge.

The Demise of AIP and Filmways

Samuel Z. Arkoff (president of American International Pictures): "I like the business. I like the people in the business. It's a business of rogues. I say it nicely. But it's a business of rogues."
Interviewer: "And you're a rogue?"
Arkoff: "No, I'm the only one who's not."[28]

The consolidation of power by the six major film studios in the early 1980s is further evinced in the story of the demise of American International Pictures (AIP). Throughout the last half of the 1950s, the 1960s, and the first half of the 1970s, AIP was an all-American success story. Led by the iconoclast Samuel Z. Arkoff and his low-profile partner, James Nicholson, AIP emerged as an efficient if at times artless "independent" B movie factory, producing such memorable films as *Wild in the Streets, I Was a Teenage Werewolf,* and *Three in the Attic.*

But by the mid-1970s, Arkoff's B pictures had become anachronistic. Due in large part to the blockbuster success of *auteurs* like Coppola, Martin Scorsese, and Peter Bogdanovich—all of whom apprenticed in the B movie business—distributors and exhibitors no longer seemed interested in smaller pictures. In the late 1970s, the independent studios faced a dilemma: while films had begun to cost a lot more to make, theatrical box office revenues remained unpredictable. Moreover, given many exhibitors' preference for "holding over" blockbuster pictures, it had become more difficult than ever to secure theatrical venues to show B pictures.[29]

The simultaneous emergence of the prerecorded videocassette and pay television markets did provide an alternative source of profits for the smaller studios. But while the new ancillary markets guaranteed at least a modest return on lower-budget films, most of the independents, unlike the majors, were not in a strong enough cash position to take full advantage of the situation. Even if an independent studio managed to retain the ancillary rights to its films, the wait for ancillary revenues was often a year or more— too long, given the exorbitant short-term interest rates on the loans these studios routinely used to fund film production.

In the spring of 1980, Arkoff assessed the difficulties inherent in remaining independent in Hollywood: "The industry is entering a different period. People are not interested in lesser pictures, so the picture business is becoming the province of well funded companies. The independents that can't keep up with the escalating costs of production and marketing will get hurt savagely in the marketplace."[30] Arkoff reminded *Variety* readers that in 1969, the last time production budgets increased dramatically and film starts declined, the motion picture subsidiaries of both ABC and CBS television corporations, along with Cinerama and National General, all went under because they couldn't maintain sufficient capital reserves. Arkoff warned that much the same fate awaited the smaller film companies in late-1970s Hollywood. As readers of *Variety* no doubt appreciated, in 1979, Arkoff himself had been forced to merge AIP with Filmways, a deal that eventually forced him to surrender control of "his" company.

Arkoff first announced his intention to merge AIP with Filmways in March 1979. At the time, both companies hoped that by combining their credit lines with the banks—AIP's credit ceiling was $10 million, Filmways's $25 million—the united companies could become a mini-major and continue to do business in the new Hollywood.

On July 17, 1979, the two formally merged, but within six months, AIP and Filmways found themselves at an ideological impasse. Arkoff wanted to continue making exploitation pictures, and the executive team at Filmways wanted to establish a position in the "prestige picture" market. The situation seemed irresolvable until Richard Bloch, a senior executive at Filmways, discovered that Arkoff had—or so it was alleged—deliberately overstated AIP's asset base during the merger negotiations. As a result of Bloch's allegations, Arkoff was forced first to resign as CEO of AIP and then to relinquish his seat on the Filmways corporate board.[31]

In March 1980, with Arkoff out of the loop at Filmways, Bloch announced the retirement of the AIP name. Soon after liquidating AIP, Filmways boasted record box office figures with *The Amityville Horror, Love at First Bite,* and *Dressed to Kill.* But while the box office success seemed to bode well for the new Filmways, it was nevertheless worrisome that all three pictures originated with Arkoff at pre-Filmways AIP.

With the retirement of AIP and the ouster of Arkoff, the strong box office figures set in motion what would become a year-long decline in stock prices at Filmways, a decline that would eventually make the company an attractive takeover target. The Filmways board predictably took the market prices more seriously than the box office figures and cleaned house, firing two of its senior executives, Raphael Etkes and Jeff Young. The two men were largely responsible for Filmways's commitment to several prestige, high-profile films, including Arthur Penn's *Four Friends* (in postproduction), Brian De-Palma's *Blowout* (in production) and (with Dino DeLaurentiis) Milos Forman's *Ragtime* (also in production).

Filmways held domestic distribution rights on all three films, which at first glance seemed to bode well. But as Filmways' executive Robert Grundburg soon realized, the company did not have adequate capital reserves to take all three to term. In order to maintain control over the films, Grundburg sold Filmways's insurance subsidiary, the Union Fidelity Corporation. But the sale bought Grundburg and Bloch nothing but trouble.

Several major stockholders publicly chided Filmways' management for first firing Etkes and Young and then selling off a lucrative subsidiary in order to maintain control over their films. In addition to *Four Friends, Blowout,* and *Ragtime,* in various stages of development at Filmways at the time were Ridley Scott's *Blade Runner,* Sergio Leone's *Once upon a Time in America,* Lee Grant's *Tell Me a Riddle, The Gangs of New York* (to be directed by Martin Scorsese), *Links* (with Diane Keaton, to be directed by Arthur Penn), *Huey* (a biopic on Huey Long, scripted by Gore Vidal), *Fire on the Mountain* (to be directed by Tony Scott), *Good Company* (to be directed by John Avildsen), remakes of Leo McCarey's *An Affair to Remember* and *A Woman's Place,* and the low-budget exploitation films *Halloween II* and *The Fan.* With the ouster of Etkes and Young, all development deals were put on hold. And while Grundburg attempted to hold on to the 1980 Etkes and

Young lineup,—*Four Friends, Blowout,* and *Ragtime*—both time and money grew short.

In the third quarter of 1980, Filmways announced $10.6 million in losses and announced its intention to suspend paying out stock dividends. In protest, Arkoff, who had held onto his 9 percent share in the company, sold his stock to Tandem Productions, at the time owned and run by Norman Lear, Bud Yorkin, and Jerry Perenchio.

While the deal officially got Arkoff out of the company for good, Filmways had little cause for celebration. Arkoff had sat rather quietly on his shares and had made no effort to parlay his stock into additional control over the company. Tandem, on the other hand, had a history of meddling and, worse, had expressed interest in owning a studio of its own. In November 1979, for example, Tandem had offered to pay Kerkorian $163 million for his 24 percent stake in Columbia Pictures. When Kerkorian began to make moves on CPI himself, Tandem backed off, only to precede Kerkorian in pursuit of Chris-Craft's stake in Twentieth Century Fox. Failing that deal as well, a takeover of Filmways seemed not only well within the scope of Tandem's interests but well within its financial capabilities as well.

No doubt hoping to have the last laugh at Filmways's expense, Arkoff told the trades that he was "genuinely relieved" to be through with the company, "where I spent my time giving them advice they now realize they should have taken."[32] Arkoff's exit seemed to mark the end for not only AIP but for Filmways as well. Despite selling off various assets and streamlining its management—moves *Variety* described as "a Stockmanesque axing of projects and re-evaluation of product"[33]—Filmways announced fourth quarter losses totaling over $66 million and a stock price decline of $11.71 per share.

As 1981 came to a close, Filmways became the object of considerable takeover speculation. Foremost in the rumor mill was not Tandem but Orion, whose distribution deal with Warner Brothers was about to expire. At the time, Orion resembled Filmways in both size and interest. But unlike Filmways, which was having a very difficult time taking its projects to term, Orion had successfully mounted the production and release (through Warner Brothers) of two very successful films, *Arthur* and *Excalibur.*

Amid rumors that corporate raider Saul Steinberg had an interest in taking over the company, Filmways sold out to Orion and its partners, the Warren Pincus Capital Corporation and, in what now seems a foreshadowing of things to come, a fledgling pay TV outfit called Home Box Office (HBO). HBO's role in the deal was made clear when Orion's Arthur Krim announced that the company hoped to bring the remaining Filmways projects to term by licensing (i.e., selling off) cable television broadcast rights to its partner HBO in advance. From the start, Orion-Filmways-HBO walked and talked like a trust; in other words, it seemed prepared to at least try to do business in the new Hollywood.

But Orion underestimated the extent of Filmways's debt. After just one week, Orion was forced to sell off the former Filmways publishing subsidiary Grosset and Dunlap. A second subsidiary, the Pic-Mount corporation, was "spun off," and then a third, Broadcast Electronics, was put up for sale. By August, the name Filmways had been retired, and eventually all three of Etkes and Young's projects had been sold to one of the major studios.

It wasn't until the August Orion stockholders' meeting that the Filmways deal was formally announced, and by then Filmways, in effect, no longer existed. The meeting itself was altogether anticlimactic, a quiet end to a very significant new Hollywood story. The August 4, 1982, issue of *Variety* characterized it: "Sparsely attended meeting at the Plaza Hotel drew little gadfly action and virtually no discussion reinforcing *fait accompli* sensibility going in. Holders did suggest women and minority representation on the board, and the prospect of a small token gift from the company at the next meet. Both suggestions were taken under advisement."[34]

Why Not Zoetrope?

It's a fascinating world to watch. A kind of Disneyland. But that's the nature of movies, which is art and commerce, only [in Hollywood] the commerce is God. . . . You sit in New York and say "That's a piece of junk. Why do they make movies like that?" Then you come out [to Hollywood], and you can begin to understand. . . . "
—Brian DePalma, director, 1991[35]

The Hollywood that Coppola hoped to revolutionize, to "bring to its knees" in 1980 with the purchase of Hollywood General, was then in the process of redefining, indeed revolutionizing, itself. Higher interest rates and bigger budgets and profits led to further vertical integration and multinationalization on the part of the studios, which subsequently led to a greater centralization of power and capital. By 1981 the industry seemed to have completely closed ranks, and in doing so managed to put *auteurism* behind it. Thus, despite good intentions and, eventually, several terrific movies, Zoetrope was doomed before it ever got off the ground.

Still, one can hardly blame Coppola for going ahead with his studio project. Given the success of *Apocalypse Now* in 1979—given the success of virtually every film he either directed or produced in the 1970s—Coppola had every reason to believe that he could extend *auteurism* to include control over at least the means of producing his films and, if he got lucky, the technology to distribute them as well. Even if he had followed the trade accounts of the Kerkorian-CPI battle, the actors' strike, the Disney-Universal versus Sony lawsuit, and the demise of AIP and Filmways, Coppola probably believed that these stories had nothing to do with him.

But in the final analysis, they all did. The Justice Department's failure to define Kerkorian's dual interest in MGM and CPI as a trust further licensed the growing conglomeratization of the industry and indirectly encouraged corporate raiders and investment bankers to target film studios. The practice of leveraging such purchases against the assets of the company in question led directly to the dismantling of MGM and Fox and upped the capitalization needed to maintain a reasonable level of production at a major studio. That Kerkorian, despite a considerable personal fortune—well in excess of Coppola's—was unable to keep MGM afloat indicated how hard it would be for Coppola to make Zoetrope competitive in the new entertainment marketplace.

The 1980 actors' strike and its resolution in management's favor revealed just how diversified and powerful the major studios had become. Throughout the conflict the studios successfully exploited growing public disillusionment with unions in general and high-priced talent (like Coppola) in particular and thus gained an implied public endorsement for their particular style of doing business. The resolution of the strike and the suit against Sony further established parameters for studio control over the new ancillary markets of pay television and prerecorded videocassettes, two markets Coppola needed to exploit in order to succeed at Zoetrope.

The AIP and Filmways stories likely hit the closest to home, but alas, they played out too slowly and too late to do Coppola much good. Once again, the message was the importance of capital reserves and diversification. If one wanted to be in the film business, one had to be in a position, like the majors, to ride out the bad times. But even in the good times one would have to survive long enough to meet short-term debt payments. That AIP and Filmways were unable to survive the good times was a message Coppola might not have wanted to hear, but it was one that might have saved him a lot of money and trouble.

Coppola and Lucas

When we were kids building [American] Zoetrope [in the late 1960s], we needed a copier. George's dad was a 3M representative, and I asked George if we could get a 3M machine at cost. George said: "My father would never do that." George comes from a very conservative Northern California family where money is a kind of serious business. . . . My attitude towards money is that it's something to be used."—Francis Coppola, 1981[36]

When George Lucas received a special Academy Award in 1992, he thanked his parents, his teachers, and his mentor, Francis Coppola. For those who know both men, the tribute was hardly a surprise. Despite a shift in position in Hollywood—Lucas is certainly the more powerful player today—the two men have remained friends since Lucas first worked with Coppola in the 1960s. And though the films they have produced and/or directed since then seem quite different, both have taken significant steps to distance, or at least protect, themselves from corporate Hollywood.

Lucas's continued success with his production/distribution unit (Lucasfilm) and his state-of-the-art postproduction facility (Industrial Light and Magic), both founded at approximately the same time as Coppola's Zoetrope Studios, is a kind of object lesson on exactly how to successfully establish a position on the near margins of Hollywood. In retrospect, it seems clear that, quite unlike Coppola, Lucas understood the emerging "new Hollywood," or at least that Lucas's particular interests (in the postproduction of high-concept films) posed less of a threat to the studio establishment than Coppola's far grander plans at Zoetrope.

Since Lucas has made the studios a lot of money, he has secured a reputation for being a cooperative studio player. But he is a pragmatist, not a true believer. Dating back to the halcyon days at American Zoetrope in San Francisco, Lucas has consistently expressed his antipathy for studio Hollywood. For example, when executives at Warner Brothers failed to appreciate the first script for *American Graffiti*, Lucas bristled: "The studios . . . don't understand scripts . . . that [scripts] should be more like blueprints than novels. They don't even know who McLuhan is over there."[37]

In 1981, as Lucasfilm and Industrial Light and Magic were beginning to take shape, Lucas explained his desire to circumvent the studio system in terms reminiscent of his former mentor: "LA is where they make deals, do business in the classic corporate way, which is screw everybody and do whatever you can to turn the biggest profit. They don't care about people. It's incredible the way they treat filmmakers. . . . I don't want anything to do with them."[38]

That Lucas proved to be the more successful of the two in the long run is a fact of life in the new Hollywood that Coppola has had to learn to deal with. Both men have sought independence from the studio mainstream, but it is clear that they have different ideas about exactly where the margins of Hollywood are located and what, financially and artistically, can be sacrificed in order to survive there.

Clearly it was Lucas who read the trades more astutely in 1980. And thus it was Lucas who played the game more carefully. As early as 1981, a year before Coppola had released a picture at Zoetrope Studios, Lucas doubted Coppola's ability to succeed: "I disagreed with Francis when he said he was going to Los Angeles. We both have the same goals, we both have the same ideas and we both have the same ambitions. . . . [We have] a disagreement in the way it should be done. . . . Being down there in Hollywood, you're just asking for trouble, because you're trying to change a system that will never change." As to Coppola's electronic cinema method and his plans for research and development at the studio, Lucas predicted trouble in the simplest of terms: "The studios will never come to understand it at all."

Comparing Lucasfilm with Zoetrope Studios, Lucas aptly characterized a fundamental difference in temperament and management style: "It's going to take six years for me to get my facility functioning the way his is right now," Lucas remarked in 1981. "He just went 'Boop' and it was done. . . . I'll have mine, and it will take a lot longer to get it built, but I don't think it will ever collapse."[39]

Even before the release of *One from the Heart,* Coppola seemed inclined to agree; Lucas was indeed the one more likely to succeed. "If I'm like America," Coppola mused, "George was my Japan—he saw what I did wrong, and he perfected what I did right." As the gap between them seemed to widen after the release of *Star Wars* in 1977, Coppola put their relative stock in the industry in perspective: "George is so wealthy now, he doesn't need a partner anymore. And he's a practical person who doesn't want to be saddled with a diseased organ."[40]

Three *One from the Heart*

I sent a telex to Francis telling him that because I loved him, I would tell him what no one else was willing to say, that he was setting up his own Vietnam with his supply lines of wine and steaks and air conditioners, creating the very situation he went there to expose. That with his staff of hundreds of people carrying out his every request, he was turning into Kurtz—going too far.—Eleanor Coppola[1]

In September 1978, Francis Coppola screened a rough cut of *Apocalypse Now* for a room full of United Artists (UA) executives. He had hoped the screening would buy him more time from the studio, but it had the opposite effect. The screening of the still incomplete film—which was already a year overdue and reportedly well over budget (rumor had it topping $70 million)—went so badly that one executive dubbed the film "Apocalypse Never."[2]

What made the screening all the more frustrating for the studio executives was the fact that on some deep level they had to realize that they had gotten exactly what they had bargained for. In 1976, when UA executives first gave the project the green light, all they had in front of them was a right-wing script for a $1.5 million, 16-mm Vietnam movie written by John Milius for George Lucas and American Zoetrope in 1968—a project, it is well worth noting, that Warner Brothers had turned down eight years earlier. When Coppola brought the same project to UA in 1976, the executives were anxious to make a deal with *him* to direct virtually anything, and thus they provisionally budgeted $12 million, a completely arbitrary figure.

There were obvious problems with the development deal. Coppola certainly had to rewrite the script (to make it a big studio feature, to make it more politically correct for 1976), and, once he rewrote it, the production was certain to cost significantly more than $12 million. Because Coppola had been so successful in the past, the script and budget problems struck UA executives as minor details to be ironed out once the project was under way.

When the development deal was signed, UA, in terms both parties no doubt understood, implied a willingness to finance (at any budget) any Coppola film, sight unseen, titled *Apocalypse Now*, about Vietnam. But while the studio was prepared to pay more than $12 million in order to cash in on Coppola's box office appeal, no one could ever have predicted the amount of bad luck the project would meet on location in the Philippines and, as a result, the degree to which the budget would increase.

By any standard the location shoot was a disaster. Poor weather followed by Martin Sheen's near-fatal heart attack and then a civil war in the Philippines, events obviously beyond Coppola's ability to control, all conspired to hold up production.[3] But even under those extraordinary circumstances, the bottom line numbers were alarming. By the time principal photography had been completed, the shoot had covered an astounding 238 days spread over fifteen months.

When the United Artists executives met after the preview screening of *Apocalypse Now* to discuss what to do about the film and about Coppola, they agreed on two things: they didn't much like the movie, and they blamed themselves for losing control over the project. Had cooler heads prevailed at the meeting, the executives would have realized that they had far less to lose than they thought. They still were in the first position on an "event film" by America's most famous movie director. It would be hard, under such circumstances, not to make money. But cooler heads did not prevail, and the executives at United Artists decided to cut the studio's principal investment in the film to $7.5 million. Their reasoning was simple: since they did not control the project, the *auteur* should shoulder the risk.

Since the studio was bargaining from strength—Coppola had virtually no chance of completing and releasing the film without the studio's cooperation—United Artists got its way. In exchange for a principal investment of $7.5 million, UA retained domestic distribution rights to the film. As to the remaining budget expenses, UA agreed to *loan* Coppola sufficient funds to complete the picture. In what turned out to be a backhanded affirmation of *auteurism*, UA turned the film over to its *auteur*.

By the time the film was in the can, UA had loaned Coppola approximately $25 million, a sum partially secured by Coppola's considerable profit interest in the two *Godfather* films as well as certain other assets held in his own and American Zoetrope's name. But though the deal left him deep in debt and obliged to United Artists, the bottom line revealed that Coppola ostensibly owned the project—to the same extent that one "owns" a house or a car one purchases with a bank loan—and thus, within very few limits, he could do with the film what he pleased. As a result of his revised deal with United

Artists, Coppola ended up shouldering much of the risk for the film's future performance at the box office. But he also secured a degree of control over his own destiny that neither he nor any other director of his generation had ever enjoyed.

In their haste to alter the conditions of their deal with Coppola, the UA executives failed to appreciate how little they stood to gain financially by limiting their investment in the picture. By loaning Coppola the money to complete the film, they unintentionally set him up either to fail and subsequently default on the $25 million loan, or to succeed and in doing so humiliate UA in the eyes of the rest of the industry.

If the film went on to lose money, UA's only option if it wanted to get its $25 million back would be to foreclose on Coppola's corporate and personal assets. The studio would then have to weigh the immediate financial advantages of foreclosing on, for example, Coppola's house, against the very negative public relations such a move would no doubt engender. Moreover, even if the studio decided to seize *all* of the director's assets, the executives were well aware that the collateral Coppola put up to secure the loan was worth significantly less than $25 million. As a result—and this is the most ironic cut of all—the lion's share of the principal was essentially collateralized by Coppola's newest "asset," *Apocalypse Now,* the very film UA executives believed would bomb at the box office.

Coppola could continue to increase the budget with no regard for his own ability to pay UA back because the studio, as a condition of the renegotiation, had surrendered control over the amount of money Coppola could spend on the film. More problematic still for the studio, it could no longer enforce a firm completion date for the movie. Thus, like some endless nightmare baseball game, the production phase of *Apocalypse Now* slogged on and on. All UA could do was sit in the stands, so to speak, and watch the game.

Complicating matters further for UA was that Coppola's ability to pay the studio back hinged primarily on future profits from foreign distribution and various ancillary sales. But the studio executives' decision to cut their investment in the film implied that *they* thought the film was no good. This significantly compromised Coppola's ability to negotiate with foreign distributors and network and pay television executives—all of whom realized that UA had already bailed out on the picture.

In yet another Catch-22, the amount of money Coppola was likely to net from the disadvantageous foreign distribution and television exhibition deals once the film was in release was in direct proportion to the picture's domestic box office. Thus, once the film was completed, executives at UA had two choices. If they still hated the final cut, they could save money on the front end by stinting on the advertising budget and releasing the picture only to selected big city venues. But doing so would virtually guarantee that Coppola would default on the loan since a poor showing domestically would adversely affect foreign sales as well as ancillary deals with pay and network television.

The studio executives' second option, whether they liked the final cut or not, was to finance a major nationwide release with advertising appropriate for such a blockbuster. The second option at least allowed for the possibility of success at the box office, but it carried with it an even more daunting scenario: What if the public actually liked the film? The studio would get its money back, yes, but Coppola would get the last laugh. The UA executives had to decide which possibility was the more onerous: losing $32.5 million on one film or looking stupid while Coppola reaped the benefits of the film's box office success.

While the trades kept track of the various power struggles between UA and Coppola, Transamerica, UA's parent company based in San Francisco, watched from the periphery. Transamerica's primary concern at the time was not how well the film might do at the box office but how all the publicity about the film and Coppola's deals with the studio might affect Transamerica stock's price. Despite what emerged as an interesting little Hollywood story—regarding Coppola and UA, and *Apocalypse Now* and *auteurism*—Transamerica executives soon came to realize that in the larger scheme of things, one film, no matter how much it cost, and ultimately no matter how much negative press it received, had little or no effect on net stock value.

This, too, worked to Coppola's advantage. Even though UA had put itself in an untenable position with regard to the film, Transamerica simply couldn't be bothered to intervene. Thus, in a particularly lighthearted and self-mocking move, to commemorate the film's third year of production, Coppola bought his friend James Harvey, a Transamerica senior executive, a telescope and had it set it up in Harvey's office so he could focus on a plaque on Coppola's North Beach office building that read: "To Jim Harvey, from Francis Coppola, so you can keep an eye on me."[4] The gift struck Harvey as whimsical, but it sent a message back to the executives at UA that Coppola was essentially through dealing with them. The gift reminded UA executives of Coppola's friendship with their boss, James Harvey and at the same time seemed to indicate that Coppola believed that the movie was so good he could afford to make the joke.

When *Apocalypse Now* was finally ready for release, Coppola had yet another surprise for the industry. Despite all the problems he faced completing the film, the cost of making it was not, by 1979 standards at least, outrageously expensive. It cost less, for example, than *Moonraker, Flash Gordon,* and *Star Trek,* all of which were released the same year. But despite the *real* numbers, public perception—fueled by media hype—suggested otherwise. By the time *Apocalypse Now* opened nationwide, the production, as opposed to the film, had become the subject of virtually every article and review.

At the time, UA had to feel somewhat ambivalent when the press began to regard *Apocalypse Now* as a symptom of an industry out of control. Unsure whether or not it wanted the film to succeed—the studio seemed to lose either way—UA marketing executives never agreed on a way to release the picture. As a result, though it was well within their ability to change or at least redirect the press "line" on the film, UA did nothing to protect "their" property.

Though in many ways the pre- and postrelease critical and public response to *Apocalypse Now* was unfair, it did indicate that *auteurism* was at a sort of crossroads. In the early days of the so-called Hollywood *auteurist* renaissance, movies like *The Godfather* and *Jaws* not only signaled the "arrival" of university-educated *auteurs,* they also revealed the new guard's willingness—even anxiousness—to shoot Hollywood-style genre films. These were not rebels or artistes, but savvy players subtly updating the safe studio genre package. The big budgets were merely a product of the age; the *auteurs* were in many ways the lucky beneficiaries of such soft and high times.

But the amount of money invested in the director as commodity—the director as an insurance of box office success—seemed from the start to hinge on a fundamental capital risk: Times change, and one day, one of the studios would be caught with its money tied up in the last *auteur* movie. Certainly such a fear fueled UA's panic over *Apocalypse Now.* Given the film's production history and UA's various deals with Coppola along the way, the studio had every reason to believe that *Apocalypse Now* would mark the end of the *auteur* era.

Fortunately for Coppola, UA was wrong about *Apocalypse Now.* Unfortunately for UA, its next big project, *Heaven's Gate,* fulfilled the industry's worst fears about the *auteurist* blockbuster and all but put United Artists out of the movie business.

Heaven's Gate

Nobody really controls a production now; the director is on his own, even if he's insecure, careless or nuts. There has always been a megalomaniac potential in moviemaking, and in this period of stupor, when values have been so thoroughly undermined that even the finest directors and the ones with the most freedom aren't sure what they want to do, they often become obsessive and grandiloquent—like mad royalty. Perpetually dissatisfied with the footage they're compulsively piling up, they keep shooting—adding rooms to the palace.—Pauline Kael, 1980[5]

It isn't only in retrospect that *Apocalypse Now* and *Heaven's Gate* seem somehow connected. At the very same meeting during which the UA executives decided to cut their investment in *Apocalypse Now,* they made their first move toward mounting a "new Western" focusing on the Johnson County Wars.

The story behind UA's funding of *Heaven's Gate* goes something like this. In August 1978, as prerelease hype mounted around Michael Cimino's *The Deer Hunter,* Stan Kamen, Cimino's agent at William Morris, proposed a movie package to UA: *The Johnson County War,* an action-adventure western directed by Cimino and starring Kris Kristopherson. It is important to note that Kamen was not shopping for a development deal; in other words, he was not looking for seed money to begin work on a project. Instead he was asking for an immediate "go" commitment with "pay or play" options that obliged the studio to pay fees amounting to $1.7 million whether the film was produced or not.

The most attractive aspects of Kamen's proposal were the opportunity it presented for UA to produce Cimino's follow-up to *The Deer Hunter*—a film which, even before its release, had generated a lot of excitement in Hollywood—and Cimino's pre–Academy Award asking price, $500,000, a relatively modest director's fee for 1978. Additionally attractive was the film's relatively low projected budget ($7.5 million) and the fact that much of the preproduction would be handled by Kamen, who represented not only the director but many of the proposed cast members as well.

The Johnson County War was one of several projects discussed at that September meeting. Given that the meeting was essentially a wake over the rough cut of *Apocalypse Now,* Kamen's proposal was evaluated with regard to Coppola's ever forthcoming film. Ironically, the executives warmed to *The Johnson County War* because it seemed so unlike *Apocalypse Now.* Moreover, when the executives looked at their slate for the next few years, they saw that for 1979 they had two blockbuster films, *Moonraker* and *Rocky II,* and as things were set at that time, two potential blockbusters scheduled for release in 1981, both sequels to sequels: *For Your Eyes Only* and *Rocky III.* Exactly where *Apocalypse Now* fit in UA's future remained a mystery; after all, in

September 1978 the picture still seemed a long way from release and an even longer way from being a box office success.[6]

In retrospect, it is fair to assume that *The Johnson County War* seemed so good primarily because *Apocalypse Now* seemed so bad. In fact, UA gave Cimino's film the green light in order to fill the "blockbuster gap" created by *Apocalypse Now.* Of course, as fate would have it, it was the five-hour-and-twenty-minute *Heaven's Gate,* and not *Apocalypse Now,* that turned out to be unreleasable. And when a two-and-a-half hour version of *Heaven's Gate* was finally prepared for release, at a cost of approximately $36 million (though the press reported that the production cost as much as $100 million), it became *the* box office disaster of all time.

But while it is true that UA lost a great deal of money on *Heaven's Gate*—if we factor in advertising and distribution costs, the net loss approached $44 million—and made back more than its investment in *Apocalypse Now,* the industry as a whole suffered more from the success of Coppola's film than from Cimino's box office failure. After 1981, the studios were able to reclaim control over the "product" from powerful directors, all of whom, after *Heaven's Gate,* were potential Michael Ciminos.

The filmmakers themselves were at least partly to blame. They had so upped the stakes and the costs—they had so focused on making big movies—that they had, in effect, collectively risked their status on each and every prestige *auteurist* package. In the aftermath of *Heaven's Gate,* 1970s *auteurs* like Martin Scorsese, Robert Altman, Peter Bogdanovich, and William Friedkin, along with Cimino and Coppola, all proved unable to make a smooth transition into 1980s Hollywood.

Coppola's ruminations on the *Heaven's Gate* fiasco were at once sympathetic and philosophical and are worth repeating here. In an interview conducted, ironically, during the production of *One from the Heart,* his own *Heaven's Gate,* Coppola opined:

> I think what happened to *Heaven's Gate* has to do with much bigger, more fundamental problems about making a movie today. Traditionally, what happens is the director embarks on an adventure, and he's basically frightened of the so-called studio because he knows the people he's dealing with are not the kind of people with whom he wants to sit and discuss what he's really going for. So what he does is use his strength as a viable director to get all the rights: [especially] right of final cut. . . . As a result the studio is without much control. The director goes out and starts making his film. Realizing his life is going

to be affected with one throw of the dice the director starts protecting himself by trying to make it beautiful, spectacular, and one of a kind—almost without regard for what were the original priorities of the piece.[7]

In the immediate aftermath of the release of *Heaven's Gate*, even the most sympathetic in the media were hard-pressed to defend *auteur* Hollywood. The *Wall Street Journal*'s Joy Gould Boyum, for example, wrote: "The industry has to a degree abdicated to its directors. This is the victory those of us who care about films have always wished for, but it turns out now not to be precisely what we had in mind."[8] Striking a similar note, Vincent Canby of the *New York Times* added: "*Heaven's Gate*—the phenomenon not the movie—has been a long time coming, but to blame it on any one director or corporate management is vastly to oversimplify what's been happening to commercial American movies over the last several decades . . . the cost of making a movie, even a modest one, has soared even faster than the cost of everything else in the economy . . . the hits make more money than ever, while people won't even go to see a flop if it's free."[9]

While the *auteur* Hollywood renaissance seemed to come to a close with *Apocalypse Now* and then *Heaven's Gate*, it is important to note that Transamerica, which owned UA during the development and release of both films, emerged for the most part unaffected. Revenues at the insurance conglomerate rose to $4.04 billion in 1979, and in 1981, when *Heaven's Gate* realized the very blockbuster box office failure UA executives feared when they first viewed a rough cut of *Apocalypse Now*, Transamerica stock took an inconsequential and temporary dip of three-eighths of a point.

The Critics

Apocalypse Now is a failed quest—a common modern form—a search for the holy grail that doesn't exist. Like some topological puzzle, the end of the river brings one back to the beginning, although in a distorted and exaggerated, yet distilled and purified guise. . . . *Apocalypse Now* is about failure, and its quest could not responsibly end in success.—Ronald Bogue, academic film critic[10]

On May 11, 1979, with United Artists's approval, Francis Coppola sneak-previewed *Apocalypse Now* at Mann's Bruin Theater in Westwood (Los Angeles). Tickets, priced at $7.50, were to go on sale at 6:00 P.M. for an 8:00 P.M. show, but people began lining up at 9:30 A.M. Crowd control was provided by the legendary rock promoter Bill Graham, who had a small part in the

2 and 3. Before and after Zoetrope: *Apocalypse Now* (United Artists, 1979) and *Gardens of Stone* (Tri-Star Pictures, 1987).

film, and the excitement surrounding the screening prompted Larry Glea-son, the president of Mann Theaters, to announce (with glee, no doubt): "This is insanity. It's pandemonium."[11] From the second it hit the theaters, *Apocalypse Now* was exactly what Coppola had promised it would be: an event.

What should have been a triumphant moment for Coppola was muted by memories of the difficulties he had faced getting the film financed and finished and by the very strange, often personal, and deeply contradictory preliminary critical response to the film. It was as if no one, including Coppola himself, could get past all the hardware, all the time, all the money. "We made [the film] the way America made war in Vietnam," Coppola mused. "There were too many of us, too much money and equipment and little by little we went insane. I thought I was making a war film and it developed that the film was making me."[12]

Failing to read the temperature of the press, Coppola repeatedly empha-sized the myriad connections between the film and his life: "I found that many of the ideas and images with which I was working as a film director began to coincide with the realities of my own life, and that I, like Captain Willard, was moving up river in a faraway jungle, looking for answers and hoping for some kind of catharsis."[13] With *auteurism* nearing its end, Cop-pola's tendency to view filmmaking in grandiose terms—as an adventure, as a journey up the Mekong River—struck many critics as the worst kind of Hollywood egoistic hype.

Even those who rather liked the movie, *Sight and Sound*'s Michael Dempsey, for example, were concerned by the personal stakes Coppola seemed to raise with every film. "The gradiosity of Coppola," Dempsey wrote on the film's release, "is a matter of colossal fantasies of art, fantasies which only a particular kind of film director can possibly hope to challenge." For Dempsey, the problem with *Apocalypse Now* wasn't its politics or even its ending (cited by so many other critics), but rather the stakes of all so-called ultimate movies. "People like Coppola are expected to produce masterpieces at will each time they make a movie," Dempsey concluded. "They expect it of themselves; anything less is considered a disgrace, a betrayal."[14]

For the vast majority of those writing for the popular press, what was principally at stake was whether or not *Apocalypse Now* lived up to all the hype. On that score, only one major reviewer seemed willing to say that it had. Jack Kroll, writing for *Newsweek,* wrote: "The most important thing about Francis Coppola is that he is a wonderfully gifted filmmaker, and the miracle is that after all this madness he has brought us a stunning and unforgettable film."[15]

The rest of the reviews, even those in narrower-interest publications, seem all of a kind. In the *Nation,* for example, Robert Hatch complained that "Coppola seem[ed] to be achieving a bizarre public relations divinity, with attention shifting from the work itself to traumas attendant upon his accomplishing a haven of megalomania."[16] Stanley Kauffmann, in the *New Republic,* called the film's "jungle discotheque" look "hideously fantastic" and concluded that the blame for the film's failure lay with Coppola's egotistical need to make the "ultimate picture" on Vietnam. "[Coppola] likes size and he can use it," Kauffmann wrote. "Of course it can be argued that other American directors, given $30 million to pour, might also produce scenes of sweep and flourish, and Coppola simply couldn't have done it without money."[17]

When reviewers finished talking about the money, they focused on the ending, though in many cases different reviewers had seen different final scenes. By the end of 1979, four endings had been screened. The first, shown on early rough cuts for the industry and the press, presented a ground and air assault on the Kurtz compound stylized to look like the apocalypse in the film's title. Coppola eventually abandoned this ending because it seemed to undercut some of the film's more important moral gestures. Coppola rightly feared that this Milius-inspired *Gotterdammerung*-style finale with special effects worthy of a $30 million state-of-the-art Hollywood production seemed to highlight just how much the film depended on style at the expense of substance.

The second version of the ending appeared on the Cannes Film Festival answer print. In this ending, Willard kills Kurtz, but instead of ordering an air assault on the compound, he remains entranced by Kurtz's handiwork and contemplates taking the colonel's place. At the film's American premiere and through some of its first run screened in 70 mm, Coppola tried a third ending that shows Willard exiting the compound forlorn, unwilling to take Kurtz's place but unable to do much else besides head back downriver. Finally, by the time the 35-mm print of the film hit most theaters, and now in the video version of the film, Willard's exit is followed by credits superimposed over napalm explosions taken from the first, rough-cut finale.

Coppola's indecisiveness about the ending—a problem that would haunt virtually every Zoetrope Studio film over the next four years—seemed to indicate his political ambivalence.[18] If *Apocalypse Now* was the ultimate Vietnam picture,[19] the critics seemed to say, it had to make the ultimate political statement as well.

The one thing that the critics could not challenge was that all the money was "up there" on screen. But instead of applauding the film's scope and grandeur, they attacked Coppola for spending too much time and money getting the look and feel as opposed to the politics of the times right. Because Coppola seemed to ignore politics—because he seemed unable or uninterested in making a liberal Hollywood statement—many of the critics argued that the film was deeply conservative. One critic went so far as to call the film "monstrously illiberal"; a second argued that it was "as conservative as *Birth of a Nation*."[20] And, in what has become one of the most frequently cited attacks on Coppola and the film, former American Zoetrope member and *Apocalypse Now* scenarist John Milius called his onetime mentor "a raving fascist, the Bay Area Mussolini."[21]

In virtually every review, the critics assessed what the film meant in relation to the economic conditions of the new Hollywood. In doing so, they unintentionally met the film on its own terms. When critics attacked the film for its autobiographical subtext, they foregrounded the industry's growing disinterest in the personal; when they attacked Coppola for being apolitical or worse, politically conservative, and for paying too much attention to style and not enough to content—a lament that has come to characterize the critical line on Coppola for the past fifteen years—the critics stumbled on just how completely Coppola had embraced the notion of *auteurism* as it had been discussed when he was a student at UCLA. For Coppola, working in a genre-based cinema like Hollywood, style *was* the determining factor of authorship. By affirming Coppola's attention to style, the critics were merely remarking that Coppola was, despite all the money and all the battles with the studio, still an *auteur*.

The Memorandum

The question of whether Coppola had a breakdown on *Apocalypse Now* is prime gossip material. But it only veils the grim truth that the movie director in America is rarely adult enough to lose his mind.—David Thomson, film critic[22]

On April 30, 1977, during the production of *Apocalypse Now*, Francis Coppola sent a memo to his fellow workers at American Zoetrope in San Francisco which, even by Hollywood standards, was astonishingly fatuous and paranoid. The memo was eventually leaked to *Esquire* magazine and subsequently reprinted in its entirety some six months later.[23] Coppola later tried to put the memo into perspective, noting that he wrote it just days after Sheen suffered his heart attack and the news of Coppola's affair with a younger woman on location in the Philippines reached his wife, Eleanor, in San Francisco. Additionally, he pointed out that the memo resulted from political infighting at American Zoetrope. As Coppola put it in a 1992 interview, "I felt my own staff was jockeying for political position, trying to bring my wife into it. And I wanted to organize things more clearly, and I wrote this memo to set things straight—and they published it. And everyone made fun of me, and I was very embarrassed."[24]

Coppola's apparent paranoia was only part of the story; indeed, to paraphrase William Burroughs, sometimes being paranoid means simply that you have all the facts. Things were going wrong in Coppola's life and in his work, and at the time he was far less willing (than his wife, for example) to blame himself than some mystical force that seemed to be mounting against him. In the grandiose scheme of things that had come to characterize Coppola's world vision at the time—which, too, seems a result of the scale and scope of things at the far end of *auteurism*—the things that kept going wrong with *Apocalypse Now* had less to do with artistic vision than they had to do with the Fates. He saw himself as a tragic hero, a role for which he seemed a natural.

The first line of the memo set the tone: "This company [then called Zoetrope] will be known as American Zoetrope and, purely and simply, it is me and my work." Coppola then further clarified his position: "We will not be in the service business . . . but rather will maintain these facilities in order to better realize my own projects. Therefore you really are not employees of a company—instead, the staff of an artist, very much like the crew of a motion picture."[25] "Wherever I am," Coppola concluded unselfconsciously, "will be considered the headquarters of the company."[26]

Much of the memo attended to the issue of money. Knowing that a showdown was imminent between himself and UA over the cost of the movie, Coppola explained: "I am cavalier about money because I have to be in order not to be terrified every time I make an artistic decision. Remember, the major studios have only one thing a filmmaker needs: capital." In response to reports that the budget was spiralling toward $70 million, Coppola decided not to simply dismiss the rumors as outrageous exaggerations, which they were, but instead chose to reestablish his adversarial position vis-à-vis the industry establishment: "My flamboyant disregard for the rules of capital and business is one of my major strengths when dealing with [the studios]. It evens the score, so to speak."[27]

To even his most loyal employees, Coppola must have seemed mad (like Kurtz? like Willard?); to those in power in the industry, he sounded an awful lot like a man spoiling for a fight. Either way, the memo reveals Coppola's instability at the precise moment he seemed committed to taking on the studio establishment.

Though the memo was never meant for public purview, its publication in

Esquire gave the moviegoing public its first real indication of just how out of control the film and its director were. For those with even a cursory understanding of abnormal human psychology, Coppola seemed deeply paranoid. "Please remember," he noted near the end of the memo, "my name is Francis Coppola. I am dropping the Ford. This comes from a statement I once heard: 'Never trust a man who has three names.' "[28] Stranger still were the various tragic heroic postures he saved for the memo's conclusion. "I've heard that success is as difficult to deal with as failure—perhaps more so," Coppola mused, "Euripides, the Greek playwright said thousands of years ago: 'Whom God wishes to destroy, he first makes successful in show business.' "[29]

One from the Heart: What's $25 Million More or Less in the New Hollywood?

When we announced *One from the Heart* at a press conference, we talked about technology, about methods, about talent. . . . But all they wanted to know about was the problem with the money.—Francis Coppola, 1981[30]

At the 1979 Academy Awards, with *Apocalypse Now* basically complete but not yet released, Coppola was called on to present the Oscar for Best Director. On-stage, Coppola eschewed the cue cards and instead took the opportunity to make a prediction about the future of the industry, a future in which he planned to remain an important player. "I can see a communications revolution that's about movies and art and music and digital electronics and satellites but above all, human talent," he announced. "It's going to make the masters of the cinema, from whom we've inherited the business, believe things they would have thought impossible."[31]

With the purchase of Hollywood General a little over a year later, Coppola set about making good on his prediction. By the time shooting began on *One from the Heart* on February 2, 1981, Coppola had already mapped out a new "electronic cinema" process, a truly revolutionary method for shooting a movie employing state-of-the-art video technology. *One from the Heart,* Coppola mused, would succeed because of the method; and conversely, the method would catch on once the film succeeded at the box office. "On one level," he told novelist Gay Talese in an *Esquire* interview, "*One from the Heart* is a thrust into a new technology . . . it's different from anything I've done before—anything anyone's done before."[32]

Though such hyperbole was characteristic of Coppola and seemed in line with the prerelease hype on all of the "ultimate movies" coming out at that time, Coppola's emphasis on technologies that might force the other studios to retool or regroup focused a kind of industrywide attention on *One from the Heart* that the film itself could ill afford. Additionally, the film and the technological revolution it seemed to herald came at a particularly bad time for the studios. They had just begun to deal with the "revolutionary" videocassette and cable television technologies (and markets) and thus felt particularly threatened by talk about yet another new, new Hollywood.

Though the studios had historically eschewed research and development, their battle with Sony seemed to suggest a need to at least start thinking about the future. Coppola's continued focus on that future made the studios nervous, even though, financially speaking, he had little chance of ever realizing his ambition.

The primary problem posed by Zoetrope Studios was that Coppola had considerable access to (and was of considerable interest in) the mass media. Though *One from the Heart* was just a film, and Zoetrope just a small and severely undercapitalized studio, the press seemed inclined to *promote* Coppola's plans.[33] And the more the press repeated Coppola's version of the future of Hollywood, the more possible it seemed to become.

Coppola's focus on distribution and exhibition technologies—the very disturbing aspect of the home box office debate that the studios had hoped they put behind them after successfully dealing with the Screen Actors Guild and then with Sony in 1980—no doubt made all the press attention to *One from the Heart* particularly rankling. In order to protect their position—in order to maintain control over the distribution and exhibition of motion pictures in the United States—and in order to send a message about the shape of things to come in the industry, it was necessary for the studios to make sure that Coppola would not be able to fund his research. In order to do that, the studios had to make sure that *One from the Heart,* the film on which the entire studio depended, bombed at the box office. And that, alas, was easy for them to do.

Though it is tempting to wax conspiratorial here, there is no evidence of any accord among the studios to "get Coppola." But the production problems that plagued the film—all of which, more or less, had to do with capital secured through the major studio–big bank apparatus—seem at the very least to indicate an unstated industrywide decision to make the movie as difficult to produce as possible.

Coppola's first big problem with the studios came about early on, when he began negotiating for production financing for the film. MGM, after expressing significant interest in the project, mysteriously balked at providing a completion guarantee.[34] On the heels of the MGM rebuff, the Chase Manhattan Bank refused to float Zoetrope a loan underwriting the production, thus, for the time being, at least, forcing Coppola to suspend preproduction.

Though it did not make much sense at the time (unless one took into account the larger issues raised by One from the Heart), MGM's treatment of Coppola was hardly unprecedented; studios regularly get cold feet over projects they previously promise to support. Though he may have not understood exactly why MGM decided to back out, Coppola responded rather calmly to the snub and simply resumed shopping the film around.

He found a buyer rather quickly in Barry Diller at Paramount,[35] the distributor of both Godfather films, but the deal was hardly sweet. While Diller expressed a desire to distribute the film, he offered no cash up front and no completion guarantee either. What Diller did promise was that Paramount would, on its completion (and, one gathers, approval), release six hundred prints of the film domestically on a specified date (February 10, 1982) and at that time spend $4 million to advertise the movie. Since no footage had yet been shot, a release date was provided solely to symbolize Paramount's earnest interest, but in reality neither Coppola nor Paramount could be held to the specifics of the agreement.

In the meantime, Coppola continued to map out the production of One from the Heart, and despite cool major studio interest in the project, the preliminary budget kept getting higher. Before a single foot of film had been shot, the movie's proposed budget soared from $15 to $23 million. Having been stung in different ways by Apocalypse Now and Heaven's Gate, the majors, which in the business climate at the start of the 1980s had already begun to think collusively if not collectively, were hardly anxious to invest in yet another prestige auteur film. And Coppola's hype that One from the Heart was a kind of trial run for his new technology just made matters worse. No studio wanted to fund Zoetrope's research and development without a stake in the technologies' future use and revenues.

The studios' reluctance to support Coppola's Zoetrope project was, of course, understandable. But the studios had more to fear from themselves than from Coppola. Without studio production financing—and, far more importantly, studio distribution for One from the Heart—Coppola had virtually no chance of realizing his goals. (Even with their financing, his success still seemed doubtful.) But what if Coppola somehow got One from the Heart made and it was not only the next Godfather but the next Raiders of the Lost Ark, too? Could Paramount, for example, trust Columbia not to opt for the considerable short-term profits earned by such a film despite the possibility that the film's success might eventually adversely affect the studios' long-term future? Ironically, Coppola's only real chance to get *One from the Heart* shot and into the theaters was to play on the studios' short-term thinking and greed, which was precisely what he had hoped to get away from when he purchased Hollywood General. Of course, in order to exploit the studios' greed, he would have to make a movie like *Raiders of the Lost Ark,* which at the time was not at all what he wanted to do.

Production began on *One from the Heart* without any real guarantee that completion funds would ever be available. Paramount, unlike UA during the production of *Apocalypse Now,* held a strategic advantage. While UA had to release *Apocalypse Now* in order to recoup its investment and enable Coppola to pay them back,[36] Paramount had wisely set up what in industry argot is termed a "back-end deal," in which the studio can withhold production funds until after a film is complete and approved. In terms the *men* who run the industry readily understand, such a deal brings to mind a rather graphic sexual image that illustrates not only this type of arrangement but the power relations inherent in virtually all studio-artist relationships.

Given that the Paramount deal was little better than MGM's, Chase Manhattan remained unwilling to float a production loan. That Coppola went ahead and began the production phase of the film anyway epitomized what he termed in the *Apocalypse Now* memo a "flamboyant disregard for the rules of capital." In what would be, alas, his last bit of bombast on the subject of *One from the Heart,* just days before Paramount all but destroyed its chances at the box office, Coppola offered the following account of the financing of the film: "We had maybe one scary week [during the production] but what I did was sit down and say, 'Lookit, I got this movie and if I can bluff my way through two weeks I'm going to have so much movie done the question will be, who will step forward to stop me?' Once I had it going, it was a potential something—to the bank a potential asset, to the industry a new film—I knew that it would take a lot of energy to stop me. That's exactly what happened. We bluffed our way. We started production without the money. After two weeks we had enough of a movie completed to be in forward drive."[37]

According to Zoetrope Studios president Robert Spiotta, the film finally cost just under $27 million to produce; this after a preliminary budget of $15 million and a "final" production budget of $23 million. As Coppola had hoped, the money surfaced once (and because) the film was under way. First Chase Manhattan lent $8 million; then, as production costs mounted, the bank added another $4 million; and then, on the strength of foreign presales of distribution rights, the bank provided another $7 million. Smaller loans—in the $1 million vicinity—were provided by Norman Lear (who at the time asked to remain anonymous), Barry Diller and Michael Eisner at Paramount,[38] and the Security Pacific National Bank (already one of several lien holders on the studio).

An additional $3 million came from Canadian real estate tycoon Jack Singer, a relative newcomer to the entertainment business. The Calgary-based financier's show business experience at the time was limited to an investment in the still unreleased Canadian film *Surfacing* and a failed attempt with his brother Hymie to outbid Gulf and Western for control of Canada's largest theater chain, Famous Players.

Little in Singer's portfolio prepared anyone in the industry for his emergence as Coppola's white knight. But those who knew Singer realized that he had long wanted to become a player in Hollywood. As he told *Variety* in March 1981, he invested in *One from the Heart* not only because of his long-standing interest in the entertainment business but also because it gave him a chance to start at the top.

Singer proved to be a natural for Hollywood. Announcing his decision to invest in *One from the Heart,* he gushed: "Coppola's the kind of person I really like. He's like a national treasure. If they let a guy like that go down the tubes, it would be a tragedy. I'm interested in the person. He's my type of guy."[39] But as Coppola and the rest of the industry would soon discover, Singer knew enough not to invest much in hype. From the very start he was prepared to make his move should *One from the Heart* bomb. As his brother Hymie glibly put it in a subsequent interview in *Variety:* "If *One from the Heart* doesn't pay, we will wind up with the studio."[40]

Also in March 1981, just as Singer's $3 million seemed to clear up the film production picture, Coppola again pressed his luck. First he added thirty-two days to the shooting schedule, and then he began to rethink and redesign what would become the film's signature scene: the dazzling opening credit sequence which simulates, in a moment of pure cinematic postmodernism, a flight through deserted Las Vegas streets, exaggerating the big sign–little building architecture described in Robert Venturi, Denise Brown, and Steve Izenour's postmodern primer, *Learning from Las Vegas.*[41]

To pay for the additional shooting days and the special effects required to execute the sequence, Coppola planned to turn to Paramount, which had stipulated in the most nebulous of terms that it might provide up to $4 million in additional production funds should Coppola require them. But in what turned out to be a major strategic error, Coppola decided to shoot the footage first and ask for the money later. By the time Coppola went to Diller to ask for the additional $4 million, the footage was already in the can and the money already spent. Miffed that he was not consulted in advance about the budget overage, Diller took a first step toward backing out of the film and refused to front Coppola the cash.

At the time, Coppola contended that he had waited until the film was complete before going to Diller because he wanted to know precisely how much money to ask for. But Diller, for reasons that went beyond his evaluation of the movie and its potential at the box office, was simply seizing an opportunity to obstruct the film's production. Having already "spent" money he didn't have, Coppola turned again to the Chase Manhattan Bank.[42] He was dangerously overextended, but after he agreed to put up both his Napa Valley winery and the studio as collateral,[43] Chase Manhattan provided sufficient funds to complete the picture.

The Electronic Cinema Method

Every time I make a movie, every time I want to make a film, every time I want to sponsor a filmmaker, I have to go, hat in hand, to a series of studio executives who don't have my background and my experience. [And then] when a good film comes along, one that they think will work with the public, they act a little bit like Danton, who when the rabble rushed by his house to make a revolution ran out behind them to lead them.—Francis Coppola, 1982[44]

Though the $27 million production cost of *One from the Heart* belied Coppola's claims that it streamlined the production process and cut costs, the electronic cinema method, in theory, still seems a viable, perhaps even a revolutionary method.[45] First, the entire screenplay is composed in paragraph (as opposed to standard script) form and entered into a computer. Storyboard sketches are then added to accompany the script paragraphs. (In *One from the Heart*, for example, there were more than five hundred such sketches.) The storyboard entries are transferred to video, then duplicated and distributed to a variety of production departments (for wardrobe, set design, etc.).

The actors are then called in to read their lines (like a radio play). Their recorded dialogue is synched to the storyboard sketches, and then sound effects and songs are added. The sketches are subsequently reshot on Polaroid stills with the actors standing in front of the sets, thus completing a process Coppola termed "previsualization." Previsualization enables a director to edit an entire movie before committing anything to 35-mm film, thus

4. Coppola in his trailer, the Silverfish, the headquarters of his electronic cinema process. Photo by Ralph Nelson Jr. (Lucasfilm, 1988).

extending the boundaries of "development" and streamlining the production phase into a "simple" execution of a preconceived, previsualized look.

Postproduction is similarly streamlined. All of the processed film—in other words, all the scenes that are shot and developed in 35 mm—are routinely transferred to videotape and the tape is then coded. A rough cut is executed in video and subsequently turned over to a film editor, who matches the coded tape to the negative. An added benefit of such a postproduction method is that a completely edited film can be made available for release quite soon after the production phase is complete. Since all films are financed with bank loans, a reduction in lag time can save the distributor of a picture a significant amount of money in interest charges.

As things began to unravel at Zoetrope—after the first couple of weeks of filming *One from the Heart*—Zoetrope's electronic cinema division director (and former Lucasfilm special effects chief), Thomas Brown, was working on a light pen that would enable illustrators to draw straight onto the previsualized sketches. He had in mind a huge database onto which the various hands that affect a film could literally draw onto the previsualized text. Ultimately, Brown promised, "[we] will take the film out of filmmaking altogether."[46]

But despite the practicality and promise of the electronic cinema method, Coppola's inability to resist making yet another "ultimate film" undermined the process. By 1981, the whole concept of cost cutting was absurd once a Coppola production got rolling.

The sets on *One from the Heart* cost over $4 million, and the opening credit sequence by itself added another $4 million to the budget. Coppola took an additional $3 million as compensation for directing the movie, and thus, even before he paid the actors, the cinematographer and art director, and the Teamsters, he had already spent what amounted to the studio average for a completed feature movie.

Coppola's specific and uncompromised sense of how the film should look led to a seemingly endless set of difficult production problems, which further escalated costs. For example, in order to create a look similar to 1930s and 1940s film musicals, he insisted on shooting the film in the "square-r," or Academy aspect ratio (1.33: 1), which produces a square-ish (as opposed to the more conventional rectangular) image. But once he began shooting, he discovered that the tops of the sets (which more than two hundred carpenters were needed to make) were visible. The problem was solved when the ceilings were painted and heavy netting was applied to create a more three-dimensional (and theatrical) feel. When Coppola viewed the dailies on video, however, he realized that the netting needed to be painted blue, not black. Set designer Dean Tavoularis then had the nets painted blue, but the second coat of paint was too heavy and the ceilings began to sag. After replacing and repainting the ceilings, Tavoularis decided that it would be nice if there were stars on the ceilings as well, and given the scale of the production no one seemed willing to tell him not to bother. After five tries, the ceilings were finally ready and production continued, until the next problem . . .

Coppola's plans for the film—his sense of what the film was, what it should be—were never clear. In one interview, he claimed that he wanted to make a little relationship film, but then he added that he wanted to experiment with a radically different theatrical style. He succeeded in establishing a method in which production tasks were better coordinated, but then he hired cinematographer Vittorio Storaro and art designer Dean Tavoularis, both of whom had worked on *Apocalypse Now* and were hardly accustomed to worrying about production costs. Coppola no doubt appreciated Storaro's and Tavoularis's ability to help him achieve the film's breathtaking look, but their participation also contributed to the film's $27 million budget.

Even after it was completed, Coppola seemed singularly incapable of talking about *One from the Heart* coherently or even rationally:

> I thought, what would happen if you just took the story—a guy, a girl, another guy, another girl (as simple as it could be, dumb but sweet)— and set it in Las Vegas? And I'm walking down the Ginza—the Ginza's in the heart of Tokyo, and it looks just like Las Vegas—thinking that Las Vegas is the last frontier of America. When they ran out of land, they built Las Vegas, and it was built on those notions of life and chance— which to me, are sort of like love. You know how things come together when what you're interested in and emotionally attached to, just by accident, kind of hits a resounding thing in you? So I said, why . . . not make it like one of those films that they make a series out of—relationship films—but make it kind of like a Kabuki play set in Las Vegas![47]

In the early 1980s, the studios were turning their attention to high-concept pictures, projects that could be reduced to a single tag line. Coppola's *One from the Heart* seemed hardly to fit that trend. That the film can't be described in a single sentence—or at least a single sentence that makes any sense—not only reveals its unmarketability but the director's ongoing confusion about the picture. *One from the Heart* is a terrific movie, I think, because of all its confusion, because of Coppola's refusal or inability to scale things down. But it was not the film he needed to make in 1981, and as a result, his studio, his career, and the electronic cinema method suffered.

One from the Heart: What's One Studio More or Less in the New Hollywood?

One from the Heart suffered from the perception of me as some wild, egomaniac, Donald Trump type of guy, and once they think about you that way, it's just so many months before you're brought down.—Francis Coppola, 1992[48]

In order to satisfy complicated state film-exhibition regulations, on August 19, 1982, Paramount held a screening of a rough cut of *One from the Heart*. Coppola had not yet synched the evocative, narrative music track onto the print, and many of the elegant dissolves from one theatrical setpiece to another were not yet in evidence. With two such essential stylistic elements missing from a film that so depended on style, it is hardly surprising that the exhibitors' reaction was cold. One exhibitor broke with protocol and revealed his reaction to the *San Francisco Examiner*'s film critic, Judy Stone, who then further broke with industry-press ethics by quoting (but not naming) the exhibitor in her column. The exhibitor's response was damning: "I almost think the film is unreleasable. How can these talented Big People be so wrong. . . . Does Francis have people all around him mesmerized so that they can't even tell him the truth?"[49]

The exhibitors' reaction to the film had an immediate effect on Coppola's already uneasy relationship with Diller and Paramount. *One from the Heart* was not—as Diller had once hoped or, perhaps, as he had once feared—a potential blockbuster. Thus, there was no longer any reason for Paramount to hold onto the picture. Since Diller had insisted on a back-end deal when he contracted for domestic distribution rights to *One from the Heart*, the studio was not obliged to "pay or play"; it could, at any time, simply refuse to distribute the picture.

At the same time, Diller was under no pressure to discuss the studio's position with Coppola and he was under no obligation to act (to nix the deal) in a timely fashion. Diller took full advantage and decided to wait as long as possible before telling Coppola about his plans to drop the picture. It was a particularly callous move designed not only to protect the studio but to completely undermine the film's chances at the box office and, by extension, the feasibility of the studio collateralized against its revenues.

Unaware of the extent of Paramount's dissatisfaction with the picture, Coppola turned to the trades to vent his frustration, alleging that the studio previewed the film without his permission. It was an offensive strategy that would have been effective only had the film been so good that the studio could not afford not to release it. At the time, he seemed genuinely unaware of just how much Diller and Eisner disliked the movie and just how badly they wanted an excuse to nix the distribution deal. By going public with his dissatisfaction, Coppola invited Paramount to snub him publicly, and it did.

On January 15, 1982, to counter the bad press accompanying the Paramount exhibitors' screening of the rough cut, Coppola previewed a far more polished print himself (without Paramount's advance permission) to two sold-out audiences at the Radio City Music Hall Theater in New York. The Radio City previews became the subject of considerable industry speculation when, three days later, Paramount finally announced that it had decided to terminate its distribution deal with Zoetrope.

Many in the industry suspected that Coppola's grandstand move at Radio City had embarrassed the studio. But at the time, Diller told the press that the deal had been torn up the day before the Radio City screenings and that he had delayed the announcement of Paramount's decision not to distribute *One from the Heart* in deference to Coppola's planned New York preview.[50] Though Coppola later argued that he had screened the film in order to show Paramount that the San Francisco previews were misleading, and that he had hoped to convince Diller that the film could indeed be an event if handled properly, Paramount unloaded the movie and in doing so effectively destroyed its chances at the box office.

In retrospect, Coppola's Radio City ploy seems a clumsy, foolhardy maneuver. But at the time it struck many in the industry as both bold and strategically sound. For example, writer-director Paul Schrader dubbed Coppola's decision to preview the picture at Radio City "a brilliant move," then added, "If [*One from the Heart*] is a hit [Coppola] can wipe out a year of bad publicity." A "writer friend" of Coppola's similarly seemed unwilling to count the director out: "Francis is a genius at manipulating the media, and I'll bet he pulls it off again. Just remember: this isn't the story of a little guy against the system. Francis *is* the system." Finally, even a "Paramount insider" allowed that the Radio City previews might save the picture. "We might well have backed the idea," he confessed to the press, "if Francis had come to us with it."

In his own defense, Coppola summed up the situation as follows: "As soon as things started going bad with Paramount I decided to open the film. . . . It's like being rejected by your lover; it gives you an excuse to call someone else . . . so I thought, let's have a perfect screening—a big screen, good projection, a 1.33 ratio [the pre-CinemaScope screen shape, 1.33 times as wide as it is high] so the heads don't get chopped off. Let 6,000 people see it, not six exhibitors. Besides, I own the picture, not Paramount. It's up to me to make it a success. If it is, we'll be able to make eight to ten pictures a year. If not, the banks get the studio."[51]

Once the euphoria attending the gala premiere died away, Coppola began to more realistically consider the film's box office potential. The situation, he soon realized, was grim. Finding himself with no distributor for *One from the Heart* less than a month before its scheduled release, Coppola faced the fact that, before his first Zoetrope picture ever reached the theaters, the banks would indeed get the studio.

Soon after Paramount's decision to back out, Coppola began talking about not distributing the picture at all. "The best thing with this movie might be to make it impossible for people to see it," Coppola told the press, "and let people imagine what it is. Maybe I'll just withdraw the picture. Five years from now, I'll show it."[52]

However interesting such a strategy might have sounded, Coppola simply couldn't afford to wait. Though it was "his" film (even more so than *Apocalypse Now*), the bottom line was that he owed Chase Manhattan Bank and Jack Singer almost $27 million. The longer he waited to release the film, the more interest accrued on the loans.

Because Zoetrope (and Coppola personally) was in no position to carry the debt load, Robert Spiotta immediately began fielding alternative distribution offers from other studios. But as the Zoetrope president glibly told an interviewer at the time: "In this industry, the greater your need the worse your deal."[53] And Zoetrope was in dire need. Thus, the best Spiotta could manage on such short notice was the following five options: (1) a two-picture deal with Warners for both *One from the Heart* and (the as yet "undeveloped") *The Outsiders,* (2) a distribution deal with Columbia for a limited release of *One from the Heart,* (3) a distribution deal for *One from the Heart* with Orion (under the Filmways banner), (4) a deal for *One from the Heart* with Universal, or (5) a distribution deal with either Columbia or Warners for just *The Outsiders.*

Each choice posed a different kind of problem. The two-picture deal from Warner Brothers, which on the surface sounded the sweetest, stemmed from the studio's keen interest in the teen movie project, *The Outsiders.* Though Coppola and Spiotta had reason to be optimistic about how Warners would handle the release of the teen picture, it was unclear exactly how the studio planned to handle the distribution of *One from the Heart.*

The Columbia deal at least identified *One from the Heart* as the picture of interest. But given all the bad publicity attending the film's production and Coppola's problems with Paramount, the proposed limited opening, which would expand only if the film caught on immediately, sounded at least as bad as Warners's halfhearted offer to release the film nationwide.

The problem with the Orion deal was a little more complicated. Orion, like Zoetrope, was another so-called alternative studio. With some luck Orion might have afforded Coppola the chance to market *One from the*

Heart as a radically new movie of a sort the big studios were too conservative to understand. But while going with Orion sounded good in theory, Orion was still in the process of taking over Filmways, the banner under which it had proposed to release *One from the Heart*. Thus, despite his considerable interest in working with the smaller studio, Coppola simply could not afford to wait until the Orion-Filmways deal was finalized and the studio was in a position to release the picture.

The terms of the Universal offer were considerably worse than the original Paramount deal. Universal offered $6 million for the domestic distribution rights and the network and pay television and videocassette rights as well. That is, for just $2 million more than Paramount had offered, Universal wanted to control the film in every available domestic venue.

At the time, the possibility of receiving up-front cash in a distribution deal for just *The Outsiders* with either Warners or Columbia seemed to have potential because Zoetrope would then be able to use the development money to mount a limited release of *One from the Heart*. But while that option sounded inviting, Coppola realized just how small such a release would have to be and how little time he had before his creditors started placing liens against his assets.

One thing was clear in all the offers: no one was all that interested in distributing *One from the Heart*. Spiotta had hoped to secure a deal similar to the one that had been nixed by Paramount: a six hundred print release and $4 million in advertising in exchange for the right to distribute the film domestically. Failing that, he had hoped at least to find a studio that could be enthusiastic about the movie. But after Paramount's decision to pull out, no one in the industry seemed willing to fake it.

In the meantime, rumors leaked from Zoetrope that Coppola had decided to release the film himself without first selling off the rights to *The Outsiders*. In response to these rumors—which were most likely disseminated by Spiotta or Coppola to test exhibitor interest—several big-city venues contacted the studio. The Plitt and Loews chains both vied for exclusivity, and several key theaters in Denver, Las Vegas, Chicago, Boston, Washington, and Long Island placed bids.

At first, Spiotta hoped to use the considerable exhibitor interest in the film to negotiate a sweeter deal with one of the major studios. Instead, ironically, the arrangement Spiotta was most inclined to accept in the first place—the two-picture deal with Warners that promised some kind of release for *One from the Heart* and up-front cash for the rights to *The Outsiders*—fell apart precisely because of the rumor that Zoetrope might release *One from the Heart* itself. Because all of the other deals were unacceptable, Spiotta was forced to act on a rumor he had made up himself. In frustration, Spiotta confessed to the press: "From a practical point of view, distributing this film beyond an initial release without a distribution organization [is] madness."[54]

In preparation for a Zoetrope limited release, Spiotta ordered twenty-five (as opposed to Paramount's promised six hundred) prints. By the time the prints were ready, a deal had been struck with Columbia. Unlike Warners, which wanted *The Outsiders* as well, or Universal, which insisted on protecting itself by demanding all the ancillary rights to the film, Columbia seemed willing to take a chance so long as it didn't have to put much money up front. Additionally, Columbia expressed interest in a long-term relationship with Coppola despite the distinct possibility that *One from the Heart* would not do well at the box office.

After signing the deal with Columbia, Coppola and Spiotta remained concerned about the studio's lack of enthusiasm. To placate them, Columbia issued a press release that both announced the distribution deal and further claimed that after a recent screening of the movie (the second such screening for most of them), executives at the studio had all quite suddenly fallen in love with *One from the Heart*.[55] It is hard to imagine that anyone in the business, including Coppola and Spiotta, believed them.

Columbia decided to meet what had been Paramount's, and had become Zoetrope's, commitment to release the film in time for Valentine's Day. But since Columbia had not agreed to distribute the film until late in January, there was no time to get a trailer into the theaters or ads into the papers. Indeed, there was no time to turn the film into the kind of event it had to be in order to make money.

Moreover, Columbia proved unwilling or unable to manage the press's reaction to the whole distribution controversy. Paramount's exit seemed to indicate that the film was, as the article in the *San Francisco Examiner* suggested, "unreleasable." The press focused mercilessly on Zoetrope's financial problems and Coppola's seeming carelessness with money. As a result, by the time the film was set for release, it was the wrong kind of event—a film *not* to be seen.

Then there were the initial reviews, many of which were vicious. Vincent Canby of the *New York Times* wrote: "Nothing had quite prepared me for the staggering number of wrong choices made by one of our most talented and adventurous filmmakers."[56] Other reviewers followed suit, and Columbia panicked. To solve the film's image problem, the studio turned to Cambridge Survey Research, a market research firm that had gained prominence from its work on Jimmy Carter's 1976 presidential campaign. But it was already too late.

Exit surveys—which should have been done before the film was officially in release and before an ad campaign was designed—revealed that the film did best with a narrow audience: college-educated single white men between the ages of twenty-six and thirty-five. The market research company suggested that Columbia should stick with its limited, primarily urban opening in order to exploit that audience but was unable to come up with a useful plan to reach anybody else.

The Cambridge team then proposed three advertising pitches: the first banking on Coppola's "name recognition," the second touting *One from the Heart* as an "innovative" project like Coppola's previous work, and the third defining the film as a love story "captured by the extraordinary atmosphere of fantasy-photography, scenery, lighting and music."[57] Cambridge further suggested that Coppola should make a personal appeal for the film on radio and television explaining why people should go to see *One from the Heart*.

What the Cambridge market researchers failed to understand was that the problem with the film *was* Coppola; people had tired of his bombast, and they were put off by all the money it cost to make his movies. The less *he* said about the film the better. Had they taken the time to check the kinds of things Coppola told the press whenever reporters asked for his opinion, the market researchers would have told him to keep his mouth shut.

Given the uselessness of the market researchers' suggestions, Columbia turned to its own distribution department for help. Predictably, instead of trying to come up with an original strategy to reach the mass audience, they simply plugged *One from the Heart* into a release package that had proven successful for a supposedly similar movie. While Columbia claimed in the trades that it was going to use new marketing methods, it instead began to advertise *One from the Heart* the same way it had just successfully marketed Roman Polanski's *Tess*. In other words, the studio attempted to define *One from the Heart* as an art movie with a potentially wider than usual appeal. Since it had opened *Tess* in the major urban markets and then rode positive word of mouth to some box office success, Columbia executives continued to talk themselves into a limited-release strategy, screening *One from the Heart* in just twenty-five theaters in nine cities.

The strategy was a bust. After just seven weeks, *One from the Heart* was dying—playing at just one theater. Instead of mounting an expensive and embarrassing national release, at the end of April 1982, with Coppola's consent, Columbia pulled the film.

Though *One from the Heart* rather quickly took its place as one of the biggest box office failures in modern cinema history, the big news at Columbia at

5. Nastassia Kinski in Coppola's ill-fated *One from the Heart* (Columbia Pictures, 1982).

the time was not *One from the Heart* but rather the purchase of the studio by Coca Cola. The $4 million Columbia lost on *One from the Heart* seems inconsequential in light of the $700 million the studio grossed in 1982 and the $5.9 billion made by Coca-Cola.

But for Coppola, whose assets were tied to loans supporting the studio and the film, the failure of *One from the Heart* was devastating. In the wake of the dismal showing at the box office, Coppola announced that, after less than two years in operation, Zoetrope Studios was for sale.

The Critics

In Sweden, they really seem to like the movie.—Francis Coppola, 1982[58]

On January 20, 1982, still almost two weeks before the film was scheduled to premiere, *Variety* ran its review of *One from the Heart*. Since at the time the film was without a distributor, the review was read with real interest throughout the industry.

Unfortunately for Coppola, the piece, subtitled "Dazzling body, empty heart," did little to change the industry line on the still unreleased movie. Like many of the press reviews that would follow over the next month, the *Variety* review contextualized its critique in terms of the film's $27 million or so price tag. Thus, an overall assessment of the film as "frequently funny, tuneful and occasionally engaging" was qualified by an ongoing critique of the dazzling technological effects that made it a potential event film.

According to *Variety, One from the Heart* was a "modest, amiable small picture" overwhelmed and undermined by a gaudy, sensational visual style. The review acknowledged "the lensing achievement of Vittorio Storaro" (which created "the most stunningly atmospheric photography and magical lighting conceivable"), as well as Robert Swarthe's special effects and Arne Goursand and Rudi Fehr's editing, but only in order to elaborate its argument that such technical-stylistic achievements were a liability to the movie.

The review concluded, ominously, that "the necessary next step would be finding a strong enough narrative substance to live up to the stylistic and technological genius that can obviously surround it."[59] Before *One from the Heart* had played in a single theater, *Variety* was already talking about Coppola's next picture, as if the failure of this one was a *fait accompli*.

In the February 17, 1982, issue of *Variety*—published approximately one week after the film opened nationwide—there was more bad news. The initial critical response from the influential New York critics (noted in a *Variety* section called the "New York Critics Scorecard") resulted in two favorable, ten unfavorable, and three inconclusive reviews.[60] Moreover, the bad reviews were truly scathing and more often than not echoed *Variety*'s argument about money and technology overwhelming a thin narrative.

The most damning and in a way the most indicative of these reviews was written by Pauline Kael for the *New Yorker*. It appeared in print, like so many of the bad reviews, more than a week before the film opened theatrically. "This movie isn't from the heart," Kael argued, "or from the head, either; it's from the lab. It's all tricked out with dissolves and scrim effects and superimpositions, and even aural superimpositions. . . . *One from the Heart* is like a jewelled version of a film student's experimental pastiche—the kind set in a magical junkyard; there's nothing underneath the devices but a hope of distilling the essences of movie romance."

For Kael, *One from the Heart* was the nadir of *auteurism*. Coppola had finally managed to become the "star of his movie" and in the process had lost touch with his audience. In *One from the Heart,* Kael bristled, the audience would no doubt "realize that there is nothing—literally nothing—happening except pretty images gliding into each other."[61] *One from the Heart* seemed to be the realization of David Thomson's tongue-in-cheek prophecy of a near-future cinema that would "be less narrative than atmospheric . . . whatever keeps the walls from being inert or boring—color shifts, pattern making, the ebb and flow of light."[62]

Such a cinema, Kael seemed willing to concede, could (and in this case did) look good. She acknowledged that the sets "had a wonderful grandiloquence," like "some child's vision of a world's fair of the past." But though the film *looked* good, Kael simply could not forgive Coppola for all the prerelease hype, and she made him pay for his frequently cited remark that *One from the Heart* would "make the Industrial Revolution look like a small, out of town tryout."[63]

Kael found the film's beauty quite literally superficial: "This movie feels like something directed from a trailer.[64] It's cold and mechanized; it's at a remove from the action. . . . Some directors have begun to use video as a tool . . . but Coppola has got to the point of talking as if the video equipment itself would direct his movies." As to the film's potential audience, "it could be popular with kids who grow up addicted to video games, and they could use it to get high."[65] Kael's review, along with caustic pieces by Vincent Canby, *New York* magazine's David Denby, and the *Today Show*'s Gene Shalit, buried the film before it had a chance in the theaters.[66]

There were eventually a number of positive reviews, but Columbia proved unable to take advantage of them. The first "important" positive review came from Sheila Benson in the *Los Angeles Times*. "*One from the Heart* is so daring," Benson wrote, "it takes away your breath while staggering you visually. It's so easy to love *One from the Heart,* you just let yourself relax and float away with it. A work of constant astonishment. . . . Sumptuous, sensuous, stunning."[67] Both Richard Corliss at *Time* (who dubbed the film "spectacular") and David Ansen at *Newsweek* (who called it "sensuous, gaudy, dreamlike [and] baroque") offered laudatory reviews, as did Janet Maslin, in counterpoint to Vincent Canby, in the *New York Times*.[68]

Unfortunately for Coppola and Columbia, the actual reviews were far less important to the box office of the film than the way the public perceived the reviews. The management of the critical response to a film is the job of the distributor, but since *One from the Heart* was "between distributors" immediately before its nationwide release, there was no one in a position to protect the film. And it obviously needed a protector. Virtually every negative review focused on economic and *auteurist* matters, and it would have been well within the ability of any major studio to alter that spin.

When Columbia took over the distribution of the picture, it did so halfheartedly. Discouraged by the *Variety* review and the initial "New York Critics Scorecard," the studio simply cut its losses and let the film die at the box office.

Four The Zoetrope Legacy

At this moment the personal fortunes of Francis Coppola would appear to be in serious jeopardy—but the industry at large will benefit hugely from the technical innovativeness that he has explored in *One from the Heart*. It's ridiculous to think of it, but perhaps the studios each could make a couple of million in contributions towards the cost of *One from the Heart* as an expression of gratitude for boldness in doing research and development they have failed to understand over the years. —Thomas Pryor, industry journalist, two weeks *before* the release of *One from the Heart*[1]

On April 20, 1982, approximately two months after *One from the Heart* was released, Francis Coppola announced that Zoetrope Studios was on the auction block: minimum bid, $20 million. Though Coppola had purchased the property less than two years earlier for approximately $6.7 million, the asking price was hardly unreasonable. Just a few months earlier, a comparable property, the old Samuel Goldwyn Studio, was sold at auction. The bidding began at $18 million and ended when Warner Brothers acquired the property for $35 million. But what even an astonishingly advantageous sale of the lot could do for Coppola by April 1982 was unclear. By then, the studio owed a long list of lien holders well over $20 million. Moreover, Coppola's personal fortune was still tied up in *One from the Heart*, and it was already too late to save the film.

In the very same press release that announced the studio auction, Coppola, with a weird optimism, took the opportunity to reaffirm Zoetrope's commitment to its 1982 slate of features: the re-release of *One from the Heart*; *The Escape Artist* (directed by *Black Stallion* cinematographer Caleb Deschanel); Wim Wenders's *Hammett*; a sequel to Zoetrope's pre-studio hit, *The Black Stallion Returns* (directed by Robert Dalva, who was with Coppola at American Zoetrope in the late 1960s); and two negative pickups: a TV movie called *Too Far to Go* (directed by Fielder Cook) and a German film (based on the Wagner opera) *Parsifal*, directed by Hans-Jurgen Syberberg (whose epic *Our Hitler* had previously reached the American market thanks to Coppola and Zoetrope special projects chief Tom Luddy).[2]

To the casual observer it must have seemed as if Coppola was living in a dream world. But to those who follow the trades, the press release indicated just how well Coppola understood the situation. By accepting the inevitability of foreclosure—by accepting the fact that it was too late to save the studio—Coppola ironically found himself in an enviable position. Though he was basically out of money, he still controlled several very interesting films. And since he was sure to eventually lose the studio to the bank or to one of his other creditors, he was free to develop and produce any or all of these films without any real concern for their marketability.

Moreover, Coppola was well justified in banking on a lengthy negotiation process preceding the sale of the studio. The list of lien holders was long, and the amount of money owed, significant. It was thus to several of the more "junior" lien holders' distinct advantage to show patience, to allow sufficient time for Coppola to arrange for a sale price somewhere in the neighborhood of the $35 million Warners had paid for the Goldwyn studio.

Even the lien holders who at first contemplated forcing a quick sale were soon convinced to watch and wait. Jack Singer, for example, the fifth lien holder, filed foreclosure papers as early as April 1982 and could have forced a sale at any time ninety days after the notice was served. But Singer was convinced by Zoetrope president Robert Spiotta to wait until after the first auction bids were opened (on May 26) so that a deal covering his position could be made.[3]

The first round of bids failed to contain an acceptable offer. Several bids exceeded the $20 million minimum, but none included sufficient cash up front. In public, at least, Spiotta remained optimistic, and he convinced Singer to wait for a second round of bids, scheduled for July 14. But the second round ended much like the first. When Spiotta prepared to solicit a third set of bids, Security Pacific Bank, the holder of the fourth deed of trust, filed a notice of default on its $8 million plus loan to Zoetrope. In doing so, the bank gave the studio three months to close a sale on its own, after which, if the debt remained unpaid, the bank planned to foreclose in order to sell the studio at auction.

Once Security Pacific had made its move, Singer, who stood next in line behind the bank, found himself in a difficult position. So long as the bank remained a somewhat disinterested party, as it had for more than three months, Singer could afford to wait until Spiotta and Coppola arranged a

favorable sale so that he too could get his money back. But, as Singer understood, Security Pacific was under no obligation to protect his investment. If a
bid under the $20 million minimum was made that nonetheless covered
Security Pacific's lien, the bank could sell the property and effectively leave
Singer (and all those behind him on the long list of Zoetrope creditors) out
in the cold.

Security Pacific's move to foreclose was the fourth such filing against the
studio. In addition to Singer, the first and third lien holders, James Nasser
and Glen Speidel, had also served foreclosure papers, but they were quickly
paid off with $250,000 apiece to cover their expenses in maintaining the
Zoetrope debt.[4]

Nasser and Speidel, along with the second lien holder, Texas oilman
Ellison Miles (whose investment was a mere $350,000), were virtually as-
sured of recovering their investment in almost any sale or auction scenario.
They remained willing to wait and see because the longer the sale was
delayed, the more interest accrued on Zoetrope's debt to them.

Singer was in a uniquely lousy position; the longer things dragged on, the
more likely it was that he would either have to write off his investment or
buy the studio himself. The only significant lien holder behind him was
Chase Manhattan Bank.[5] But unlike Singer, the bank had secured its loan
against Coppola's personal holdings and the slate of 1982 Zoetrope releases.[6]
Thus, the longer the sale was delayed—and, correspondingly, the more time
Coppola had to bring the various Zoetrope projects to term—the better
Chase's chances were of being paid back. Moreover, even after the dust
settled from a sale or auction of Zoetrope, Chase still had someplace else to
go to get its money. Singer did not.

The first foreclosure auction set up by Security Pacific Bank was announced for February 11, 1983, one year to the day after the national release
of *One from the Heart*. But although Security Pacific had lowered the minimum bid, demanded less cash up front than Spiotta had in the first three
Zoetrope sealed-bid auctions, and had the right and ability to foreclose on
the property, it too had difficulty putting Zoetrope out of business. First, due
to scheduling problems, the auction was delayed for three days to the even
more appropriate Valentine's Day. Then the sale was put off again, to February 28, as two old negotiations (dating back to the original May 26, 1982,
Zoetrope-run sale involving bids in excess of $20 million) were reopened.

On February 16, 1983, Spiotta announced in *Variety* that the "studio
[would] be sold before any of the other mortgagers' sales dates mature." In
other words, the sale of the studio would be closed before anyone, including

Security Pacific and Jack Singer, could stop it. But while Spiotta was telling the press that he was still optimistic about negotiating a sale of the property, industry rumors began to circulate that Spiotta planned to file for Chapter 11 bankruptcy on behalf of the studio.[7]

As things played out, Spiotta decided against declaring bankruptcy. But when it came time for Security Pacific to hold a foreclosure auction, the bank mysteriously granted the studio a thirty-day extension. Thirty days later, when again no sale materialized, the bank granted another extension, and then, thirty days later, yet another.

During the sixth thirty-day extension, a *Variety* piece titled "Zoetrope Escapes Again" leaked inside information on a potential buyer: Nova, a new Columbia-HBO-CBS coventure. Nova at the time was, as *Variety* described it, "a studio without a studio," and at $20 million, Zoetrope was well within Nova's price range. But just as Nova entered the picture, and Security Pacific and even Jack Singer started to feel confident that they would finally get their money, first lien holder James Nasser emerged from his year-long silence and promised to force the issue if things dragged on much longer. "It's got to be settled after this [latest extension]," he told *Variety*. "It can't go on any longer."[8]

The Nova deal never materialized and Nasser made good on his promise. Considering that Security Pacific's most recent thirty-day extension ended on April 15, Nasser set a foreclosure auction date for three days later. Nasser maintained that while he did not want to have to go through the trouble of auctioning the property himself, if the bank failed to act, he would.

Nasser's announcement forced the bank's hand. Security Pacific could not afford to let Nasser auction the property since he was under no obligation to protect the bank's position. Nasser, the bankers realized, was in a position to accept almost any bid at all, and he had made it clear that so long as it covered *his* lien, he would. Because it had no choice, Security Pacific planned to go ahead with the foreclosure auction on April 15. But fifteen minutes before the auction was set to begin, Joseph Kanter, a Miami Beach investor, paid Nasser $268,000 (which covered Zoetrope's delinquent account) and effectively stalled the proceedings once again. With Nasser off its back, Security Pacific rescheduled foreclosure for May 9 in order to see what Kanter intended to do.

Kanter, primarily a real estate developer, had the money to make the deal and had just formed his own film production company in Florida. But what he or his fledgling Kanter Productions needed with a state-of-the-art $20 million Hollywood studio was anybody's guess. Though he bought Coppola and Zoetrope another two months, a realistic offer from Kanter never materialized. And though Glen Speidel, the third lien holder, had to be bought off in the interim (with 100 percent of Zoetrope's basically worthless stock), as late as July 1983, after an astonishing twelve foreclosure postponements, Coppola still had "his" studio.

The thirteenth scheduled Security Pacific foreclosure auction, scheduled for July 28, 1983, seemed finally to spell the end of Coppola's control at Zoetrope Studios. But before Security Pacific could convene the auction, Jack Singer, along with a number of "minor creditors," including a roofer, a carpet company, and an electrical distributor, forced Zoetrope's holding company, Hollywood General, into involuntary bankruptcy and took matters once again out of the bank's hands.

Singer's strategy was obvious to everyone concerned. The bankruptcy petition effectively stalled the auction and bought Singer at least an additional month to secure adequate financing to buy the studio himself. Of course, it also bought Coppola and Zoetrope and the other lien holders more time as well.

Though no deal had yet been negotiated, as early as the August 3, 1983, issue of *Variety,* Singer began talking publicly as if he already owned the property. "I want to make it a viable studio again," he told reporter David Robb. "I will run it like it should be run." Claiming that he forced the studio into bankruptcy only in order to prevent other parties from "stealing it" from him—a strange argument in that there were no pending offers at the time—Singer avoided the more obvious point: that he had filed suit and planned to buy the property because if he didn't, he'd be out $4 million.[9]

Nasser mused: "It was the bank who decided the thing . . . the bank was insisting on an auction and that's what caused Singer to force the bankruptcy.[10] I guess the bank didn't think Singer would do it." Third lien holder Glen Speidel had a different slant on things. In *Variety,* Speidel openly doubted Singer's ability to raise enough money to purchase the studio and predicted that the bankruptcy maneuver would result only "in more legal bills without accomplishing anything."[11]

Speidel's remark seemed prescient when, well before Singer's bankruptcy petition could be heard, yet another potential buyer emerged: New York–based mortgage banker and real estate investor Robert Sonnenblick. The first mention of Sonnenblick's interest in the studio appeared in the September 7, 1983, issue of *Variety.*[12] Two weeks later, a Zoetrope press release announced that Spiotta and Sonnenblick had "agreed [to a deal] in principle" for $16.5 million. But, as Spiotta and Sonnenblick soon discovered, no deal could be closed without the approval of the bankruptcy judge, who made it clear that he would not consider either Singer's suit or Sonnenblick's offer until October 11, 1983, the date set for the bankruptcy hearing.

Singer's public reaction to Sonnenblick's offer, which did not cover his interests, was predictable: "As far as I'm concerned it's not a valid sale."[13] And lucky for him, it wasn't. In the fall of 1983, largely in response to Sonnenblick's offer, executives at Zoetrope began acting as if it were really, finally the end. Spiotta resigned as president, and Coppola resumed control of yet another "new" Zoetrope headquartered in San Francisco. But it was not until February 10, 1984, one day shy of two years after the release of *One from the Heart*, that Security Pacific National Bank and Jack Singer finally forced the sale of the studio.

This time around, the minimum bid was dropped to $12.2 million. At that figure, Nasser, Miles, and Speidel would all be paid in full and Security Pacific stood to lose approximately $2 million (a sum the bank felt it could collect from other properties tied to the loan).[14]

Singer's willingness to let the bank auction the property made it clear to anyone who didn't already know that he planned to purchase the studio himself. When the gavel dropped for the first and last time on February 10, 1984, Singer emerged as the only interested party and "stole" the studio with a bid of $12.3 million. Singer later told reporters that he had thought the studio might go for as high as $20 million. Industry insiders guessed closer to $15 million. But no one, especially the bank, thought the lot would go so cheaply.

At least publicly, Singer was a good winner. "I'm very happy," he told David Robb of *Variety*. "The studio is a historic site. Hopefully we're going to bring it up to its old standards. We're going to do our best to make it a beautiful, viable studio."[15] Singer immediately renamed the facility Singer Studios. Coppola took the Zoetrope name north, and though films continue to bear the Zoetrope Studios banner, there is, alas, no longer a studio.

Upon acquiring the property, Singer promised to run the studio like a business and immediately began to clean house, firing everyone left on the lot, including the unionized janitors and security guards. When the unions squawked and promised to pursue legal action against him, Singer turned to the trades and in a classic bit of 1980s business-speak put the whole matter in perspective: "We didn't fire anybody. We bought an empty lot."[16]

Though Singer had pledged on more than one occasion to make Zoetrope a viable studio again, within a month of his taking over, Singer Studios became exclusively a rental production facility. And then, on March 10, in a move that had become all too common in the new Hollywood,[17] in order to meet his obligation to the bank, Singer set about making additional cash by publicly auctioning Zoetrope memorabilia. For Singer—as for so many who took over in the new Hollywood—there was no room for sentiment. By 1990, Singer Studios was in disrepair—so much so that, in what seems an apt piece of irony, in 1992, when Robert Altman used the site to shoot *The Player,* his scathing parody of the new Hollywood, he had to renovate before he could work there.

Before the Fall

I worked for Western Union one summer when I was 14 and for some unknown reason—I still don't know why—I wrote a phony telegram to my father telling him he'd landed a job writing the musical score for such and such a film. I signed it with the name of a guy who was in charge of music at Paramount Pictures. My father was overjoyed and yelled, "It's my break." And I had to tell him it wasn't true. He was heartbroken. Is that a terrible story?—Francis Coppola, 1975[18]

Given his seemingly instinctive understanding of the marketplace in the 1970s, Coppola's rather sudden failure at the box office in the 1980s took many in the industry by surprise. After all, Coppola had not only made *The Godfather* into the highest-grossing film of its time, he had followed it up with both popular and critical success with a much more complex sequel two years later. And then, as the decade came to a close, he hit again with *Apocalypse Now,* a film United Artists foolishly thought was unreleasable.

Coppola's record as a producer of other directors' films in the 1970s was just as impressive. Less than a year after the first run of *The Godfather,* Coppola convinced Universal to release George Lucas's nostalgic teen picture, *American Graffiti.* For his trouble, despite virtually no participation in the making of the film, Coppola received above-the-title credit as the film's producer and a chunk of the film's profits, which, to date, are the largest in the history of American "independent" cinema. Seven years later, Coppola's instincts seemed sharp again when he produced Carroll Ballard's *The Black Stallion,* another film that did considerably better at the box office than anyone in the industry thought it would.

But Coppola's most surprising move as a producer—and yet another signal of his box office savvy—occurred just as the 1970s came to a close when he turned the re-release of the restored silent classic *Napoleon,* directed by Abel Gance, into a worldwide motion picture event. The success of *Napoleon* seems, even in retrospect, a bit implausible. In 1980, when the

6. One of Coppola's biggest successes as a producer, Carroll Ballard's *The Black Stallion* (United Artists, 1979).

reconstructed film began its second American run, it was fifty-six years old, silent, and over four hours long. Nevertheless, Coppola figured out a way to market the film. In reissue, *Napoleon* played to standing-room-only audiences in enormous theaters like New York's Radio City Music Hall, the 3,000-seat O'Keefe Center in Toronto, and the Ohio Theater in Columbus, in each case at $25 or more per seat.

The box office success of *Napoleon,* two years before the release of *One from the Heart,* seemed to indicate that Coppola had the Midas touch, that there was no limit to how far he could exploit his prestige as an *auteur.* But despite its success at the box office, "Coppola's" *Napoleon* met with significant criticism from the very community that had once embraced the *auteur* theory, posting for the first time a kind of warning that, in the 1980s, his prestige and success might eventually become something of a liability.

Coppola first saw Kevin Brownlow's reconstruction of *Napoleon* (in rough-cut form) in 1973 in London. Projected at its proper silent speed, the Brownlow version was almost five hours long, an hour and a half longer than Gance's own 1927 release print and three and a half hours longer than the version of the film that premiered in the United States in the late 1920s. It wasn't until November 1980, at the London Film Festival, that the Brownlow reconstruction of *Napoleon* premiered theatrically. After a decade of work reproducing the most authentic version of the picture possible, the British Film Institute (BFI) commissioned Carl Davis to compose a score based on available material dating back to the film's first run.

Despite the length and relative obscurity of the film, Coppola purchased the distribution rights to *Napoleon* after its London premiere. The rights were held by Claude Lelouch, and the deal the French cineaste held out for was hardly sweet: $400,000 plus 50 percent of the gross.[19] But Coppola knew what he wanted. In the first place, though it sounds somewhat clichéd, Coppola was anxious to "give something back" to the industry and the moviegoing public. Though he had been famous and successful for only about eight years, he seemed already interested in posterity and in establishing some sort of legacy as not only an *auteur* but a patron of the cinematic arts as well.

More selfishly, but no less conscious of his position in film history, Coppola seemed to want his involvement in the American release of *Napoleon* to appear consistent with his own future work. By 1980, Coppola had already begun developing a multiscreen version of Goethe's *Elective Affinities*, in which he planned to allude to the dazzling triptych effect Gance had achieved in the last reel of *Napoleon*. He had also begun developing *One from the Heart*, which, like *Napoleon*, he hoped would take shape through technological innovation.

For *Napoleon*'s American re-release, Coppola literally took the film on the road, and in doing so cleverly transformed a prestige project into an event. In the larger venues, the screening featured, much to the BFI's and Carl Davis's chagrin, a small orchestra conducted and playing a score written by Carmine Coppola, Francis's father. At the better facilities, the true triptych effect was performed with three synched 35-mm projectors. At the others, the effect was simulated in 70 mm.

To follow *Napoleon*'s successful opening run, Coppola signed a distribution deal with the newly formed Universal Classics, which mounted a nationwide release. Universal did a masterful job of marketing, opening the picture at the Cinerama Dome Theater in Hollywood the day after *E.T.: The Extra-Terrestrial* completed its triumphant first run. To celebrate the film's Los Angeles opening, the marketing department at Universal printed and sold programs (to simulate a more heady theatrical experience) and T-shirts (which made screenings feel just a little like a rock concert). The 70-mm Dolby stereo Universal release print nearly matched the look and sound of the first-run performances, and with ticket prices cut from $25 to $7.50, those in attendance were made to feel that they were getting a deal.

The American release was so successful that Brownlow publicly applauded Coppola and Zoetrope special projects director Tom Luddy for "mounting a miraculous campaign."[20] But despite Brownlow's approval, many at the British Film Institute, where the film was restored, bristled that Coppola's success had upstaged their hard work. In America, they argued, *Napoleon* was just another product bearing the logo "Francis Ford Coppola Presents." Coppola, they argued, had somehow become the *auteur* of not only Gance's but also *their* film.

What really irked the BFI was a court ruling that elaborated the international distribution rights to the film. By 1982, the "authentic" BFI version was licensed for exhibition only in the United Kingdom. The "Coppola version," on the other hand, could be shown anywhere, though Coppola conceded that the net proceeds of UK shows of the "Coppola version" would go to the BFI.

To defuse the situation, Coppola offered to donate the profits from the UK premiere of *One from the Heart* to the British National Film Archives. But Coppola's largess wasn't enough for some at the BFI, who argued that the real problem with Coppola's *Napoleon* was that it was inauthentic, especially in its use of the Carmine Coppola score. The whole point of reconstructing the film, they argued, was to establish authenticity. Coppola's insensitivity to such an important aspect of authorship struck many at the archive as at the very least paradoxical.

After the release of *One from the Heart* in 1982, Coppola continued to point out the similarities between his film and Gance's *Napoleon*. This too struck the BFI as presumptuous, but today the connections between the two films seem undeniable. At the time of their respective releases, both films were technologically innovative and thus seemed primarily stylistic achievements. As a result, both were widely misunderstood and unappreciated. Thanks to Coppola (and to the BFI and Brownlow), Gance and his audacious work have finally gotten a worldwide audience and long overdue recognition. At present, the best Coppola can hope for is that some cine-entrepreneur in the not so distant future will return the favor.

Apocalypse 1980

My family had an 8-mm projector, and a tape recorder, and let me play with them. I used to synchronize soundtracks to their home movies, and started a business of showing such films. . . . I used to cut up the home movies and make stories out of them, with myself as the hero. I have some of them still. But I was just fooling around, and was more interested in the exhibition end.—Francis Coppola, 1968[21]

After the successful release of *Napoleon,* Coppola's fortunes took a rather sudden and dramatic turn for the worse. If one believed in fate, it seemed as if Coppola was being taken to account for all of his good fortune. Perhaps the success he had enjoyed in the 1970s doomed him to failure on a similar scale in the following decade.

The decade indeed began ominously when, in 1980, Coppola offered to produce a thirty-minute high-tech political rally for then presidential candidate Jerry Brown on the campus of the University of Wisconsin, Madison. In concert with Brown's campaign, which purported to look to the future for solutions to contemporary problems, the live event was dubbed "The Shape of Things to Come," a title that proved more ironic than appropriate. The $150,000 live event was a complicated production. And though Coppola had virtually no television experience, he committed himself to shooting the rally live. The shoot required the difficult task of intercutting Brown's speech not only with the usual reaction shots of the crowd but with slides and videotape simultaneously projected on a twelve-by-twenty-foot screen.

The event was broadcast on March 29, 1980, and was, by all accounts, a disaster.[22] A litany of embarrassing technical problems, including misspelled titles, a dead microphone, and a "hole" in the image (most likely caused by a faulty tube in one the cameras), drew attention away from the candidate and seemed to indicate that while Coppola had invested a lot in the relationship between new technologies and the new Hollywood, he had no idea himself how any of the new equipment actually worked. The future, it seemed, was a place in which everything was broken.

By the time *One from the Heart* bombed at the box office, it was clear that Coppola could master the technology, but no one seemed all that interested anymore. To understand the magnitude of Coppola's declining fortunes, one need only look to Zoetrope's first negative pickup after the release of the studio's ill-fated debut and compare it with the astonishing success of *Napoleon.*

Too Far to Go was an adaptation of a series of stories by John Updike that played to a small TV audience in 1979 and bowed commercially two months after the release of *One from the Heart.* Purchased for $250,000, *Too Far to Go,* despite the fact that it was made for TV, was platformed by Luddy and Coppola as a prestige project, a little film along the lines of surprise Academy Award winner *Chariots of Fire.* Robert Geller, the film's producer, hyped *Too Far to Go* as the beginning of an alternative cinema at Zoetrope. "There's a place out there for smaller films," Geller told *Variety,* "and maybe you don't have to go through the big studios' front and back doors to get somewhere."[23]

While it was Coppola's plan to someday turn Zoetrope into just such an alternative studio distributing titles the majors would no longer bother with, the pickup of *Too Far to Go* revealed to the industry just how bad things had gotten at the studio after the release of *One from the Heart.* Luddy himself put things in the proper perspective when he said that "though in one sense it's a sacrifice we can ill afford, we believe [*Too Far to Go*] can be an income producing arrangement for us *very quickly.*"[24] Quite suddenly, the scale of things to come at Zoetrope had markedly shrunk, and faster profit revenues became a priority.

Hammett

One week Francis and company will be sweating out a last-minute re-write of a script that's only a few days from production; the week after, everyone else will be filming and Coppola will be up on some satellite somewhere plotting how to beam high-resolution video features direct to your neighborhood theater from outer space.
—Tim Hunter, journalist, screenwriter, director (*River's Edge*)[25]

The second most important film produced at Zoetrope Studios (after *One from the Heart*) was Wim Wenders's *Hammett,* which was originally scheduled to be the studio's first release. But two directors, five writers, and some five years in development all delayed its debut, and the film was not released until after *One from the Heart* had already bombed, and thus it was widely seen as yet another example of just how out of touch Coppola had become.

In many ways the film was the quintessential Zoetrope production in that Coppola tried to produce it according to the repertory principles he had laid out in press releases in 1980 when he first purchased the studio. The film's failure—it did poorly at the box office and with critics—seems in retrospect to reveal not only Coppola's inability to understand the 1980s audience but also his unwillingness to compromise *his* Zoetrope project.

In 1975, Fred Roos, the former casting agent and producer of *The Godfather* and *The Godfather, Part II,* read a novel by a former detective named Joe Gores, loosely based on the life and writing of Dashiell Hammett. By then a producer working exclusively for Zoetrope (San Francisco), Roos optioned the property and convinced British director Nicholas Roeg to develop it. With Roeg already attached to the project, Roos then went to Coppola, who, on the strength of Roeg's reputation and without ever reading the book, gave the project the green light.

Predictably, the first problems facing *Hammett* were legal ones. It took an entire year to get the proper releases and to convince Hammett's ex-lover (and the executrix of his estate), Lillian Hellman, to become what in Hollywood is known as a "friend of the film." In the meantime, Gores, who had been hired to adapt his novel into a screenplay, and Roeg worked separately "developing" the picture. After almost a year apart, Roeg flew to San Francisco to begin working with Gores but discovered that he and the screenwriter had envisioned different films. As Gores relates the story, "Nick said we start with a book, then gradually move a little away from it, and a little more, and all of a sudden it's a script—but really it's still the book."[26] Gores, predictably, saw his screenplay and novel as more than a mere outline. But he understood that he was, in effect, hired to write the script for Roeg.

In February 1977 Gores finished a first draft of the screenplay. Roeg loved it. Actor Frederic Forrest, whom Coppola had wanted to play Dashiell Hammett in the movie, didn't quite agree. He thought it was "the most violent script he had ever read."[27] While Gores went to work on a second draft of the screenplay, further incorporating Roeg's ideas, Coppola and Roos began trying to convince United Artists, which had offered to pay $8 million in exchange for domestic distribution rights to the film, to cast Forrest in the lead. The studio vetoed Forrest and proposed instead that Coppola cast a major star for the title role. Concerned that UA and Coppola might never agree, Roeg dropped out of the film.

With the second draft (written specifically for Roeg) in hand, Coppola set out to find another director. First, he offered the script to François Truffaut, who said it was "the best American script" he'd ever read but turned down the project anyway. Meanwhile, Robert DeNiro, who had won a Best Supporting Actor Oscar for his performance in Coppola's *The Godfather, Part II* in 1974, began expressing an interest in playing the title role. DeNiro's participation, Coppola knew, would not only meet with UA's approval but would make the task of finding another director considerably easier. But DeNiro went hot and cold on the project, and Coppola couldn't get the actor's name on the dotted line.[28] With neither a commitment from DeNiro nor a star director attached to the project, several executives at UA began to suggest to Coppola that he ought to shelve the project for a while.

But just as *Hammett* seemed destined for turnaround,[29] the resolution of a three-year-old power struggle at United Artists gave the film a new life. When United Artists first agreed to fund *Hammett* in exchange for distribution rights to the film, the studio was run by Arthur Krim and Robert Benjamin, two New York attorneys who had purchased the studio from Charles Chaplin and Mary Pickford in the mid-1950s, and owned by Transamerica, which bought UA in 1967 from Krim and Benjamin in order to boost its own sluggish stock.

Krim and Benjamin profited nicely by selling out to Transamerica; they retained significant control over the studio, and as a result of the deal their UA stock tripled in value. Moreover, Krim and Benjamin bought themselves some peace of mind. Once it had access to Transamerica's line of credit, UA was in a good position to ride out even a horrendous run of bad luck at the box office.

At first Transamerica seemed satisfied to let Krim and Benjamin run the studio themselves. But as the 1960s wound down, executives at the insurance conglomerate began to show more and more interest in the day-to-day affairs of the studio. By 1974, Transamerica's involvement in studio management so troubled Krim and Benjamin that they offered to buy the studio back. Transamerica turned them down and then, in what many in the industry saw as a kind of retaliation, made things worse by putting Transamerica executive James Harvey in charge of the studio's day-to-day operation. After enjoying two decades of autonomy, Krim and Benjamin bitterly resented having to go to Harvey in order to get anything done.

Krim and Benjamin held on for another three years while things got progressively worse. Then, in an act of sheer frustration, in the January 16, 1978, issue of *Fortune,* Krim spoke out bitterly about his relationship with UA's multinational parent. "You will not find," Krim told the magazine, "any top officer here who feels that Transamerica has contributed anything to United Artists."[30]

Transamerica CEO John Beckett responded that if the people at United Artists didn't like it they could quit.[31] Within days, Krim and Benjamin took Beckett up on his offer and shocked the industry by quitting United Artists. Making matters worse, Eric Pleskow, UA's president, Mike Medavoy, the head of production, and Bill Bernstein, the head of business affairs, tendered their resignations as well.

On January 24, 1978, in a two-page open letter run as an advertisement in *Variety,* sixty-three producers and directors (including Robert Altman, Blake Edwards, Norman Jewison, Saul Zaentz, Martin Scorsese, Bob Fosse, and Francis Coppola) appealed to Transamerica to settle with Krim and Benjamin.[32] But Beckett stood his ground. The former UA executives then announced plans to form a new company, Orion, named for the constellation they mistakenly believed was comprised, like their company, of five stars. Moving a lot faster than Beckett thought they would, the Orion five quickly signed a distribution deal with Warner Brothers and were rather suddenly ready to do business on their own.

Transamerica responded by hiring Andy Albeck to run United Artists.

Albeck's first and last big decision at the helm of UA was to give the green light to *Heaven's Gate*. Albeck eventually quit the film business and is now growing Christmas trees somewhere in New Jersey.

The UA-Orion battle helped buy Coppola more time with *Hammett* and then bought a sympathetic ear from Mike Medavoy, who had taken the project with him to Orion. When Coppola went to Medavoy with the implausible suggestion (first brought to Coppola by Fred Roos) that German cineaste Wim Wenders should direct *Hammett,* Orion so needed product that Medavoy gave the picture a second green light.

By the time Wenders got to San Francisco, the Zoetrope research staff had assembled more information on the real Dashiell Hammett than Wenders could possibly use or digest. Gores, meanwhile, was at work on a third draft, which in essence was a first draft since Wenders wanted wholesale changes in the first two versions written for Roeg. Where Roeg had wanted a loose script that was in and of itself mysterious, Wenders wanted to know what the characters were doing every minute—what they were thinking and how they were thinking.

Roeg's signature style included an expressive use of exceedingly well-lit color; as a cinematographer he had shot Truffaut's *Fahrenheit 451* as well as his own *Performance, Walkabout,* and *Don't Look Now.* When Wenders took over, he decided to shoot the film in black and white in homage to the 1940s noir films that were so indebted to Hammett's work (a decision that prompted Gores to wryly quip that Wenders "had a nostalgia for a time he'd never seen").[33]

Wenders's stylistic reworking of the film bore significant practical consequences, as art director Dean Tavoularis, who had spent the past year working in color and in Roeg's style, had to suddenly and completely rework the design of the entire movie. Eventually, the various script changes (some of which were due to Wenders's arrival) would cause Tavoularis even more trouble. Since there were drafts set in different periods, anytime between 1903 and 1928, there was real confusion as to what exactly Tavoularis was supposed to be building.[34] Coppola's insistence on shooting the entire movie on the lot with studio-constructed sets only exacerbated the problem.

Sometime during the fourth or fifth rewrite, in September 1978, Gores quietly exited the scene and Roos and Wenders hired Tom Pope, a recent USC film school graduate, to produce a new script. Pope changed the story and the script's tone, but while both Wenders and Roos loved the screenplay, Coppola, whose level of interest in the project seemed to change daily, hated it. In order to placate Coppola, Wenders had Pope do a second draft, this time juxtaposing sequences from Hammett's novel *Red Harvest* with a fictive story depicting the novelist himself as a detective. But while that draft came closer to pleasing Coppola, it had to be discarded when the rights to *Red Harvest* proved unavailable. By the time Pope went to work on his third draft, it seemed clear to all involved that Coppola wanted to hire yet another screenwriter. But when Coppola went to Orion to tell Medavoy that he wanted to replace Pope and start all over, the studio executive instead pressured Coppola to get the film in front of the cameras.

In order to maintain Medavoy's support of the project and at the same time fire Pope, Coppola, under the pretext of "previsualizing" the script, hired Gene Hackman to read the part of Hammett and Ronnee Blakely (then Wenders's wife) and Frederic Forrest to read the other principal parts, and recorded a "radio play" version of Pope's *Hammett* screenplay on the Zoetrope lot. As Coppola had rather hoped it would, the result highlighted the problems with Pope's script, and Orion gave Coppola their OK to hire another screenwriter.

In May 1979, Pope was replaced by Dennis O'Flaherty, the holder of an Oxford Ph.D. in Russian literature. What O'Flaherty brought to the project was clear from the start. While Wenders had envisioned the picture as a film noir to be shot in black and white and played naturalistically, O'Flaherty kept talking about how the detective plot was uninteresting; the very point Coppola had made with regard to Pope's script. Much to Wenders's dismay, O'Flaherty's arrival coincided with Coppola's increased interest in and control over the film. Signed on to write the script according to Coppola's guidelines, O'Flaherty hardly made his role in the drama attending the development of the project a secret. "I'd be happy to work for Francis," O'Flaherty announced, "until I drop dead."

O'Flaherty eventually transformed the gritty detective drama into something purposefully off-center, the very kind of anti–genre piece Coppola himself would undertake in *Rumble Fish*. In O'Flaherty's version, the drama grew more existential; indeed, it became so cryptic that Hammett, the character in the film, failed in the end to figure out the plot. If detective films are about a search for truth, O'Flaherty argued, his *Hammett* was about the impossibility of such a quest. It was, in his own words, "downright Hegelian. . . . It was the antithesis."[35]

Shooting began on *Hammett* on February 4, 1980, less than a week after a twelfth and "final" draft of the screenplay was "completed." At the time, Wenders could afford to be somewhat upbeat: "I thought we'd shoot in summer 1978. I figured at the longest it would take a year. Now it's together going to be more than two and a half years. It's hard to wait for something so long. A lot of my friends in Germany, and certainly a lot of the press, thought I was more or less fucked. They thought I'd never get it off the ground."[36]

In public, Wenders took care to refer to Coppola as "more of a colleague than a producer,"[37] but from the very start things did not go smoothly on the set. The biggest problem for Wenders was that Coppola was still not satisfied with the script. Throughout the first several weeks of production, Coppola himself tried to rewrite the screenplay. Then, when other studio responsibilities demanded his attention, he hired yet another screenwriter, Dennis Jakob, who had worked as a creative consultant on *Apocalypse Now*. Jakob's inability to fix the screenplay eventually led Coppola to shut down the production. By then, the shoot had entered its tenth week and, according to Wenders, the film was 90 percent complete.

Wenders appealed to Coppola to let him try to fix things on the set. But Coppola refused and then hired yet another writer, Ross Thomas (the author of fifteen best-selling mysteries), to write a new beginning and end, hoping the two might meet someplace in the middle of the movie Wenders had already shot. Whether or not Thomas, the film's last script doctor, succeeded in "fixing the film" is a subjective matter these days, but in retrospect, it seems a miracle the film was ever completed.

Though it was intended to be Zoetrope's first in-house film, *Hammett* did not premiere until May 1982 at the Cannes Film Festival, almost four months after the release of *One from the Heart*. Still reeling from the box office disaster of his own film, Coppola soon discovered that *Hammett* would fare no better. *Hammett* opened in the United States at number twenty-five in the last week of June 1982, more than six years after the first script had been written, fell to number forty-one the following week, and then fell out of the top fifty altogether the week after that.

The *Variety* review (published before the film was released in the United States) focused, as many other reviews did, on Coppola's problems bringing the film to term—again, as if the way the movie was made was more important than the movie itself: "Now overpolished by too many script rewrites, perhaps emasculated by massive footage scraps and belated reshoots, project (all shot on interiors) emerges a rather suffocating film taking place in a rickety Chinatown." As to its box office potential, *Variety* predicted ominously: "Film might hit offshore tastes. . . . A fast playoff may get *Hammett* some attention, but it does not display holding power in its present form."[38]

The Legacy

I want to be remembered as a champion of both innovation and youth. The work I've done in technology has been overlooked. . . . Maybe when I'm an old guy I'll look at all my films and say: "I was dumb, or I was very smart."—Francis Coppola, 1987[39]

In the aftermath of the ill-fated first (and to date only) theatrical run of *One from the Heart* and the disappointing critical and box office reception to *Hammett,* Coppola remained philosophical. It was, indeed, the only rational public position he could take since he fully intended to continue making movies. "I've already learned so much from the experience in two major ways," he mused in November 1982, "first, about the filmmaking process itself, what I feel a film is; and second, various practical realizations having to do with the things that make it possible to make a film—the raising of money, relations with the press, and so on. The most important thing I've learned, actually, is to play things closer to the vest from now on."[40]

But in the years that followed, as Coppola continued to reexamine the ways the popular and trade presses had contributed to the failure of *One from the Heart* and Zoetrope Studios, he found it hard to remain so diplomatic. In retrospect, Coppola couldn't help but wonder not only how, but also why everyone in the industry—and here again we must include the popular press—had turned against him. In an interview in the *San Francisco Examiner* published in May 1987, Coppola remarked: "When you're famous and powerful, people want to get you. My own naivete gets me into trouble on this level. All the things I said came from being excited . . . the press only want to hurt my feelings. . . . Nobody who really knows me or who I care about thinks that I'm a jerk or a megalomaniac."

On the subject of his own success—and the realization that his success in the 1970s has had a lot to do with what has gone wrong since then—Coppola added: "I know the press cynically believes that if you don't want publicity, you don't go out and get it. There are others, far more successful than I, who don't get all this publicity. When you've become as notorious as I've become, they think I'm doing it to get attention. Then success becomes a gag."[41]

Given the professional difficulties Coppola faced after the release of *One from the Heart,* it is not surprising that he has had to accept that his best days may well be behind him. He is by all accounts the godfather of the 1970s Hollywood *auteur* renaissance, but his work in the 1980s as a filmmaker-producer-entrepreneur remains undervalued and for the most part critically ignored. A look back at the films released under the Zoetrope banner, however, reveals an eclectic and impressive oeuvre: Gance's *Napoleon,* Syberberg's *Our Hitler* and *Parsifal,* Jean-Luc Godard's *Every Man for Himself* and *Passion,* Akira Kurasawa's *Kagemusha* and *Ran,* Kidlat Tahimik's *The Perfumed Nightmare,* Godfrey Reggio's *Koyaanisqatsi,* Rob Nilsson's *Signal 7,* Phillip Borsos's *Grey Fox,* and three mainland Chinese films (*Street Angel, Crossroads,* and *The Spring River Runs East*) all "presented" by Coppola/ Zoetrope; *Hammett, The Escape Artist, The Black Stallion Returns,* and Paul Schrader's *Mishima,* all of which were "produced" by Coppola and developed and/or shot on the lot; and, finally, *One from the Heart, The Outsiders,* and *Rumble Fish,* all directed by Coppola during his tenure as artistic director of the studio. It would be very difficult to argue that any other American studio had as interesting a lineup through the first four years of the 1980s.

Today, one can only guess at what Coppola could have accomplished had he been able to hold onto the studio and had the various Zoetrope development deals been given a chance. By the end of 1981, Zoetrope had signed deals with Franc Roddam, Martha Coolidge, Jonathan Sanger, Carroll Ballard, Jean-Luc Godard, Paul Schrader, David Lynch, avant-garde filmmaker Scott Bartlett, and stage director Michael Bennett. Also in the works were a two-thousand-seat theater and resort hotel in the Rockies designed and built to exhibit a sixteen-hour holographic film based on Goethe's *Elective Affinities* and a motion picture theme park in Belize. Additionally, Coppola himself planned to direct *Elective Affinities, The Brotherhood of the Grape* (based on the novel by John Fante and a screenplay by Robert Towne), *The Sea of Fertility* (adapted from a tetralogy written by Yukio Mishima), *Tucker* (focusing on the ill-fated inventor-entrepreneur who took on the big car companies), *Megalopolis* (based in part on ancient Roman history and contemporary Wall Street), and an adaptation of Jack Kerouac's *On the Road.* To date only *Tucker* (released in 1988 under the title *Tucker: The Man and His Dream*) has reached the screen, due in large part to George Lucas's participation as the film's producer.

The Final Days

I was interested in the idea that as an object becomes more and more beautiful, it seeks its own destruction.—Paul Schrader, screenwriter (*Taxi Driver*) and director (*American Gigolo*)[42]

In March 1983, when Zoetrope executive John Peters told *Variety* that "[Coppola] is not a businessman first—he's motivated by things other than business,"[43] no one in the industry argued the point. Zoetrope Studios was, financially at least, a failure, and Coppola's performance as the studio's artistic director seemed primarily, perhaps even solely, to blame. But even after Coppola bankrupted the studio with *One from the Heart,* he never gave up assembling a legacy, and in many ways he saved the best for last. The final two Zoetrope projects—the negative pickup of Phillip Borsos's thirteen Genie Award winning film, *Grey Fox,* and the studio production of fellow UCLA alumnus Paul Schrader's *Mishima*—not only displayed Coppola's eclectic, global sense of things but offered one final reminder of his commitment to interesting projects independent of their potential in the marketplace.

Coppola picked up the U.S. distribution rights to the Canadian release, *Grey Fox,* because none of the majors expressed interest in distributing the picture and he thought it needed to be seen. At the time, he realized that the film would not make much at the box office—certainly it had no chance of grossing enough to rescue the studio—but he was enamored with the performance of the film's star, Richard Farnsworth.

Though it is unlikely that he purchased the rights to the film in order to do so, Coppola was able to use *Grey Fox* to publicly make amends for his supposed exploitation of *Napoleon. Grey Fox* was released under a new banner, "Zoetrope Studios Presents," which replaced the *auteurist* logo "Francis Ford Coppola Presents." Coppola also eschewed nominal production credit and profit participation in the U.S. release of the film, displaying a generosity he could hardly afford at the time.

Coppola's production of *Mishima* (released in 1985, over a year after the studio had been sold) in many ways displayed the effectiveness and economy of the Zoetrope production method and the range and beauty of the studio's evolving visual style first seen in *One from the Heart* and subsequently evident in *Hammett* and *The Escape Artist.* The project was the indirect result of Coppola's ambition to secure the rights to Mishima's tetralogy, *The Sea of Fertility,* which he had hoped to develop into a multimedia film and video project attending to contemporary Japanese-American relations.

Coppola's contact with the Mishima estate dated back to 1980, and despite considerable resistance from the Mishima family and the Japanese government, he was eventually able to secure rights to the entirety of Mishima's life and fiction. In 1982, Coppola assigned those rights to a Zoetrope subcorporation, Hot Weather Films, the production unit eventually responsible for financing Schrader's *Mishima.*

In retrospect, Schrader's production seems to be the very multimedia "film" project Coppola talked about but never got around to shooting during his tenure at the studio. The picture breaks down into three distinct parts: Mishima's life just before his public ritual suicide (told in the present tense), his coming of age as a gay man in an intolerant culture (told in a nostalgic past-tense voiceover), and his fiction (read and simultaneously staged on-screen). Each part is rendered in a different format: 35-mm color film, 35-mm black-and-white film, and one-inch color video transferred to film. The overall effect is actually more "experimental" than anything Coppola himself accomplished during the same period, and, pointedly, *Mishima* was made for less than $10 million.

A *Film Quarterly* interview with Paul Schrader published after the film's release makes no mention of Coppola's contribution to *Mishima*. His actual participation in the day-to-day production of the movie may well have been minimal; indeed, the things executive producers do vary from film to film. Coppola did secure the rights that got the film made in the first place, but Schrader seems to have enjoyed an autonomy that Wenders and Caleb Deschanel, the director of *The Escape Artist,* did not, and the film is by far the best of the three.

Nevertheless, today there is no way to look at *Mishima* and not see the Zoetrope studio look—the theatrical visual style, the expressive (as opposed to realistic) sets, the sweeping camera movement—already in evidence in *One from the Heart, Hammett,* and *The Escape Artist.* However much (or little) Coppola actually participated in the making of the movie, *Mishima* still seems in many ways a Coppola film.

Coppola's influence seems all the more significant when one considers George Lucas's participation in the project. Signing on before Coppola had even secured the rights to the Mishima estate, Lucas eventually provided postproduction expertise at his amazing facility in Marin County and helped market the film. But while a number of 1980s movies that employed Lucasfilm in such a capacity bear Lucas's *auteur* signature in one way or another—here Ron Howard's *Cocoon* seems the best example—*Mishima* seems far more in line with Coppola's Zoetrope style.

Mishima, like virtually every other Zoetrope Studios film, did not do as well as it deserved to at the box office or with the critics. But Schrader did not take it personally. Instead, he put the apparent failure of *Mishima* (and in many ways Coppola's own work in the early 1980s as well) in perspective by shrugging it off as a sign of the times: "Well, the critics are always crying, 'Give me something new. We never see anything innovative.' Then you do something they've never seen the likes of before, and they howl 'What is it?' . . . Popular criticism, like everything else [in this country], is becoming extremely conservative, or just lazy."[44]

Five Exile in Oklahoma: *The Outsiders* and *Rumble Fish*

[Adolph Zukor] was like 96 years old. They were celebrating his birthday. They were helping him chew and everything. He was telling a story, I swear to God, about screwing Samuel Clemens on a story deal.—Jerry Belson, comedy writer[1]

Francis Coppola directed three movies as artistic director at Zoetrope Studios: *One from the Heart, The Outsiders,* and *Rumble Fish,* the latter two produced and released well after the studio was put up for sale. While he foresaw the production of *One from the Heart* as a kind of watershed moment for *auteurism* in American cinema and seemed to use the films he later chose to produce or pick up for distribution as a means to establish some sort of legacy as a cine-entrepreneur, exactly what Coppola had in mind— professionally or personally—with *The Outsiders* and *Rumble Fish* is far more difficult to pin down.

Both *The Outsiders* and *Rumble Fish* are teen movies, and both were shot on location in Tulsa, Oklahoma, far from the fray that surrounded the various auctions, postponements of auctions, and lawsuits that attended the eventual demise of Zoetrope Studios. *The Outsiders* seems, even in retrospect, a calculated attempt on Coppola's part to regain his lost commercial appeal, and in its own modest way the picture succeeded on that score. *Rumble Fish,* released approximately a year after *The Outsiders,* seems just as calculated in its unmarketability. *The Outsiders* was Coppola's first pure genre picture since *The Godfather. Rumble Fish,* with its complex visual and aural structure and its allegorical, allusory narrative, seems very much like Coppola's 1974 follow-up to the two *Godfather* films, *The Conversation.* While *The Outsiders* and *Rumble Fish* share a generic heritage, on almost any other level the two films could not be more different.

The Outsiders

In cinema in this country, there's a requirement to stay realistic. . . . [But] if you do *Oklahoma*, characters can't act the same way they do in *On the Waterfront*. . . . I was afraid that if the characters were written as realistic characters there wouldn't be space for the scenery.—Francis Coppola, 1987[2]

After the release of *One from the Heart*—which lost in the neighborhood of $25 million—Coppola stopped talking about taking over Hollywood. At the time, he was so strapped for cash he could no longer afford to antagonize anybody who might someday invest in one of his films. Every week the trades had more bad news about him: failed auctions, foreclosure, bankruptcy. Exactly what Coppola might do next—exactly what he *could* do next—was anybody's guess.

He did have one thing going in his favor. There is an old industry axiom: never hire a director after a hit. Given the extent to which *One from the Heart* was perceived as a failure, Coppola must have seemed eminently hirable.

In order to reestablish a position in the industry, in the spring of 1982 Coppola began hawking a project the studios could not afford to refuse: *The Outsiders*, a teen picture based on one of the best-selling adolescent novels of all time. When Coppola began shopping the picture around in earnest, and moreover began dropping names of teen-star actors committed to the project, studio interest was considerable . . . but with one catch. In order to secure financing for the film, Coppola discovered that he would have to once again get used to keeping to a budget and a timetable, details he had learned to ignore after the release of *The Godfather* in 1972.

In order to close the deal for *The Outsiders*, Coppola took a giant step backward. Not only was he no longer a studio mogul, he was just another director with a script under his arm, a line of hype, and a short rope from the studio. After twenty years in the business, Coppola found himself once again working for someone else, out there (in Tulsa, this time), making a mainstream genre picture on the cheap.[3]

The story behind Coppola's development of *The Outsiders* is an interesting one. In March 1980, a librarian and thirty of her students at Lone Star Junior High School in Salinas, California, wrote to Coppola and asked him to make a movie based on their favorite book, *The Outsiders*. The letter, along with the novel, got passed down the food chain at Zoetrope and eventually ended up on the desk of producer Fred Roos. Roos, so the story goes, was intrigued by the letter, then read the novel and became convinced that Coppola should make the movie.

On the surface, *The Outsiders* seems hardly a Coppola project. The novel is quite thin and singularly uncinematic. What little interest an adult can find in the all too familiar story of greasers and rich kids fighting it out on the mean streets of Tulsa, Oklahoma, stems from the novel's occasionally intriguing point of view. The narration, provided by one of the more sensitive young hoods, plays off the reader's image of the book's author, Susan (S. E.) Hinton, who was all of seventeen when she wrote the novel and probably hung out with the characters depicted in the book. What makes the novel "work" is its authentic voice, something quite difficult to translate to the screen.

But Roos, a savvy Hollywood businessman and former casting agent, understood that the novel's principal attraction was not its plot or style but its cast of characters. After reading the book, Roos foresaw a "package" featuring Coppola and a number of bankable young male stars. When Roos brought the property to Coppola's attention, he made sure to emphasize the film's potential box office appeal. At the time—well before the release of *Hammett* and *One from the Heart*—Coppola realized that in order to continue to meet the payments on the studio, he would need at least one big box office picture before the end of 1982. Thus, even before he had time to write a screenplay, Coppola began hyping *The Outsiders*, eventually dubbing the project "a *Gone with the Wind* for fourteen year old girls."[4]

By the time Coppola began work on the film, he was hardly in a position, on his own, at least, to make it. He and Roos had envisioned *The Outsiders* as a proper 1980s package, which, especially after the release of *One from the Heart* and *Hammett*, could be mounted only with significant financing from one of the major studios. Zoetrope's role in the film's production would involve little more than a nominal production credit; by the spring of 1982 the company was already bankrupt and the lot up for sale.

Coppola's tendency at the time to talk as if he was actually making the picture anyway—on his own, at Zoetrope—struck many in the industry as rather sad. Coppola, they knew, was so strapped for cash that when Susan Hinton asked for a mere $5,000 for the rights to the novel, he was unable to meet her price.

In order to option the book and mount a production of the film, Coppola shopped the project around and eventually signed a distribution deal with Warners. Though the smart money had the film going to Columbia as a payback for their pickup of *One from the Heart*, at the time Coppola could hardly afford to be so sentimental, and he went with the sweetest deal and the studio most likely to be enthusiastic about the film.

To anyone aware of recent history, the Warner Brothers deal was a surprise for several reasons. The studio had expressed some interest in *The Outsiders* when, in January 1982, it halfheartedly bid on the domestic distribution rights to *One from the Heart*, but Coppola and Warners had dealt with each other before, and in the past it had never turned out particularly well for either party. Back in the late 1960s, it was Warner Brothers that lent Coppola $600,000 to set up American Zoetrope in San Francisco and then, approximately a year later, demanded its money back. Warners was also the studio of record on Coppola's first three A features: *You're a Big Boy Now*, *Finian's Rainbow*, and *The Rain People*, none of which did well at the box office. Most recently, in 1981, it was Warners that had secured domestic distribution rights for both *Hammett* and *The Escape Artist*, two films that by 1982 seemed to suggest that Coppola could no longer behave reasonably or predictably as a movie producer.[5] In sum, of all the studios Coppola had dealt with in the past, Warners seemed to have the best justification for not working with him again. But in Hollywood, it's best to have a short memory.

After closing the Warners deal, Coppola was able to secure a completion guarantee from Britain's National Film Finance Corporation, which he used to obtain production financing from Chemical Bank. *The Outsiders* went into principal photography securely financed with virtually all the collateral tied into the picture. For the first time since 1974, Coppola was able to finance a production without mortgaging his studio or personal property, much of which, by the spring of 1982, could hardly be called *his* any longer. Ironically, it took a failure of the magnitude of *One from the Heart* to put Coppola into a position to finally shoot a movie using other people's money.

But the price of using the studio's money was clear at the outset. Though the deal with Warners enabled Coppola to secure funds to shoot the picture—and nominally, at least, placed the production under the Zoetrope Studios banner (since it was Zoetrope and not Warners that, technically speaking, borrowed the production funds from Chemical Bank)—it also severely limited how much Coppola could spend and exactly what he could and could not do while shooting and editing the picture.

The production budget for *The Outsiders* was just under $10 million, approximately a third of what it took to make *One from the Heart*. To keep to that budget, Coppola made some significant concessions. For example, while planning the production, he decided not to hire cinematographer Vittorio Storaro, who had shot both *Apocalypse Now* and *One from the Heart*, and instead engaged *Apocalypse Now* second unit lenser Stephen Burum.

Coppola then negotiated with the film's teen stars—Matt Dillon, Rob Lowe, Ralph Macchio, Patrick Swayze, and Tom Cruise—and convinced each to work well below his usual salary. The stars agreed to work for less in order to get a chance to work with the director of *The Godfather*. For the young actors, at least, Coppola's reputation was still worth something.

For reasons that had less to do with the budget than with his peace of mind, Coppola decided to shoot *The Outsiders* on location in Tulsa, where the novel is set in 1966, mostly to physically remove himself from the many distractions attending the various sales and foreclosures of his studio. As Coppola told *New York Times* feature writer Aljean Harmetz, "It was chaos incorporated at Zoetrope, like fighting a war. I used to be a great camp counselor, and the idea of being with half a dozen kids in the country making a movie seemed like being a camp counselor again. It would be a breath of fresh air. I'd forget my troubles and have some laughs again."[6]

Though shooting on location often unduly increases a picture's budget, when Coppola took his electronic cinema method on the road, he proved once and for all that it was a cost-effective process. First, before shooting a single foot of film, Coppola videotaped a dress rehearsal in a local college gym with all the actors reading in front of a blue screen. Coppola then went into a kind of pre-postproduction and superimposed images from the rehearsal over appropriate shots of Tulsa and the Dean Tavoularis sets in order to previsualize the entire picture. The result was just as Coppola had predicted during the production of *One from the Heart:* by the time he got around to shooting on film, he already knew what each and every scene was supposed to look like. As a result, he reduced the amount of time wasted on the set and in the editing room.

After the film was finished, Coppola told the press that, despite its sub-$10 million budget, *The Outsiders* was not "a little film."[7] But in retrospect, only Coppola's evocative use of wide-screen Panavision—an obvious allusion to the genre's hallmark work, *Rebel Without a Cause*—supports such a view. Today, *The Outsiders* seems Coppola's least original and least satisfying film. Its production was a calculated and very conservative attempt to make a commercial picture at the very moment those in power in the industry doubted his ability to do so.

Because he had to, Coppola hyped the film (as if he meant it) in the press. For example, while discussing his attraction to the story, Coppola mused: "As I was reading the book, I realized that I wanted to make a film about young people and about belonging. Belonging to a peer group with whom one can identify and for whom one feels real love. And even though these boys are poor and to a certain extent insignificant, the story gives them a kind of beauty and nobility."[8] In order to place *The Outsiders* within his oeuvre, Coppola made the picture sound like *One from the Heart:* sentimental, epic, even operatic.

Once the film was safely out of his hands and its first run completed, Coppola put *The Outsiders* in perspective: "People expect me to demonstrate more of my own style. Many directors make movies in the same style as *The Outsiders.* The actors are good; the story was the story and that's it. Yet when I do a film like that, people now expect it to have some loaded trap door. People expect me to be nutty, weird or at least a little unusual or strange."[9]

Though Warners had planned to release *The Outsiders* in the fall of 1982 to accompany its target audience's return to school, relatively minor production and postproduction delays put it off until the spring of 1983,[10] a little over a year after the release of *One from the Heart.* The film was essentially complete in time for a Christmas release, but Warners wisely decided to premiere *The Outsiders* in March, banking on the strategy that *The Outsiders* would have the off-peak season to itself. And, for a couple of weeks, it did. Though the studio spent comparatively little to promote *The Outsiders*—it was the first Coppola film in more than a decade to receive no formal advance publicity—it nevertheless opened big. In its first weekend, *The Outsiders* grossed over $5 million, more than five times what *One from the Heart* had earned in its entire first run. In its first week in release, the film topped the *Variety* box office chart.

Despite scathing reviews—only one favorable notice (from Joseph Gelmis at *Newsday*) out of eleven from the New York critics—the film held the top spot for over a month.[11] It was not until its fifth week in general release that it was replaced at the top of the list by another youth-market picture, *Flashdance,* which eventually grossed over $90 million and placed third overall for the year. Fortunately for Warners, *The Outsiders*' strong initial box office allowed them to ignore the poor reviews. Instead of blurbs touting the picture or its stars—and even after the second wave of reviews came out, the studio would have been hard-pressed to find much that could be used to promote the picture—the marketing team at Warner Brothers headlined the ad campaign with box office figures. In doing so, they defined *The Outsiders* as an event film, or at least as a picture film audiences (as opposed to critics) seemed to like.

The Outsiders remained on *Variety*'s top fifty list for almost three months. By the time its first run was over it proved to be Coppola's most successful outing in almost five years. But while the box office success put Coppola in a stronger position for his next film deal, he found it hard to ignore the bad notices: "The New York critics have come down as hard as they can on everything I've done since *The Godfather, Part II*," Coppola reflected. "I've never had a bone from those guys. Sometimes I think: 'Are my movies that bad or are they exaggerating?' "[12]

After years of attacking his grandiose epics for their bloated budgets and obnoxious prerelease hype, the critics instead chastised Coppola for making such a silly, unpretentious, and unambitious little film. Vincent Canby of the *New York Times* wrote: "Francis Coppola's *The Outsiders* coming on the heels, so to speak, of *One from the Heart*, leads one to suspect that Mr. Coppola is no longer with us, but up with his entourage observing the world from a space platform."[13] David Denby, in *New York* magazine, called the film "a frightening failure," and Gary Arnold of the *Washington Post* wrote that Coppola seemed to be "in a state of artistic convalescence."[14]

For Warner Brothers and the industry as a whole, the box office success of *The Outsiders* carried a lot more weight than the critical consensus that the film was Coppola's worst ever. But for Coppola, the financial success of the film was a pyrrhic victory. *The Outsiders* was exactly what the audience seemed to want in 1983. But it clearly was not the kind of picture he ever wanted to make again.

Rumble Fish

Rumble Fish is Coppola's best film, the most emotional, the most revolutionary and the most clearly in love with the 1940's movies. It has a mood from Camus and the French Existentialists, but it looks and feels like Welles and Cocteau. . . . It is deliberately an American art film—as full of the heart's creaking sound as *Kane.*—David Thomson and Lucy Gray, film critics[15]

I was scared. I couldn't understand any of it.—Robert Evans, producer (*The Godfather, Love Story, Chinatown*)[16]

A little over a year after *The Outsiders* was released, Coppola had a second S. E. Hinton adaptation in theaters nationwide. The film, *Rumble Fish*, Coppola's most audacious, stylized, and uncommercial work since *The Conversation*, reminded the industry and the critics just how little of his own creative talent had gone into the production of *The Outsiders*.

Fully aware that *The Outsiders* seemed to suggest that the various failures at Zoetrope had taken their toll on his ability as a director, Coppola used

8. Coppola's emphasis on set design in *Rumble Fish:* William Smith, Matt Dillon, Mickey Rourke, and a giant clock (Hot Weather Films and Universal Studios, 1983).

Rumble Fish to reestablish his authorial/artistic signature. At the time Coppola seemed to appreciate the fact that *The Outsiders* had improved his position in the industry at the expense of his standing as an *auteur* and as an artist.

In interviews Coppola has consistently pointed out that he began planning *Rumble Fish* even before he was finished shooting *The Outsiders*. In 1984, for example, Coppola reflected: "While I was filming *The Outsiders*, I decided to make another movie, in a different spirit. I wanted to show that with or without stars, with or without new techniques, whatever I did was still Coppola."[17] Three years later, in another interview, Coppola added: "I really started to use *Rumble Fish* as my carrot . . . for what I promised myself when I finished *The Outsiders*."[18]

Though he had won twice at Cannes in the 1970s (with *The Conversation* and *Apocalypse Now*), Coppola had never placed one of his own films on the New York Film Festival program until *Rumble Fish* in 1983. Coppola's work as a producer or cine-entrepreneur had been featured, of course; no less than five Coppola/Zoetrope pictures had made the cut, including *The Black Stallion, Napoleon, Every Man for Himself, Koyaanisqatsi,* and *Kagemusha*. But in 1983, Coppola and Universal, the distributor of *Rumble Fish,* decided that if they were to make any money at all on the picture, they had to target the art house audience. The New York Film Festival seemed as good a place as any to start.

But the studio's plans for the picture were immediately upset when both the critics and the festival audience hated the film. Stanley Kauffmann of the *New Republic* characterized the screening as follows: "*Passion* [the Godard film which was shown immediately before *Rumble Fish* at the festival] is released here in connection with Zoetrope Studios; the American print bears the title 'Francis Ford Coppola Presents.' Coppola also presents a new film of his own, called *Rumble Fish*. That logo at the start is the only relation to Godard: comparison of the two films would be senseless. Comparison of *Rumble Fish* with Coppola's own past films is sad enough."[19] Kauffmann dubbed *Rumble Fish* "a ridiculously trite configuration of adolescent heroics." As to the film's central symbol—the rumble fish themselves, who fight until they die or kill their mate—Kauffmann concluded: "I suppose there's a moral in all this, but it's not about those poor fish, it's about Coppola."[20]

On October 19, 1983, *Variety*'s critics' scorecord on the film noted nine unfavorable and one inconclusive review.[21] The film's poor showing with the mainstream reviewers along with reports on the screening at the New York Film Festival effectively killed the picture's chances at the box office. Quite unlike the up-market *Outsiders,* which opened big and thus allowed Coppola and Warners to ignore the reviews, *Rumble Fish* needed the critics to make an impact on the art-house circuit.

Rumble Fish opened at number 29 in its first week of release, rose briefly to 16, then 11, then fell to 15, 22, and 47, and then, after just seven weeks in distribution, fell out of the top fifty altogether. Less than a year after the simply awful teen picture *Porky's* grossed over $100 million, *Rumble Fish* dropped out of sight after earning a little over a million.

To be fair to Universal, *Rumble Fish* was a very difficult film to market. Though it followed *The Outsiders* both thematically and chronologically, *Rumble Fish* could hardly be categorized or marketed as a sequel. And while the teen audience was a prodigious market at the time—audience studies indicated that four out of every ten teenagers went to the movies at least once a month and that 73 percent of all ticket sales could be attributed to the twelve-to-twenty-nine-year-old target market[23]—*Rumble Fish* seemed hardly like, for example, the 1982 teen audience hit *Porky's,* or the lighthearted, upbeat John Hughes film *Sixteen Candles,* which did quite well at the box office in 1984.

Indeed, *Rumble Fish* seemed intentionally unmarketable, so much so that *Time* reviewer Richard Corliss concluded at its release: "Pressed to the wall by his failures with *One from the Heart* and Zoetrope Studios, prodded by a Hollywood that wants one of its pedigreed talents to make a 'good picture,' [Francis Coppola] keeps slipping away into stylistic eccentricity. In one sense, then, *Rumble Fish* is Coppola's professional suicide note to the movie industry, a warning against employing him to find the golden gross. No doubt, this is his most baroque and self-indulgent film. It may also be his bravest."[23]

Further complicating Universal's marketing attempts was the film's evocative, eccentric, and eclectic score, written and performed by former Police percussionist Stewart Copeland. Much to Universal's disappointment, the score (and the record pressed from that score) didn't sound anything like the still-popular pop trio, the Police. Consistent with the film's mixing and matching of styles, Copeland's music seemed to defy genre categories; it wasn't rock, jazz, *or* classical. As a result, though record albums were being used to support releases of many of its other titles, Universal had no idea how to use the *Rumble Fish* soundtrack to help market the movie.

Universal also had to deal with the fact that, by 1983, Coppola's name alone was no longer enough to get people to see the film. Thus, when Coppola told the press that he was more satisfied with *Rumble Fish* than with anything else he had ever made—he still says so now, a decade later—such hype was widely disregarded at the time as absurd.

Principal photography on *Rumble Fish* commenced in July 1982, less than a month after the production phase on *The Outsiders* was complete and less than half a year after the disastrous first run of *One from the Heart.* In preparation for the retro look of *Rumble Fish,* Coppola, set designer Dean Tavoularis, and cinematographer Stephen Burum studied German expressionist films and then paid particular attention to the visual strategies employed in Anatole Litvak's *Decision Before Dawn.*

San Francisco Ballet director Michael Smuin, who along with Copeland was added to the creative team that had produced *The Outsiders,* provided the film's signature scene: the dazzling rumble set down by the tracks that introduces the film's antihero, the Motorcycle Boy. Smuin's work moves the film not so much toward musical theater (and *West Side Story,* which, of course, also features choreographed violence) but, along with the photography and sets, toward a kind of antirealism seldom if ever seen before in a teen film.[24]

Burum, whose wide-screen color photography for *The Outsiders* seemed perfect for that film's various allusions to *Gone with the Wind* and *Rebel Without a Cause,* was called on to shoot *Rumble Fish* in a style more in

9. Matt Dillon in *Rumble Fish* (Hot Weather Films and Universal Studios, 1983).

keeping with the silent films of 1920s Germany that he and Coppola had watched while developing the picture. In order to achieve that look, Burum opted to shoot *Rumble Fish* in an unusual focal length (14 mm) and almost entirely in black and white (with the exception of a few color special effects denoting the significance of the rumble fish the Motorcycle Boy frees in the river).

Much like Storaro's work in *One from the Heart,* which was shot in the square-r aspect ratio, Burum's *Rumble Fish* seemed to dramatically reshape the visual field. Indeed, both films call attention to camera work, and moreover to the ways the camera reveals action on-screen. *One from the Heart,* because of the square-r aspect ratio and its use of theatrical scrimlike transitions, is an almost entirely vertical film. The camera travels through space up and down as opposed to side to side. *Rumble Fish,* on the other hand, is almost exclusively horizontal. And while *One from the Heart* was shot to look like high-resolution video (that is to say, perfectly lit and always in focus), *Rumble Fish* eschews all but high key light, and the entirety of the frame is almost never visually accessible (much like, for example, Orson Welles's *Touch of Evil*).

In integrating the electronic cinema method into the production of *Rumble Fish,* Coppola showed, as he did in *One from the Heart,* how a film's soundtrack can be used to propel and interpret as opposed to simply punctuating a film's narrative. Copeland fashioned a music track for *Rumble Fish* that includes much of the sound-effects loop within it; amidst the occasional reggae and zydeco riffs, one hears the sounds of the streets . . . the sounds of characters walking, breathing, even dreaming. The Copeland score was then synched by sound engineer Richard Beggs using a "revolutionary" technological device called Musynch, which allowed Coppola to digitalize the score and then record it frame by frame onto a videotape of the film (which had previously been time coded and already contained the image and dialogue tracks).

By "looping" approximately 90 percent of the picture in the controlled environment of the postproduction studio, Coppola not only saved time and money but also dramatically asserted his total control over every aspect of the production. In seeming response to Pauline Kael's sarcastic quip about *One from the Heart,*[25] *Rumble Fish* was truly a film that deliberately looked and sounded as if it *were* directed from a trailer parked somewhere off the set.

A Few Last Claims at Genius

And what is genius anyway if not a certain combination of unquestionably personal talents, a gift from the fairies, and a moment in history?"—André Bazin, film theorist and historian[26]

They throw the word genius around: Bertolucci is a genius; Francis is a genius after doing three or four films. I think they have a genius association and you get a genius card."—John Milius, screenwriter, director, and founding member of American Zoetrope[27]

With both *The Outsiders* and *Rumble Fish* shot and in theaters in the space of a year and a half, Coppola turned to the press to once again promote the Zoetrope method. "Movies have always been thought of in three stages," he remarked in an interview in the *San Francisco Chronicle.* "There's preproduction, production and the postproduction, where you actually put the movie together. The whole point of our system is to make it possible to do all that at once—cheaper, faster and better. Someday, for example, we'll be making movies with no sets at all. We'll work with only a stage. And it will look totally realistic."[28]

In retrospect, Coppola's high hopes for *Rumble Fish* seem to reveal just how dramatically he overestimated the 1980s film audience. Its dense style and the conspicuous absence of realistic depictions of sex or violence made *Rumble Fish* unattractive to teenagers. Additionally, the film was not strictly nostalgic (like, for example *American Graffiti* or *The Wanderers*) and thus missed with the twenty-five-to-forty-year-old crowd. The picture is dedicated to Coppola's elder brother, August, a college professor, and, ironically, it is on college campuses today (in film courses) that *Rumble Fish* is finally being seen and appreciated. But in its initial release, on virtually every front that matters to the industry, the film was a failure.

Though most of the reviewers for the popular press hated the picture, a few important critics applauded Coppola's audacity, his artistic courage, and his style. But even those who loved *Rumble Fish* realized just how unpopular it was bound to be. Jack Kroll at *Newsweek*, for example, opened his review ruefully: "Despite financial problems that would choke Lee Iacocca's carburetor, savage reviews of his recent films and his current status as the media's favorite movie-biz whipping boy, Francis Coppola keeps on going. His new film, *Rumble Fish*, is his most personal work and an act of courage."

Focusing on the film's unrelentingly dark vision of contemporary youth, Kroll dubbed it "a brilliant tone poem of [teendom's] inner exile." As to the evocative music track: "[It] heaves and hisses and wails like our country giving birth to a monstrous mutation of city and nature." Burum's cinematography, Kroll added, "turns Tulsa into a city vibrating with fatality." As to the performances—all of which were expressionistic, as opposed to the more naturalistic Hollywood style—Kroll found Matt Dillon's and Mickey Rourke's evocation of the inner turmoil of youth "a relief," especially in comparison with the simplistic portrayal of teenagers in the recently released *Porky's, Risky Business,* and *Eddie and the Cruisers.* In conclusion, Kroll called *Rumble Fish* "a welcome reach for beauty and honesty by an artist who won't surrender."[29]

In *MacLeans,* Lawrence O'Toole was equally enthusiastic. "For all its frantic movement and pessimism," O'Toole gushed, "the film has odd moments of poetry that are like benedictions." Regarding the film's postmodern ennui—its ability to capture the mood if not the melodramatic trappings of teen anomie—O'Toole acknowledged *Rumble Fish*'s "inky ode to nothingness." O'Toole did concede that there were narrative sections of *Rumble Fish* that didn't quite hold together: "[But] such oversights seem little reason for the invective hurled at the film. It is as though the backlash from Coppola's two previous mistakes (*The Outsiders,* also from a Hinton novel, and *One from the Heart*) still has not lost its momentum." Finally, O'Toole blamed the critical community and the public it serves for its impatience with style, its insistence on simpler, dare we say more "Reaganite" entertainment. "The real reason [for the critical and box office failure of the film]," O'Toole concluded, "may be that in 1983 extreme style is a form of abrasiveness. Truly unique, dark-minded moviemaking such as *Rumble Fish, The Moon in the Gutter* or even *Daniel,* in an era that cleaves to what is safe and innocuous, is an increasingly risky business."[30]

But while both Kroll and O'Toole were satisfied to deal with the film on its own terms—as an original and highly stylized work—the vast majority of the reviewers writing for the popular press found the picture pretentious and hopelessly obscure. For them, *Rumble Fish* seemed to reveal Coppola's foolish abandonment of narrative and his misguided descent into style after the release of *Apocalypse Now.*

Six *The Cotton Club*

Every putz thinks he can produce a movie. There isn't anybody who's asked me what I do who doesn't think, after I try to explain it, that they could do it too. . . . Producing is bullshit work. It's a bunch of silly people running around trying to take credit for other people's stuff.—Art Linson, producer of *Dick Tracy*[1]

In the spring of 1983, when Francis Coppola first became involved in "the Robert Evans Production" of *The Cotton Club*, both men clung to the old Hollywood adage that it is best to have a short memory. The two were extremely unlikely bedfellows with hard feelings dating back more than ten years.

In 1971, Evans was in charge of production at Paramount, and it was his responsibility to oversee the production of *The Godfather*. Throughout the film's development, production and postproduction, Evans posed a series of challenges to Coppola's control over the picture. First, Evans did not like Coppola's casting choices; he thought that Marlon Brando was too expensive and difficult and that Al Pacino was too short. During the shoot, Evans argued that the lighting was too dark, the pace too slow, the film too long. Once the picture was shot, Evans praised the film's look and Pacino's and Brando's performances, but found the plot too fragmented, and astonishingly, the running time too short. Coppola and Evans continued to argue up until the film's release. But when *The Godfather* won an Academy Award for Best Picture and then became the biggest box office film of all time (until *The Exorcist* supplanted it in 1973), Evans did what all good producers do in such circumstances: he made himself available to the press in order to take credit for the picture's success.

The Evans-Coppola feud continued long after the release of *The Godfather*. In a *Playboy* interview in 1975, Coppola told William Murray that "a lot of energy that went into [*The Godfather*] went into simply trying to convince the people who held the power [read here, Evans] to let [me] do the film [my] way."[2] Almost ten years later, as he began work on the screenplay for Evans's *Cotton Club,* Coppola told another interviewer: "I'm terrified of being in a situation where I have people second-guessing me. If I have to fight for everything, like I had to fight for Al Pacino and Marlon Brando, I don't have the energy anymore."[3]

In a 1984 interview, Evans continued to tell his side of the story regarding the production of *The Godfather.* According to Evans, Coppola's final cut "looked like a section out of *The Untouchables,*"; it was so bad, *he* had to recut and "[change] the picture around entirely."[4]

When Evans first began to develop *The Cotton Club* in 1980, he and Coppola seemed to be headed in two very different directions. *Apocalypse Now* had just become a box office hit, and with its profits Coppola closed the deal for Hollywood General. Evans, in contrast, seemed to be on his last legs; he hadn't had a hit in years, and a series of well-publicized personal and professional problems had all but cut him off from the industry subculture.

Evans's predicament in 1980 seems all the more dramatic when one considers just how far and how fast he fell. At Paramount in the 1970s, Evans had the Midas touch. In addition to *The Godfather,* he produced several other big box office movies, including *Rosemary's Baby, The Odd Couple,* and *Love Story.* When Gulf and Western CEO Charles Bluhdorn gave him the chance to produce his own films at Paramount under the Robert Evans Productions banner, Evans continued to enjoy considerable success. Within months of signing the production deal with Bluhdorn, Evans emerged as the central player in the deal for *Chinatown.*

But as the 1970s wound down, Evans's luck seemed to run out; first there was *Black Sunday,* then *Players,* and then, in 1979, *Urban Cowboy.* In an effort to regain the status and power he had achieved in the early 1970s, Evans decided to make one last play with one last property. For some fateful and strange reason, he optioned a nonfiction book by James Haskins about the Cotton Club and proposed to make a movie about Harlem in the 1920s.

Exactly what drew Evans to the property remains unclear. He was neither an expert on, nor even all that familiar with, jazz, African-American culture, or, more specifically, the Harlem renaissance. But Evans *was* an expert at the high-concept pitch. Thus, despite the famous nightclub's colorful history and the complex issues of race and class inherent in the Roaring Twenties' Harlem subculture, Evans glibly summed up *The Cotton Club* in three words: "gangsters, music, pussy."[5]

Evans optioned the property for $350,000 and then, in a very surprising move, announced his intention not only to produce but to also direct the film.[6] If *The Cotton Club* failed, Evans surmised, he was through in the business. If it hit, his run of bad luck would be forgotten. With that in mind, he decided that the only person he could trust to direct the picture was himself.

Dealing the Picture

A deal . . . it's like chasing a girl. You work at it until she says yes. . . . You keep putting pressure on them. Hit 'em right between the eyes . . . you kill 'em.—Wayne Huizenga, CEO of Blockbuster Video[7]

In order to get things rolling, Evans went about putting the film together like a producer; that is, he began by concentrating on packaging the product long before he had a story or a script. To make the project attractive to potential investors, he came up with a high-concept slogan: "Its violence startled the nation; its music startled the world." First, Evans shopped the idea around at the major studios. But they all passed on the project for two reasons: Evans's well-publicized drug arrest and conventional wisdom that it is impossible to make a mass-market film about African Americans.

After failing to interest the major studios, Evans began to explore ways of raising the money outside the industry. His first break came through a chance meeting with an actress named Melissa Prophet. When Evans told Prophet about the *Cotton Club* project and his difficulties raising money, Prophet dropped the name of a friend who might be able to help: Adnan Khashoggi, the Arab arms dealer who would eventually gain wider recognition through his involvement in the Iran-Contra affair.

Evans understood that Khashoggi could fund the film by himself if he wanted to and hoped that the aura of Hollywood would be enough to get him hooked. Prophet hoped to convince Khashoggi to underwrite *The Cotton Club* so that she could collect a finder's fee, which, if Khashoggi backed the entire project, would top six figures. Khashoggi stood to gain the least in the bargain. The best he could hope for was second position on a film the major studios had all turned down.[8]

Prophet made the first move (on Evans's behalf) and met with Khashoggi in Las Vegas. She pitched the project and Khashoggi expressed interest. But when Prophet suggested that Khashoggi should fly to Los Angeles to meet with Evans, Khashoggi countered by dispatching Prophet in his private 727 to fetch Evans and fly him back to Las Vegas. Khashoggi's insistence on holding the meeting on his turf and Evans's willingness to meet him there established, in terms both men understood, the power dynamics of their relationship.

10 and 11. Richard Gere and Diane Lane, the two young, white lovers in *The Cotton Club*. Photos by Adger W. Cowans (Orion Pictures, 1984).

When the two men met, Khashoggi continued to press his advantage. Evans had hoped that Khashoggi, who was not in the film business, would prefer to be a silent partner. But it became clear from the very start of their first meeting that while Khashoggi had no interest in taking a screen credit, he did want to play an active role in the development of the movie. Worse yet, Khashoggi balked at funding the film outright and instead offered Evans $2 million in seed money, making it clear that he had no intention of investing any more until he saw a completed script.

Evans turned Khashoggi down high-handedly, cooly rejecting what was clearly a development deal. Khashoggi, he suggested, simply didn't understand how the entertainment industry worked. Khashoggi didn't much care how the industry worked and told Evans to take the offer or leave it. Evans, who had to turn Khashoggi down in order to save face, exited empty-handed.

With Evans safely en route back to Los Angeles, Khashoggi privately told Prophet not to worry about her cut; Evans would be back. And on April 30, 1981, Evans indeed did return to Las Vegas and took Khashoggi's $2 million to begin to develop *The Cotton Club*. Two strings were attached to the money: Prophet would get a producer's credit should the film get made, and Khashoggi's investment in the project was to be kept secret.

With Khashoggi's seed money, Evans hired Mario Puzo to write the script. When a first draft was complete, Khashoggi invited Evans and Puzo to Las Vegas for a party at the Dunes Hotel in their honor. The following morning, Khashoggi dispatched his brother Essam to draw up a contract adding another $10 million to fund the production. But a few days later the deal fell through when Adnan Khashoggi expressed reservations about the script, which he had finally found time to read. After reading the Puzo script, Adnan Khashoggi instructed his brother to ask for 55 percent of the picture in exchange for the $10 million. It was a deal the Khashoggis knew Evans had to refuse.[9]

Ironically, just as Khashoggi pulled out—ostensibly *because* of the Puzo script—several studios called Evans to express interest in the project. So far as the studios were concerned, with Puzo's participation, *The Cotton Club* no longer looked so much like a "black picture" as it looked like another *Godfather.*

With the possibility of a big studio backing the film, Evans set about packaging the Puzo script with a major star. He offered the lead to Al Pacino, but Pacino turned him down. Then Evans offered the role to Sylvester

Stallone, who was interested. Evans met with Stallone's agent and they agreed on a figure: $2 million. Evans then flew to the Cannes Film Festival intending to peddle *The Cotton Club* as an Evans-Puzo-Stallone package. But before Evans could set up a single meeting, Stallone's agent upped the star's asking price to $4 million and Evans canceled the deal.

Evans, trying to assemble "the package" (before doing much else on the film) began to court Richard Pryor. At first, Pryor wouldn't even meet with him. At the time Pryor was in the process of splitting up with his wife and didn't want to talk business. In order to get Pryor to discuss the film, Evans tried to take advantage of Pryor's rumored desire to save his marriage by setting up an informal dinner with Pryor, Pryor's estranged wife, himself, and Ali MacGraw (his own ex-wife).

Pryor at first agreed—maybe the social arrangement sounded too weird to miss—then backed out of the dinner. As to *The Cotton Club,* Pryor promised to consider the project and told Evans he'd have his lawyer take care of the matter. But when Pryor's lawyer got back to Evans he too asked for $4 million, the very figure Evans had refused to pay Stallone. Pryor later confessed that his attorney had recommended against appearing in any film directed by Evans. "I was advised [that the film] would be a disaster," Pryor recalled, "and the best thing was to get out of it. And the best way to get out of something is to ask for money, and that's what I did."[10]

After the Pryor deal unraveled, Gregory Hines, then a Broadway star with no real film record, approached Evans. Unlike Pryor, Hines actually could sing and dance and thus could participate in the musical numbers set onstage at the Cotton Club. But while Hines suited the part, his participation in the project altered the nature of the package. Without Pryor (or Stallone or Pacino), the studios' interest in the project waned and Evans once again faced an uphill fight to finance the film.

In January 1983, Evans's *Cotton Club* project turned three years old. But though he had worked hard, he had little to show for his efforts. He had made what seemed like the right moves, but he still had no financing, no star, and, according to a number of Hollywood insiders, no script. Moreover, what could have taken shape as a Stallone-Pryor-Puzo package had instead, as the studios had suspected all along, evolved into a movie about African Americans and a couple of white gangsters with no stars and a first-time director.

Undaunted, Evans continued to plug away; in the purest sense of the term, he continued to "develop" *The Cotton Club.* But he did so on his own dime. Then, finally, after yet another deal to finance the movie fell through, Melissa

Prophet put Evans in touch with the Los Angeles Lakers's owner, Jerry Buss, who in turn introduced Evans to Ed and Fred Doumani, two brothers who owned the Tropicana Hotel, the La Concha Motel, and the El Morocco Casino in Las Vegas.

Though the glamour of Hollywood had failed to seduce Adnan Khashoggi, the Doumanis seemed far more inclined to be swayed by Evans's hype. First, at a preliminary meeting set up by Buss and Prophet, Evans pitched the concept. The Doumanis seemed interested. Then Evans sent them the Puzo script. Though he would later confess that he had no idea what he was reading, Ed Doumani called Evans to tell him that he liked the screenplay. Evans realized that he had the Doumanis sold and moved quickly to close the deal.

Just as he reached an accord with the Doumani brothers and their limited partner, Denver insurance magnate Victor Sayyah, Evans signed Richard Gere to play the white male lead. The casting of Gere, who had just appeared in *An Officer and a Gentleman* and seemed ready to become a major star, was arranged by Paramount and seemed to signal the studio's interest in producing and/or distributing the film. It also significantly redefined the project. Gere's participation in the production meant that the film would focus less on the African American performers and by necessity evolve into a star vehicle for him.

At first, the casting of Gere worked very much to Evans's advantage. Evans understood that the more he deemphasized the Harlem subculture plot, the better chance he had of getting a distribution deal with a major studio. Moreover, though Evans was aware that Gere had a reputation for being difficult on the set, Evans also realized that Gere could be controlled in ways a star of Stallone's magnitude could not. And with Gere instead of Stallone in the lead role, Evans felt secure that *The Cotton Club* would remain a Robert Evans picture.

The one significant problem posed by Gere's participation in the film was, ironically, his sudden stardom. Because of the success of *An Officer and a Gentleman*, Gere was already committed to another project (at Evans's old studio, Paramount) by the time he agreed to appear in *The Cotton Club*. As a result, Gere's agreement with Evans was contingent upon the completion of production before the end of 1983. Thus, after waiting around for over three years to get started, Evans suddenly had to hurry and get the production under way.

On the strength of the production deal with the Doumanis and Sayyah and the casting of Gere, Evans subsequently contracted with the Producers

Sales Organization to arrange for the foreign distribution of the film (in exchange for an $8 million guarantee).[11] On the domestic front, Orion Pictures promised to contribute $10 million to release and advertise the picture.[12] Though both agreements were relatively sweet, both were essentially back-end deals; in order to see any of the cash, Evans, the Doumanis, and Sayyah had to finance the production with their own money.

Having closed deals to produce and distribute the movie, Evans turned to the trades and played the public relations game with real skill. Understanding the oxymoronic nature of 1980s Hollywood hype, he talked unselfconsciously about austerity while planning to make a $20 million picture. Sounding as grandiose and melodramatic as Coppola—speaking about film production as a kind of adventure, a high-stakes gamble—Evans confessed to Variety: "I have $20,000,000 to make this picture. Anything more than that and they're going to take my house away."[13]

In order to demonstrate his commitment to cutting costs, Evans scapegoated the unions. By pointing out in the press how much union workers increase a film's budget, he successfully backed the New York Teamsters into a landmark deal which abbreviated the workday in exchange for concessions on overtime pay. Evans knew the film would cost a lot more than $20 million, even with the Teamsters deal, but he decided not to tell anyone at Orion or the Producers Sales Organization. He did so even though he understood that unless he was able to find another investor crazy enough to fund the picture in exchange for third or fourth position in the profit structure of the film, he would either have to pay for the budget overages himself, or eventually he would have to convince Orion or the Producers Sales Organization to advance him some money.

Practically speaking, Evans had only one option. He didn't have all that much cash on hand and his credibility with the banks was weak. His plans to go ahead and shoot anyway, hoping that Orion or the Producers Sales Organization would step in and pick up the additional production costs, recalled the nightmarelike scenario attending the production and release of One from the Heart, when Coppola counted on Paramount to "save" his film. Though at the time it must have seemed to Evans that his only hope of ever getting the picture started was to begin the shoot before all the money was in place, by counting on the studio or the foreign distributor to rescue the film he instead mapped out a strategy in which he was sure to lose control of the picture.

As the date for the beginning of principal photography approached, Evans turned to the trades and, in a novel public relations ploy, announced his intention to fully "integrate" the production of the film. In a short piece titled "Evans Vows Lotsa Minority Jobs on His 'Cotton Club,'" Evans promised that *The Cotton Club* would be "the first totally integrated film since *Gone with the Wind*."[14] More than four months before *The Cotton Club* shoot was scheduled to begin, Evans's concern about the "minority audience" suggested one of two things: either the film would be (just) a "black picture" after all (and in that case the $20 million budget was already too much), or Evans was confident enough in the film's *Godfather*-like appeal to white audiences that he could afford to try to expand audience awareness of the project well before the picture was due for release.

Evans's tendency to focus on preproduction hype, casting, above-the-line staffing, advertising, and distribution strategies displayed his strengths as a big-budget movie producer. But it also revealed an underlying problem with his approach to the project. Having put some of the money in place and then used a lot of it to assemble a top-rate production team—including cinematographer John Alonzo (who shot *Chinatown* for Evans in 1974), production designer Richard Sylbert, and music producer Jerry Wexler—Evans seemed to have no idea how to get the Puzo script ready in time for the film's July 11, 1983, start date. With all the back-end financing contingent on a release in June 1984 and, more pressing, Gere's commitment to Paramount looming in the near future, Evans was in a real bind. After well over a decade as a movie producer, Evans seemed to have no idea what a director did to get a film ready for principal photography.

In public, Evans behaved as if nothing was wrong, as if he had the situation under control. But he wasn't fooling anyone involved in the production. When it seemed likely that the film wasn't going to start on time, Gere threatened to quit. Rather than deal with Gere, Evans continued to busy himself by hyping the picture in the press. As Richard Sylbert, the film's veteran production designer, recalled, "[Evans] was behaving like the steward on the *Titanic*, who went into the dining room and said, 'Don't worry folks, we're only stopping for some more ice.'"[15]

Behind the scenes, Evans was justifiably panicked, so much so that in March 1983 he hired his former nemesis Francis Coppola to fix the Puzo script.[16] After reading the screenplay, Coppola told Evans that he thought Puzo's script was "unworkable" and then offered to rewrite it. Without considering how Coppola's increased participation in the movie might change the delicate dynamics of "the package," Evans took him up on his offer. As Evans would soon discover, by turning to Coppola he had effectively given the movie away.

More Money, Less Control

Throughout dinner [Coppola] regaled us with Bob Evans firing him stories, which were hilarious in their extreme sliminess.—Julia Phillips, producer (*The Sting* and *Close Encounters of the Third Kind*)[17]

Coppola produced a new script in less than a month. Quite unlike the Puzo screenplay, which adhered to Evans's original "gangsters, music, pussy" tag line, Coppola's read more or less like a historical montage of the Harlem renaissance. Evans hated it. Coppola's script, he said, was "a history lesson that read like a PBS documentary."[18]

As the July 11 start date approached, on-location preparation was in full swing. Though he didn't have a script, Evans was still managing to spend $140,000 per week. Moreover, though he found Coppola's screenplay "unworkable," Evans soon discovered that Coppola's participation in the project had become essential to Orion, which had begun to doubt Evans's ability to get the film in front of the cameras. Thus, though he would have liked to fire Coppola right then, Evans could do nothing until he was in a position to begin shooting the movie. And he would not be ready to begin shooting the movie until he had a screenplay, a task he had assigned to Coppola.

Coppola's limited role in the preproduction of *The Cotton Club* was no doubt a humbling experience. He was at best the film's second screenwriter, and it was clear to virtually everyone in the industry that he had agreed to accept the job only because he needed the money and needed to have his name associated with a respectable studio project. That he eventually had the Orion executives' confidence had less to do with their respect for him than with their distrust of Evans. Nevertheless, Coppola's connection to the project quickly paid off.

While Coppola's subsequent drafts of the screenplay continued to focus more on exploited African-American performers than on white gangsters, Orion wisely continued to hype *The Cotton Club* as a reunion of Puzo, Coppola, and Evans, the team that had produced *The Godfather*. Meanwhile, no doubt encouraged by Coppola's apparent return to the one genre he really seemed to understand, United Artists offered Coppola the chance to direct a gangster picture, *The Pope of Greenwich Village*, as part of a big-budget studio package that at the time included two stars he'd worked with in the past, Al Pacino and Mickey Rourke. For a director who had fallen so far so fast, the offer must have seemed too good to be true.

Assuming at the time that his role on *The Cotton Club* would be limited to that of script doctor—assuming, that is, that he would be available once *The*

Cotton Club shoot began on July 11—Coppola began mapping out some ideas for *The Pope of Greenwich Village*. He later reminisced: "I had several good ideas on the subject [of *The Pope of Greenwich Village*]. I had Vittorio Storaro and the desire to make a murky film in the style of George Orwell and set in New York City."[19] Because of scheduling problems, first with Pacino and then with Coppola, the deal eventually fell through. Today, we can only guess at how different Coppola's version would have been from Stuart Rosenberg's, which was released in 1984.

The scale and scope of the on-location preproduction of *The Cotton Club* quickly depleted Evans's funds. He had done well to secure production financing from the Doumanis and Sayyah and was guaranteed $18 million from Orion and the Producers Sales Organization once the film was ready for release. But the preproduction of the film in the meantime was the problem, and even after Evans sold all his Paramount stock, he didn't have enough cash or collateral to keep things going until the start of principal photography on July 11.

Though he was still unhappy with Coppola's work on the script and understood that he had to supervise preproduction in New York if he had any hope of controlling the picture's cost, Evans hit the road again looking for more money. In doing so, he lost track of the creative end of things and gave Coppola the opportunity to continue developing *The Cotton Club* on his own.

When Evans put the word out that he needed more money to get the film started, a customer of Evans's limousine service named Elaine Jacobs offered a solution. She put Evans together with Roy Radin, a retired variety show producer. Radin then set up a $35 million holding company in Puerto Rico to help finance preproduction. The deal also set up financing for four future Evans films to be named at a later date. For his efforts, Radin received 10 percent of the new corporation.

The deal sounded good, and it was certainly timely, so Evans signed on the dotted line. But he should have read the fine print. Though Radin was the middleman in the deal and received his cut off the top, a clause in the contract greatly restricted Evans's ability to do much of anything in the future without Radin's OK. After signing the deal with Radin, Evans found himself experiencing an old Hollywood lesson firsthand: "You take the money, you lose control."

As *The Cotton Club* became an increasingly complex package, Evans, the man who had put the deal together, slowly but surely found himself becoming a minor player in a scenario that had grown more interesting than the film itself. Once he and Radin agreed to terms, Elaine Jacobs demanded a percentage of Radin's end of the deal as her finder's fee. Radin balked and countered with a flat-fee offer of $50,000. Evans, who thought Radin was being cheap, sided with Jacobs, but Radin seemed intent on stiffing her. And then things got weird.

According to *New York* magazine's Michael Daly, Radin and Jacobs met in a limousine to hash out a deal. Radin had hired Demond Wilson, the former star of the television series *Sanford and Son,* to tail them. But Wilson couldn't keep up. Radin's decomposed body was eventually found in a canyon north of Los Angeles. He had been shot through the head.

Evans emerged as a suspect in the murder when news of his disadvantageous deal with Radin began to circulate. Homicide investigators from the Los Angeles Police Department interviewed the producer for four hours, but no arrest was made. According to Daly, the scene at Evans's office ended with the police heading to their car with autographed copies of the script of *Chinatown* under their arms.[20]

In *The Kid Stays in the Picture,* his 1994 memoir, Evans tells a somewhat different story about the so-called *Cotton Club* murder. As Evans tells it, he first heard about Radin's disappearance from Greg Bautzer, his attorney. At the time, Evans maintains, he was surprised by the news but did not see what it had to do with him. Bautzer did, and on Evans's behalf contacted the legendary criminal lawyer Robert Shapiro.[21]

While the district attorney's office continued to investigate (and publicize and perhaps exaggerate) Evans's relationship with Radin, John O'Grady, a private detective employed by the victim's family, discovered that Jacobs had been hired by Radin to transport a large amount of cocaine. Radin's death, according to O'Grady, was the result of a drug deal gone sour.[22] O'Grady's investigation seemed to prove once and for all that the murder had nothing to do with *The Cotton Club.* But given the apparent connection between the crime and the Hollywood drug scene, the new evidence did little to convince police of Evans's innocence.

In 1989 Jacobs (by then Jacobs-Greenberger) and three accomplices were arrested and charged with kidnapping and murder. Though several years had passed and there was still no evidence of Evans's connection to the Radin-Jacobs drug deal, the prosecution continued to refer to him as a potential suspect. Because he was still officially under investigation, Evans, on Shapiro's advice, sought protection under his Fifth Amendment rights when he was called to testify at Jacobs's preliminary hearing. "Remember,"

Shapiro cautioned, "the statute of limitations never runs out in a case like this."[23]

Jacobs and her three accomplices were all convicted of kidnapping and murder, but even though no charges were ever filed against him, Evans's name remained tied to the crime. At this writing, Evans dismisses the contention that he ever had a motive to murder Radin or that Radin's disappearance and murder had any relation to the film he was working on at the time. "This case had nothing to do with *The Cotton Club*," Evans writes, "There was no deal or money . . . just the handshake between people interested in funding a company that never came into existence."[24]

Given the scope and complexity of his legal and financial problems at the time, it is understandable that Evans continued to neglect certain key creative elements in the ongoing development of *The Cotton Club*. While Evans concerned himself with the possibility that he might be indicted for Radin's murder, Coppola continued to develop the script. Much to Evans's disappointment, Coppola's work remained sensitive to the situation of the performers at the Cotton Club at the expense of the gangster (genre) plot.

In order to get Coppola to water down the script, Evans dispatched a young African-American actress named Marilyn Matthews to reason with him. It was an interesting political move on Evans's part. He wanted Coppola to produce the screenplay he had envisioned when he first purchased the rights to the property. And he hoped Coppola would not take the moral high ground with Matthews.

But what Evans failed to consider was that whenever he focused on the problems with the screenplay, he reminded the Doumanis, Sayyah, Orion, and the Producers Sales Organization that Coppola was somehow still involved in the project. And it took little imagination on their part to think about what the film might be like if Coppola took over.

In a move that signaled their impatience with Evans, and ironically not with Coppola, the Doumanis decided to withhold financing pending the production of a more polished screenplay. The move was not merely an effort on the Doumanis' part to exert power. Instead, it seemed to reveal that the Doumanis had come to believe (along with the executive team at Orion) that the principal asset in the *Cotton Club* project was Coppola. Since Coppola was the film's screenwriter, the Doumanis made the script the focal point in their reopened negotiations with Evans.

Taking full advantage of the situation, Coppola invited Evans (and Gere, Hines, and Matthews) to his Napa Valley estate to discuss the script. By agreeing to meet on Coppola's turf, Evans repeated the mistake he had made two years earlier with Adnan Khashoggi. And Coppola, like Khashoggi, took full advantage.

Evans arrived at Coppola's estate needing an immediate solution to his problem with the Doumanis. During the story conference, Evans seemed to break under the pressure and decided that if he could get Coppola to agree to direct *The Cotton Club,* he could convince the Doumanis to resume financing the picture and, though he would no longer get to direct, he could at least hang onto his job as the movie's executive producer. When Evans gave the Doumanis the good news about Coppola, they immediately agreed to resume financing the production.

Evans had reason to be optimistic when, after the meeting, Coppola wrote another, "better" draft of the script[25]—one, importantly, agreeable to both stars and, as Evans had hoped, less politically correct and more commercially viable. But though the script was finally to his liking, Evans still had cause for concern. The Doumanis' decision to resume their financing was contingent on Coppola's agreement to direct, and though Coppola and Evans had agreed to that in principle, there was no contract binding Coppola to the project. Moreover, though Evans had used Coppola's willingness to direct to placate the Doumanis, he had no idea how much Coppola would want as compensation. After all, Coppola was, for the first time in over a decade, directing a film he himself had not developed. Given that the film's $20 million budget was unrealistically low even with Evans directing, Evans was concerned that Coppola's compensation package might not only affect the film's final cost but might also affect the way future profits would be dispensed should the film do well at the box office.

Nevertheless, Evans kept his concerns to himself. At the time, he had good reason to be far more anxious about his own uncertain role in the production. The Doumanis, who were learning about the film business on the job, so to speak, likely did not understand what they needed Evans for now that Coppola was at the helm. With that in mind, Evans made sure that they understood just how difficult Coppola could be to work with, and, though he knew better, he "assured" them that if it became necessary, he alone could "control Francis."[26]

Much to Evans's relief, Coppola's asking price was not outrageous: $2.5 million plus a reasonable percentage of the gross. But the money wasn't all Coppola wanted. In addition to the financial package, Coppola stipulated that the deal was contingent on his absolute authority over the production.[27] Evans, who was anxious for Coppola to sign, expressed confidence that he would continue to have an impact on the production even though relations were not good between the two men personally. But Coppola made sure that Evans understood exactly what his demands entailed. "I told Evans," Coppola recalled, "that as a writer I would do it any way my director instructed me to, but if I became the director, I would need to have total control and final cut."[28] Coppola knew from past experience that Evans was bound to interfere and thus did all he could to make it clear that Evans's influence on the creative side of things would be over once the contract was signed.

It took Evans over a month to come to terms with Coppola's demands. Though in public he continued to express confidence that he could work with Coppola on Coppola's terms, he seemed to understand that the agreement would push him to the periphery. And it did. Once Evans signed, Coppola exerted his power. His first big move was to fire Evans's cinematographer, John Alonzo (whose contract was eventually bought out for $160,000).[29] On Coppola's short list to replace Alonzo were Stephen Burum, whose esoteric work on *Rumble Fish* made Evans very nervous, and Stephen Goldblatt, whose one major credit at the time was Tony Scott's very stylish horror picture, *The Hunger*.

Though Coppola had effectively given Evans a choice, it was a choice between two relatively uncommercial cinematographers. Somewhat more leery of Burum, Evans opted for Goldblatt, who joined the project for less than it cost for Alonzo not to shoot the film. Coppola subsequently fired all but one of the film's production executives, all of whom had been hired by Evans.

Once Coppola set up shop on location in New York—and got his electronic cinema paraphernalia in place (including the Airstream trailer he dubbed *Silverfish*, from which he had directed *One from the Heart, The Outsiders,* and *Rumble Fish*)—he set about casting the film. But while he had allowed Evans to choose between the two cinematographers, Coppola rather quickly lost patience when Evans challenged his casting decisions. Things got particularly ugly when Coppola hired Fred Gwynne to play Owney Madden's sidekick, Frenchie. Evans vetoed Coppola's decision and stated emphatically that he didn't want to hire Herman Munster. Since it was still early in the game—early enough for him to back out if he had to—Coppola used the quarrel over the casting of Gwynne to issue an ultimatum: unless the conditions of the agreement were respected, he was quitting and going back to California. Realizing that he was in no position to win the argument, Evans backed down.

Evans took his capitulation to Coppola hard. After the casting of Gwynne, he stayed away from the set, remarking that "if you're not calling the shots, you're not the producer."[30] With Evans out of the way, Coppola set about making *The Cotton Club* his film and in the process sent the entire production spinning into chaos. He hired novelist William Kennedy to work with him on the script. Within a month, well within the preproduction time frame, they had another "final draft." But when they sent a copy of the draft to production designer Richard Sylbert, he discovered that six of the seven locations he had scouted for Evans were no longer in the screenplay, and ten of the sets he had designed and had constructed on Evans's dollar were no longer needed. With less than a month left before principal photography was set to begin, all Sylbert had to work with was a handwritten note from Coppola that read: "I haven't thought it out yet in terms of sets and settings. Try not to get too anxious."[31]

Though Evans remained in self-imposed exile, he had not completely given up on the idea of somehow regaining control of the production. Thus, when he finally got a look at how different the Coppola-Kennedy draft was from the draft produced after the meeting at Coppola's estate, Evans decided to make a move. He called Victor Sayyah, who was feuding with his partners, the Doumanis, at the time, and began to engineer a plot to take the film back from Coppola. Evans told Sayyah that not only was the new draft considerably different from the script that had been approved by him and the Doumanis, but that Coppola was talking about doing still another rewrite. Evans reminded Sayyah about the script problems that stalled the productions of both *Hammett* and *The Escape Artist,* two Coppola-produced films that bombed at the box office. Sayyah took it all in, but in the end he refused to back Evans. For the time being, at least, *The Cotton Club* was still Coppola's picture.

The Shoot

The movie was like a vampire. You'd think, "This is it, it's finally got a stake through its heart." But every day it would come out of its coffin. It didn't die. Somehow, it didn't die.—Richard Sylbert, production designer for *The Cotton Club*[32]

On August 22, 1983, a little over two months behind schedule, *The Cotton Club* shoot began. But when the crew and cast assembled at Prospect Hall in Brooklyn, something was missing. Richard Gere, who was scheduled to appear in the day's scenes at the location, had failed to show up. So as not to waste the set or the light, Coppola had Hines do an ad lib production number (which made it into the final cut of the film). While Coppola showed just how well he could still think on his feet, this opening day

12. Surrounded by (movie) gangsters: Francis Coppola on the set of *The Cotton Club*.
Photo by Adger W. Cowans (Orion Pictures, 1984).

improv on location seemed to be an omen of things to come. Gere's disappearance, it turned out, had little to do with Coppola. His dissatisfaction dated back to Evans's inability to get the film started on time and failure to keep him informed about impending production delays. Gere eventually returned to the set for a significant boost in salary—to $3 million, $1.5 million of which was taken out of Evans's 10 percent of the gross.

Opening day set the tone. But Coppola did not let the insanity of the shoot bother him; indeed he seemed to thrive on the confusion. As Richard Sylbert mused in retrospect, "Nobody knew what was going on from one minute to the next. Once I asked [Coppola], 'Why do you make all this chaos?' and he said, 'If nobody knows what's going on, nobody can discuss it with you."[33]

Though Coppola may have used the chaos to cement his authority, many of the events that eventually held up the production were beyond his control. Moreover, Coppola could afford to be oblivious to all the chaos, and, frankly, he was rather used to the hectic and often insane manner in which big films are made. None of *his* money, for a change, was tied up in the project, and as the dailies bore out, all the money that was being spent was "up there" on the screen.

But those with a significant financial stake at the front end of the production—the Doumanis, Sayyah, and Evans—saw things quite differently. With the exception of Evans, who continued to keep away from the set, none of the men financing the film had any experience in the industry. The production of *The Cotton Club* struck them as particularly slow, wasteful, and chaotic. Victor Sayyah, who had taken on the task of monitoring things on the set after Evans gave up trying to deal with Coppola, had no idea what it was he was supposed to be watching.

Though he was on the set virtually every day, Sayyah was no more successful than Evans had been in controlling Coppola. Further, Sayyah soon discovered that even if he saw something on the set that bothered him, he couldn't do anything about it. In all of his other business dealings, Sayyah had enjoyed a modicum of control, and the peculiar dynamics of *The Cotton Club* shoot were thus particularly frustrating. So much so that during a row with Melissa Prophet (who had remained involved in the production as a liaison between Coppola, Evans, and the money men), Sayyah went berserk and threw her through a plate glass window.[34]

After the Sayyah-Prophet altercation, Ed Doumani took Sayyah's place. But he was even less inclined to accept the way his money was being spent. With weekly production costs exceeding $1.2 million (about $300 a minute), Doumani decided to hire an expert to oversee the project. But rather than turn to an experienced Hollywood producer, Doumani instead hired a Lebanese B movie impresario named Sylvio Talbet, who, for $200,000 and coproducer credit, sat next to Coppola on the set and clicked a string of worry beads. Completely overwhelmed by the scale of the production and intimidated by Coppola's expertise and seeming madness, Talbet proved incapable of protecting the Doumanis' investment.

Their inability to control Coppola, and as a result the cost of the production, proved to be just one of the Doumanis' many problems in financing the film to completion. Almost immediately after the shoot began, the Doumanis had to turn their attention to the first in a series of lawsuits filed against the production. On August 24, 1983, Bud Diamond, a variety show producer, filed a restraining order against Robert Evans for using the title *The Cotton Club,* a title he had used since 1975 for a series of musical-comedy shows. Named as codefendants in the suit were the Producers Sales Organization, Mario Puzo, music producer Jerry Wexler (who was no longer part of the production team), costume designer Milena Canonero, and Totally Independent, Limited (the Doumanis' holding company).[35] The Doumanis eventually paid Diamond off after they discovered that he held a patent on the Cotton Club name.

After dispensing with Diamond, the Doumanis turned their attention back to the production and realized that they were running out of cash. With Evans in Mexico in semiretirement, the Doumanis enlisted Melissa Prophet to keep the news of their financial problems from Coppola and Orion.

Despite Prophet's campaign of disinformation, the Doumanis' position soon proved untenable. On October 3, after desperate negotiations with banks in New York and Las Vegas, the Doumanis failed to come up with enough cash to meet the production's massive payroll, and the New York unions (which had made such a sweet deal with Evans back in February) shut down the production. Complicating matters further for the Doumanis was that they still had not paid Coppola, whose contract called for additional compensation as a penalty if his salary schedule was not met.

In the October 5, 1983, issue of *Variety*, under the headline "Coppola Stays Home from 'Cotton' Shoot: No Pact or Checks," Coppola displayed his ability to play the public relations game. Cleverly sidestepping the money issue—since he was contracted to receive $2.5 million in salary alone, it was unlikely that anyone would be inclined to feel sorry for him on that score—Coppola described Evans's and the Doumanis' failure to pay him as a sign of disrespect. "I made a bargain with myself," Coppola told *Variety*, "that I would be tolerant and helpful, but now that we're beyond the halfway mark my position is getting weaker and weaker."[36]

As to the rumors about the growing strain between him and Evans, Coppola declined to comment, implicitly confirming that the rumors were true. Bobby Zarem, a spokesman for the still-exiled Evans, countered by remarking to *Variety* that so far as he knew, Evans had no immediate plans to replace Coppola, suggesting that Evans and the Doumanis had at least talked about it. Coppola responded to Zarem by deferring to his attorneys and then began talking about moving on to another project.[37] To all those in the industry used to reading between the lines, it was clear that either Evans or Coppola was through on *The Cotton Club*. And the smart money was on Coppola to come out on top.

Two weeks later, *Variety* announced an accord between Coppola, Evans, and the Doumanis.[38] Coppola received a substantial portion of his salary up front. In exchange, he forgave the cash penalty he was entitled to when the Doumanis failed to pay him in a timely fashion and sacrificed any chance he might ever have had of taking advantage of the $1 million incentive cash payment he'd receive should the film be brought in on time and under the $20 million budget.

By the seventh week of production (which marked Coppola's return to the set, cash in hand), $18 million had already been spent. Not only had it become clear that Evans's original budget was inadequate, but industry insiders began projecting that the film would cost in the neighborhood of $40 million. Thus—and this alarmed the Doumanis, who despite their investment and all the aggravation were not first in line for a percentage of the profits—*The Cotton Club* would have to gross approximately $120 million (roughly $12 million more than the number two film in 1983, *Terms of Endearment*) in order to break even.[39]

That the movie was going to go well over budget was hardly a surprise to Evans, who had arbitrarily set the budget at $20 million because that seemed to be the most he could raise to fund the production. When Coppola arrived on the scene, his participation, in and of itself, altered the nature of the project. As Barry Osborne, Orion's line producer on the film, told *Variety*, $40 million was, so far as the studio was concerned, "a normal figure for the scope of the picture . . . when you hire a director of Francis Coppola's stature, the picture will be done in a different style."[40] Osborne made it clear from the start that Orion was anxious to turn *The Cotton Club* into an event picture. But at the same time, Osborne indicated, it was not Orion's problem how, or even if, Evans and the Doumanis found the cash to complete the production. By steadfastly refusing to advance Evans and the Doumanis any cash, Osborne seemed to be sending a message to the industry at large: Orion was prepared, even with a film with as much box office potential as *The Cotton Club*, to adhere to the letter of its contracts.

While such a message had more to do with perception than reality—if the production had completely shut down, Orion would not have let the picture die; instead the movie would have been formally taken away from Evans, the Doumanis, and Sayyah and produced by Orion—the decision not to help Evans created a second, larger problem for *The Cotton Club* production team. By allowing Evans and the Doumanis to succeed or fail on their own, Orion gave the press another chance to focus on the absurdity of the Hollywood production process where so much money is spent and so little work seems to be done. While Orion should have been protecting the film, which was, after all, the studio's property once it got to the marketplace, it allowed *The Cotton Club* to begin to look much like *One from the Heart*. In doing so, Orion opened the door for the press to begin depicting *The Cotton Club* as the wrong kind of event picture.

Coppola's return to the set only partially deflected attention away from the chaotic production. Just as fences seemed to be mended—in the very *Variety* piece that had announced the Evans-Doumani-Coppola accord— someone "close to the film" leaked important and potentially embarrassing budget information, including word that the sets alone for *The Cotton Club* cost over $5 million ($1 million more than the astonishingly expensive sets for *One from the Heart*).[41] Though Evans was not identified as the source, a month later, in an interview in the *Wall Street Journal,* he blamed Coppola for taking the film's budget up to the $40 million mark.[42] Evans's decision to use the *Journal* to get back at Coppola suggested not only that he was the leak in the *Variety* piece, but also that he had still not fully accepted his diminished role on the picture.

Since he was still in control of the production, Coppola did not have to, and thus did not, respond to Evans in print. Instead, in a personal letter to Evans, he made his position clear: "You have double crossed me for the last time," he wrote. "If you want a PR war or any kind of war, nobody is better at it than me."[43]

Exactly what Evans hoped to accomplish by further antagonizing Coppola —and in doing so hurting the film's chances at the box office—was unclear at the time. It is understandable that he wanted to get back at Coppola for so completely taking over the creative end of *The Cotton Club.* But he should have known that if *The Cotton Club* struck it big at the box office, no one in the industry would care who had really produced the film. And if the film won a Best Picture Oscar—and two of Coppola's films already had—however alienated Evans felt during the production, he'd find himself on-stage thanking everyone involved for being so gracious, so helpful, so damned talented. It was in Evans's own best interest to shut up and wait for the film to do its thing at the box office.

As the revised December 23, 1983, target date for the completion of the production phase neared, yet another financial problem forced Evans back from exile. The Doumanis, who had planned on assuming less than $20 million in debt, had reached their credit limit. It was only a matter of a week or so, they told Evans, before they would once again be unable to meet *The Cotton Club* payroll. Tabling his battle with Coppola for the moment, Evans set about finding new backers. But because of all the bad publicity he found it difficult to find a decent deal. Virtually anyone willing and able to help wanted a significant profit participation and screen credit as executive producer. Even if Evans was willing to share the profits, he feared that if he shared his production credit with anyone else it would further diminish his prestige in the industry.

Evans decided that his only chance to retain credit for (if not control of) the picture was to get more money from the studio. But when he approached Orion, studio executives reminded him that they were not obliged to come up with any cash until after the film was completed. Evans argued that the film would never be completed if Orion didn't kick in immediately, but the studio held to the bottom line of the contract.

Desperate, Evans went to see Barry Diller, then in charge at Paramount. According to Evans, it was Diller who suggested that Evans should declare bankruptcy, which would enable him to tear up the contract with Orion and free him to deal the film to another studio. Once the Orion deal was voided, Diller, again according to Evans, promised to pay $15 million *up front* for domestic distribution rights to the film.

But the Evans-Diller maneuver was doomed—not because it was unethical (which it was) or illegal (which it wasn't), but because Evans's real problem with *The Cotton Club* was less money than time. If Evans declared bankruptcy and tried to back out of the deal with Orion, the studio, in order to protect its position, would have to file suit in response. Even if it did not prevail, Orion could hold up the production for several months, long enough to ensure that Evans and the Doumanis would default on the short-term loans financing the picture. In the meantime, after being advised by the Paramount legal staff that the bankruptcy court might not invalidate the Evans-Orion deal, Diller reconsidered his offer. Though the bankruptcy maneuver was his idea in the first place, Diller eventually told Evans that it didn't make sense for him to commit Paramount funds to a film he might not get to distribute.

Evans was skunked. He turned to his attorney, Alan Schwartz, who had from the start strenuously advised him against dealing with Paramount behind Orion's back.[44] By the time he decided to take Schwartz's advice, Evans had no deal with Paramount anyway. His only hope was that Orion wouldn't find out about his discussions with Diller. But information in Hollywood always finds its way to the wrong party. When the news reached the executives at Orion, industry rumors began to circulate that the studio was planning to void the distribution deal. Realizing that Orion's exit at such a late date would effectively kill the film, Ed Doumani went to Orion to apologize for Evans and plead for an advance on the distribution money. After the meeting, Doumani announced that despite Evans's shenanigans he had convinced Orion to provide the necessary completion funds.

But the following day, Doumani's lawyer called to inform his boss that this was not the deal Orion had put on the table. Doumani dispatched his lawyer to meet again with Orion executive vice president Bill Bernstein, who ultimately agreed to front the cash on the condition that Evans turn over whatever little control he had left. After four years of dealing and maneuvering, suddenly Evans was completely out of the picture.[45]

Postproduction

Morale among the editors is fine . . . all the stuff one reads in the papers doesn't affect us. I've worked on this film for 18 months and I've never seen Bob Evans.
—Barry Malkin, editor of *The Cotton Club*[46]

By the time the production phase was complete, the budget on *The Cotton Club* had reached $47 million, roughly eight times the budget of *The Godfather*. Since the Doumanis had financed the film with short-term debt, pressure was brought to bear on Coppola to finish postproduction quickly so that they could collect the $10 million distribution fee from Orion (which was contingent on delivery of the negative).

Whether or not the $47 million would be "up there" on the screen—as it always had been with Coppola's pictures, regardless of their success at the box office—was less important to the Doumanis than the amount of additional time they would have to carry the loans supporting the film. Once again, the issue was not only money but time.

On May 2, 1984, Coppola tested a 140-minute cut of *The Cotton Club* on an invited audience of "non-film people" aged eighteen to thirty-nine. On the same day, the Ladd Company tested both a 228-minute and a 180-minute cut of Sergio Leone's *Once upon a Time in America*, yet another gangster picture that had seemingly spun out of control during production. While Leone's film tested badly—and versions as short as 90 minutes were released to horrendous reviews and small audiences—Coppola's tested quite well. But just as Orion seemed prepared to finally distribute the film nationally, first Sayyah and then Evans filed separate lawsuits that postponed its release.

Sayyah's suit was strange and held little promise for success. He alleged that the Doumanis had misled him; he had invested $5 million in what he had expected to be a $20 million film directed by Robert Evans. But after the Doumanis turned the project over to Coppola—which by most accounts made it a more commercial picture—the result was a far different movie that cost somewhere in the area of $50 million.[47] Sayyah further claimed that the Doumanis employed Joey Cusumano, who, according to Sayyah was a noted organized crime figure,[48] to muscle him off the picture.

While Sayyah's accusations made for good copy, his real beef with the Doumanis was simpler than that; he realized that the film had cost so much that it was unlikely he'd recoup his investment. He needed somebody to blame, somebody to hold accountable. In the end, though, all Sayyah got for his trouble was a lesson on doing business in the new Hollywood.

Evans's suit held more promise for success and was even more acrimonious. After the secret Diller-Evans deal fell through and then became

13. Gregory Hines on stage in *The Cotton Club*. Photo by Adger W. Cowans (Orion Pictures, 1983).

public, Orion line producer Barry Osborne began mapping out an advertising and release strategy for *The Cotton Club*, taking over the only task Evans had retained after Coppola effectively maneuvered him off the set. Evans hoped to use the suit to force Osborne to allow him to participate in the release of *The Cotton Club*, thus perhaps restoring his credibility as an industry player.

The Doumanis, Orion Pictures, and Coppola were named codefendants in the suit. During the trial, Coppola seemed to be the most sensible witness, pointing out to the judge that though Evans had to a large extent developed the project himself, any action restoring power to Evans would bring instability and chaos to an already unstable and chaotic situation. By then, Coppola could afford to be practical; whether or not Evans participated in the release of the picture had little effect on his work (which was basically complete) or his stake in the profits of the film.

For those in the industry following the story in the trades, it was hardly a surprise that all of the players who took part in the production of *The Cotton Club* were determined to see each other one last time in court. Evans, of course, was the most anxious since he had the most to gain. And when his chance came, he made the most of it.

According to *Variety,* Evans broke down and cried on the stand. His testimony seemed borrowed from a bad courtroom melodrama, but it was effective. He told the court that the movie business dealt in perception as much as reality and that the Doumanis, Coppola, and Orion had unfairly tarnished his reputation. He didn't want any more money, he just wanted the prestige that went with participating in the marketing and advertising of what was once *his* movie.[49]

The court bought Evans's performance and restored various important marketing and distribution chores to him. In elaborating his decision, Judge Irving Hill of the U.S. District Court showed that jurists in Los Angeles also know their film history when he compared the testimony in the case to Akira Kurasawa's *Rashomon,* "in which every event is reported differently by every person who saw it."[50]

But Evans's victory was short-lived. On August 15, 1984, just under two months after the court decided in his favor, Evans signed a settlement agreement with the Doumanis. The Doumanis gave Evans $500,000 in cash and forgave a $1.6 million note they held on Evans's Coldwater Canyon home.[51] Evans retained producer credit on the film, but he could no longer participate in its distribution, which was scheduled for Christmastime 1984.

After the August 15, 1984, accord was announced in the trades, John Rockwell, a Los Angeles restaurateur who had helped set up the first Evans-Doumani meeting, filed suit against Evans, claiming that the producer had reneged on a $2.1 million finder's fee. Though he had no written record of the agreement, Rockwell claimed that Evans owed him 7 percent of the total amount invested by the Doumanis, which had swelled to $30 million.[52] The Doumanis, who had previously claimed that they had paid Rockwell off for $25,000,[53] were named as codefendants. While the suit seemed largely a nuisance, it added to the film's prerelease reputation as a doomed project.

And then there was Susan Mechsner. In a story titled "In Only One CC Scene, Actress, with Points, Gets 100 G," Mechsner, who in the final cut appears only briefly as a cabaret dancer who eyes Dutch Schultz, told *Variety* that she was "in shock" when she discovered that her "co-starring role" was virtually cut out of the movie. Mechsner also told *Variety* that while she received $100,000 plus two points on the net for her work—this too was disputed; the studio claimed she was only on the set for four days and that they had paid her only $7,000—she still planned to sue the usual parties (Evans, the Doumanis, Coppola . . .) when "the time [was] right." Mechsner alleged that she had suffered considerable mental anguish upon seeing the film in its completed form and discovering that her role had been virtually eliminated. Worst of all, her last name had been misspelled in the final credits.[54]

The reason Coppola had cut her out of the film, Mechsner claimed, stemmed from a row she had had with the director when he asked her to cut her hair. "With Coppola everything's the film," she told *Variety*, with no sense of irony. "It took me twelve years to grow my hair."[55] Mechsner's story seemed far-fetched until she began talking about another service she had provided for the film. Her connection to the project, she alleged, dated back to some parties Evans had thrown for the Doumani brothers, and the points she claimed she was entitled to (but most likely would never receive since they were on the picture's net profits), were "gift points" for helping Evans court the Las Vegas investors.[56]

Like Rockwell, Mechsner had no written contract and stood little chance in court. But her story further suggested that the various plots stemming from the production of *The Cotton Club* were more interesting than the picture itself.

Unlike the prerelease press on *One from the Heart,* which focused on the folly of *auteurism,* the bad press attending the release of *The Cotton Club* instead concentrated on the outrageous behavior of the film's outrageous production team. Apparently having learned from his mistakes, Coppola protected the film itself from any advance media criticism by simply refusing to show it to anyone (including not only the press but also Evans, the Doumanis, Sayyah, and Orion).

While Coppola set about the complex task of editing and mixing the sound on the film, employing eighteen editors working sixty-hour weeks, the Doumanis and Evans showed just how short memories are in Hollywood when they announced plans for more joint film ventures in the future, a relationship Ray Loynd of *Variety* characterized as a veritable "love nest." Evans unironically and gleefully referred to himself as the Doumanis' "hired gun."[57] "Through hardship," Evans told Loynd with apt melodrama, "we have become close now. In essence, I'm working for the Doumanis; it's like working for a studio."[58]

The Doumani-Evans "love nest" was good news for everyone left standing with a stake in *The Cotton Club*. Evans was no longer an independent producer and no longer nearing bankruptcy; the Doumanis could, for the time being, act like they weren't so sure they were going to lose their shirts with *The Cotton Club* and have to give up on the idea of making movies; and Coppola and Orion could finally focus on finishing and releasing the picture, the "product" that had brought them all together in the first place.

Intrigue, Anger, Blackmail, Deceit . . .

Many years ago Moss Hart told me that relationships in our business are built on such strange personal emotions that they become three-sided: your side, my side and the truth.—Robert Evans in a letter to Francis Coppola, October 1, 1984[59]

Most people in Hollywood are too insecure to tell people the truth about how they feel about them. They never know when they may need them. Sincerity is not one of Hollywood's main attractions.—Mike Medavoy, former chairman of Tri-Star Pictures[60]

Evans's 1994 memoir tells a significantly different story about the development and production of *The Cotton Club*. According to Evans, Coppola deliberately maneuvered him out of the picture as a payback for his continued insistence that he had recut *The Godfather*.

In support of his version of the story, Evans reproduces an exchange of two telegrams sent in mid-December 1983. The first, unsigned but supposedly sent by Coppola, read as follows: "Dear Bob Evans, I've been a real gentleman regarding your claims of involvement in *The Godfather*. I've never talked about your throwing out the Nino Rota music, your barring the casting of Pacino and Brando, etc. But continually your stupid babbling about cutting *The Godfather* comes back to me and angers me for its ridiculous pomposity."[61]

The second telegram was sent and signed by Evans the following day: "Thank you for your charming cable. I cannot imagine what prompted this venomous diatribe. I am both annoyed and exasperated by your fallacious accusations. . . . I am affronted by your gall in daring to send this Machiavellian epistle. The content of which is not only ludicrous, but totally misrepresents the truth." The telegram ended with a strange but nonetheless clearly stated threat: "I cannot conceive what motivated your malicious thoughts . . . however, dear Francis, do not mistake my kindness for weakness."[62]

When the battle over the casting of Fred Gwynne led Coppola to threaten to quit the film, Evans recalls that Coppola said: "This is not *The Godfather*, Evans. I've had it! Fed up with you. Tired of your second guessing. Tired of everything about you. The family's packed, we're out of here. You do it or I do it. You stay, I leave." "How," Evans asks rhetorically, "could a guy I plucked from near obscurity to superstardom vent this vitriolic hatred?" The answer was so simple he should have seen it coming. In a classic bit of Hollywood-speak, Evans concludes: "No mistake about it—it was an ingeniously conceived, ten-year-festering come shot, a royal fucking by Prince Machiavelli himself."[63]

Once he was barred from the set, Evans's next chance to see what had become of "his" film was an October 1984 preview screening of Coppola's rough cut (which Evans attended, uninvited). According to Evans, the screening seemed like "deja vu all over again"; like the director's cut of *The Godfather*, *The Cotton Club* was gorgeously shot but horrendously edited. Though he was hardly in a position to influence Coppola (as he was when he claims he reedited *The Godfather*), Evans nevertheless sent Coppola a thirty-one page critique of the editing of the picture.

Coppolla predictably refused to consider Evans's suggestions. "That December 8," Evans writes, "*The Cotton Club* had its gala premiere in New York. The Prince [Coppola] purposely had ignored my every written word, and the finished cut didn't include one of my suggestions. . . . Somber would best describe its audience reaction. Somber as well best described its box office results. Royalty always gets covered. Prince Machiavelli royally fucked all. He collected millions."[64]

The Release

It doesn't matter if [a] movie doesn't deliver. If you can create the *impression* that the movie delivers, you're fine. That's the difference between playability and marketability. When you've got playability you show it to the critics. If you've got marketability, there's enough there to cheat it or stretch it and make people believe that it really does deliver. . . . And the terrible, horrible, scary thing is that every now and then we actually make it work.—Mark Gill, senior vice president for publicity and promotion at Columbia Pictures[65]

The Cotton Club premiered on November 28, 1984, in Albany, New York, as the centerpiece of a benefit for the New York Writers Institute, then headed by *Cotton Club* scenarist William Kennedy. The national release was set for Christmas week, and Orion seemed confident that the film, despite its chaotic production history, could well be a hit.

But before *The Cotton Club* opened nationwide, *Variety*'s "New York Critics Scorecard" dampened the studio's enthusiasm. In a week when both *A Passage to India* and *Starman* netted thirteen favorable reviews apiece, *The Cotton Club* received only four, against eleven unfavorable notices.[66] By and large, the reviews offered what had become the party line on Coppola: the film cost too much money; or, more specifically, he had spent too much money on creating a distinctive look and had once again failed to pay sufficient attention to elaborating a coherent plot line.

What made the reviews truly alarming was their similarity to the notices that accompanied the release of *One from the Heart*. For example, Pauline Kael opened her review as follows: "If a whiz-kid director from the three-minute-rock-video field tried his hand at a Jazz Age musical, the result might be *The Cotton Club*. Francis Coppola, who co-wrote and directed it, seems to have skimmed the top off every twenties-thirties picture he has seen, added seltzer, stirred it up with a swizzlestick, and called it a movie. . . . His only goal seems to be to keep the imagery rushing by—for dazzle, for spectacle. The thinking (or the emotional state) behind his conception appears to be that it's all been done before, and that what remains is to feed your senses. He just wants to look at pretty lights, movement, color. He's just watching his brain cells twinkle."[67]

For Kael, *The Cotton Club*, much like *One from the Heart*, evinced the folly of *auteurism*, the vanity of the director as star: "The movie is Fellini-esque (especially in its last section, which cuts between Grand Central Station and a Grand Central set on the Cotton Club stage) and Coppola, like Fellini, assumes the role of the master of ceremonies, the eye of the hurricane. But his expansiveness has become strictly formal. Emotionally, he seems to have shrunk. The way he directs the cast here, people exist to reflect light."[68]

While Kael's review seemed to hit all the wrong notes, Orion found the more balanced critique in *Variety* only slightly more encouraging: "The arrival of a new film by Francis Coppola brings with it the anticipation of greatness. His latest, *The Cotton Club*, certainly isn't in the same league as his best pictures, but neither is it on the grim order of such recent efforts as *One from the Heart* and *Rumble Fish*." As to the film's commercial potential, while *Variety* affirmed that *The Cotton Club* was "by no means a disaster," nevertheless, given its $47 million budget, the picture would "have a tough go at recouping its cost."[69]

Though Orion had done its job promoting the film and had gotten the picture ready for a Christmas week opening, the studio took the early reviews to heart. From the very first week of *The Cotton Club*'s release, Orion concentrated on protecting its position at the expense of the film's potentially larger box office appeal. Orion was in first position in the profit structure of the film and had extended itself for only $10 million. The studio could afford to be conservative in its release of the film because it was virtually guaranteed a return on its investment in any event save a disaster on the scale of *One from the Heart* or *Heaven's Gate*. Those further down on the profit chain—Evans, the Doumanis, Sayyah, Coppola—were not only less likely to recoup their investment, they also had far less control over how the film would be marketed and distributed nationwide. Put simply, it was up to Orion to protect the other investors' and participants' positions, and the studio proved not only not interested in, but not up to, the task.

Actually, even though Orion executives panicked after reading some of the early reviews, the critical response to *The Cotton Club* was mixed. For example, Jack Kroll (*Newsweek*), David Sterret (*Christian Science Monitor*), Paul Attanasio (*Washington Post*), Andrew Sarris (*Village Voice*), Gene Siskel (*Chicago Tribune*), Roger Ebert (*Chicago Sun-Times*), Jack Matthews (*USA Today*), Sheila Benson (*Los Angeles Times*), and Tom Milne (*Sight and Sound*) all liked the film. Ian Pearson (*Newsweek*), Stanley Kauffmann (*New Republic*), David Denby (*New York*), Vincent Canby (*New York Times*), J. Hoberman (*Village Voice*), and Jeffrey Lyons (of TV's *Sneak Previews*) did not.

The Cotton Club opened at a respectable number five behind *Beverly Hills Cop, Dune, 2010,* and *City Heat*. In its second week in release it moved up to the number two spot behind the season's one true blockbuster, *Beverly Hills Cop*. Orion might well have been encouraged by the public's seeming disregard of the bad reviews, moreover, the likelihood that "word of mouth" had a lot to do with *The Cotton Club*'s move past the other studios' apparently less interesting holiday fare. But the "New York Critics Scorecard" and the *Variety* review had so dampened the studio's enthusiasm for the film that it never responded to *The Cotton Club*'s strong initial performance in the marketplace.

Coppola, in the meantime, highlighted the film's strong second week with the appropriate hype, remarking that "the public appreciates *The Cotton Club* because it's generous. It promises and delivers a lot as spectacle, as entertainment and as a story."[70] But while Coppola stood behind the picture and publicly displayed the appropriate optimism, Orion continued to cover its bottom line as if the film was surely going to bomb.

Orion's quick decision to cut its losses is even stranger when one considers how hard the studio worked and how much money it spent promoting the movie before its release. Orion's marketing and distribution team had done well to get the film into the right theaters at Christmastime and had mounted a terrific advertising campaign more than a month before the movie's nationwide release. The three *Cotton Club* ads cleverly characterized the film in three distinct and different ways: as a star vehicle for Gere, as a Coppola (*auteurist*) work of art, and as a gangster spectacle along the lines of *The Godfather*. The ads aired nationally throughout the month preceding the picture's release at a cost of $200,000 per spot.

But at the first sign of a problem with the reviewers, Orion turned its attention away from *The Cotton Club* and threw its support to *Amadeus,* a so-called prestige project the studio had once hoped to piggyback with the far more commercial Coppola picture. Once it made the decision to go with *Amadeus*—as early as January 9, 1985—Orion began talking about cutting its losses on the Coppola film.

Despite the fact that it was in release for only two weeks and at the time was the second highest grossing film in the nation, Orion turned to *Variety* and announced its intention to reedit the movie into a four-hour network television miniseries.[71] Two weeks later, executives at Orion predicted that they would lose $2 to $3 million on the project, though the picture was still the second highest grossing film in the nation and the studio's control over the movie's domestic ancillary rights suggested otherwise.[72]

Exactly what Orion had in mind at the time seems at best mysterious, at worst devious. Though the studio had set up a blockbuster release for the film, and the early box office returns seemed to support that strategy, Orion used the trades not only to hedge its bet but also to undermine the movie. When exhibitors across the country read about Orion's plans to reedit the film for a quick payoff on network television, they backed off. Reviewers also read the trades. They realized that the studio was no longer behind the film. Thus, they could pan *The Cotton Club* and not worry about losing out on some future perk at the studio. Though it is impossible to say how big a box office film *The Cotton Club* could have been, Orion's botched release seems in retrospect an apt end to Coppola's "Zoetrope period": five years of terrific movie making and truly disastrous luck in dealing with the major studios.

Seven Francis Coppola and the New New Hollywood

You hear things in weird places, you know—the sports clubs, the sales clerks that wait on these people in stores that you know—and they all want, subliminally, I suppose, to impress you with who they work with or who they know. There's a pulse, there's a sense of hearing things. If you go to lunch in Beverly Hills, or something, you'll see what I mean. You won't believe the things you'll hear.—Martin Katz, on the witness stand during the 1992 MCA insider trading trial[1]

Power in Hollywood, according to the editors of *Premiere* magazine, derives from "the ability to get [movies] made, to make them in a particular way, or to influence or manipulate those who make them with money, fear, or simple persuasiveness."[2] According to *Premiere,* the big money players these days are Warner Brothers CEO Bob Daly and COO Terry Semel, Disney chairman Michael Eisner, and the Creative Artists Agency's Michael Ovitz, the men who put the talent and the money together.

Such a definition is, of course, a bit narrow; so far as the editors of *Premiere* are concerned, Hollywood is still a place where power is in the hands of *men* who actually live and work there. Missing from *Premiere's* list of Hollywood's most powerful and influential players are TCI's John Malone, Viacom's Sumner Redstone, Blockbuster Video's Wayne Huizenga, and Sony president Norio Ohga, the men who control the industry from a distance and who stand to control a lot more than just the business of making and distributing motion pictures come the next century.

But while it fails to acknowledge the power behind the Hollywood power structure, *Premiere's* top one hundred is a useful list of who's who *in* Hollywood. In their 1993 listing, the editors of the magazine ranked Francis Coppola at number 55. Sixteen directors are listed ahead of him; Steven Spielberg, at number 13, is the first director on the list, followed by Rob Reiner (14) and then Tim Burton (20). In Coppola's neighborhood are the likes of Kit Caulkin, child star Macaulay Caulkin's manager-father, actress

Sharon Stone, and fellow *auteur* Barry Levinson, hardly the heady company Coppola traveled in fifteen years ago.

But for Coppola to be listed at all these days is something of a miracle. And while he may never make it back to where he was (or seemed to be) in 1979, his stock is on the rise again in Hollywood. In this, his second life as a studio director, Coppola has been able to demand $3 million plus 15 percent of the box office gross to produce and direct and $1 million to write *The Godfather, Part III,* and $5 million plus 10 percent of the gross to produce and direct *Bram Stoker's Dracula.*[3]

Such fees certainly put him in an elite group of working directors in Hollywood, but the money has not afforded him the autonomy he once hoped to secure when he purchased Hollywood General in 1980, nor has it gotten him out of debt. Coppola has filed for bankruptcy protection three times since 1990 in order to restructure his debts, virtually all of which date back to the purchase of the studio and the creative production financing of *One from the Heart.* Though he has been able to hold onto such assets as his 1,500-acre Napa Valley winery and estate, several apartment buildings in Los Angeles, and a resort in Belize, Coppola remains very much at he mercy of the major studios (which are willing to pay him as much as $5 million to direct a motion picture only so long as he makes the kind of picture they want him to make). Any hope of taking on the studios—which by now are significantly more complexly structured and more extensively capitalized than ever before—with the profits of one or two or even ten box office hits seems even more ridiculous now than it did in 1980.

Auteur Maudit

The day Francis Coppola abandoned realism for artifice has to rank among the saddest in film history.—David Denby, film critic[4]

It is axiomatic that when studio executives account for a director's usefulness, they look at box office receipts. Box office figures—especially the "early numbers" corresponding to a film's first weekend in release—offer the executives a misleading assurance that the business of making and distributing motion pictures can somehow be reduced to a series of numbers on a spreadsheet, that the film business could be, in the right executive's hands, no different from any other business.

In order to assess a director's talent, today's studio executives read the reviews in the popular press. They have learned not to trust their instincts; so many of them are not *film people* anyway. Instead, they defer to a group of professionals whose influence has grown in direct relation to the growing

14. The seventeenth most powerful director in Hollywood on the set of *Gardens of Stone* with cinematographer Jordan Cronenweth (Tri-Star Pictures, 1987).

conglomeratization of the industry.[5] Since 1984, the consensus view among the nation's most influential movie reviewers is that Coppola is tragically squandering a prodigious talent, one that seemed last in evidence either in 1979 in *Apocalypse Now* or even as far back as 1974 in *The Godfather, Part II*.

It is safe to assume that Coppola will continue to find work because his recent box office record—both *The Godfather, Part III* and *Bram Stoker's Dracula* made money—has been good enough to render the essentially mixed reviews irrelevant for the time being. But it is also fair to add that the very studio executives who continue to employ Coppola believe that his best days—his most creative days—are behind him. Indeed, they seem to be counting on it.

To explain why they ranked him at number fifty-five, the editors of *Premiere* glibly assessed Coppola's present industry reputation in three words: "cooperative former genius."[6] That Coppola is, and has been for the past decade, "cooperative" seems evident enough. Since 1984, he has made a series of studio films: *Peggy Sue Got Married, Gardens of Stone, Tucker: The Man and His Dream, The Godfather, Part III,* and *Bram Stoker's Dracula*. As to his status as a *former* genius, so far as the industry is concerned, the reviews speak for themselves.

At the heart of the problem with Coppola's recent work, at least according to the critics, is his seeming abandonment of narrative in favor of a signature style, an abandonment of the nuanced genre revisionism that distinguished the two *Godfather* films in favor of a reliance on the distinguishing factor of *auteurism.* According to critic Terrence Rafferty, such a shift has undermined all but an intellectual pleasure in viewing Coppola's work. In a review of *Tucker: The Man and His Dream,* Rafferty wrote: "Whatever complexities and ambiguities we find are not in the material itself but in the relationship between the movie's content and the form that the director has imposed on it. . . . *Tucker* is fascinating in a remote, intellectual way; its design is so bold and strange we spend a good deal of the picture furiously trying to puzzle out what Coppola means by it all. . . . As in all [of his] pictures since *Apocalypse Now,* [Coppola] stakes everything on style. . . . There [is] no sense of freedom in any of the shots: both people and objects seem overbearingly *designed,* so that everything has a single programmed significance and nothing is accidental."[7]

Other critics offer faint praise solely in order to make nostalgic reference to Coppola's better days. For example, Pauline Kael, in her review of *Gardens of Stone,* wrote that the Coppola movie "probably [came] closer to the confused attitudes that Americans had toward the Vietnam War than any other film."[8] But that said, Kael then went on to argue that the film as a whole disappointed; that Coppola no longer seemed to have "the daring sureness of taste" he displayed in *The Godfather* and *The Godfather, Part II.* "He used to know the difference between rich material and junkiness," Kael concluded, "but something in him has got blunted."[9]

Other critics have been even less generous. In his review of *Life Without Zoe*—Coppola's short film released as part of the omnibus picture *New York Stories*—*New Republic*'s Stanley Kauffmann suggested that Coppola should get out of the business of making movies altogether:

> Through *Apocalypse Now,* [Coppola's] films, whether successful or not, showed a director with an edge, an ambition, a large-scale identity in formation. Since then he has not only not developed, he has lost identity. It's as if the strain of *Apocalypse Now* left him stranded, grasping but not reaching. Coppola is now 50. Those who admired his earlier work and those who at least recognized the director's character will hope that some sort of self-reclamation is in order. He once said that being a director is "like running in front of a locomotive. If you stop, if you trip, if you make a mistake, you get killed." That's what seems to have been on his mind lately. Maybe he should just get off the tracks for a while and catch his breath."[10]

In the vast majority of the criticism of Coppola's post-Zoetrope films, one finds a single refrain: that his oeuvre has become both transparently and purposefully autobiographical. For example, in his review of *Life Without Zoe*, *Nation*'s Stewart Klawans wrote: "[*Life Without Zoe*] becomes explicable only if you assume the spendthrift little girl represents the studio, the fatally talented but absent father represents Coppola; the parties Zoe arranges represent such flops of the Zoetrope soundstage as *One from the Heart*. . . . Coppola has been a major filmmaker; his place in Hollywood history is secure. Like everyone else, I long to see him make full use of his talent again. That's why I'm haunted by *Life Without Zoe*, which opens up unanticipated perspectives of egomania and self-delusion. When the full effect hit me, I felt like Shelley Duvall in *The Shining*, at the moment when she sees what her husband has *really* been typing."[11]

Though Klawans seemed genuinely bewildered by Coppola's recent work, his biographical-critical approach seems on the surface fair enough; on even casual examination the films *do* resonate with various aspects of Coppola's private and public life. For reviewers, critics, and historians, the advantage to taking such an approach is that it helps establish a unifying, thematic structure to films as different as *Peggy Sue Got Married*, *Gardens of Stone*, *Tucker: The Man and His Dream*, *The Godfather Part III*, and *Bram Stoker's Dracula*.

But at the same time, this programmatically *auteurist* critical approach oversimplifies these complex and stylistically ambitious movies, all of which are, ultimately, quite different from one another. Additionally, such an approach virtually ignores the relationship between the final product, the *auteur* film on-screen, and the original conception of the project; that is, the relationship between what the director (or in some cases, the film's screenwriters or producers) originally wanted and what finally made it up there on the screen.

In his review of *Peggy Sue Got Married*, for example, *Mademoiselle*'s Ron Rosenbaum posed the argument that the film's narrative—its chronicle of a woman's journey into her past and subsequent return to the present a bit wiser but nonetheless committed to changing nothing along the way—offers a significant allegory to Coppola's own refusal to apologize for his Zoetrope films and his subsequent acceptance of a diminished status in the industry as a result.[12] Though such a reading is certainly interesting, it fails to acknowledge that Coppola signed on to direct *Peggy Sue Got Married* quite late in its development and had very little input or impact on the story or script.

That the film nevertheless seems to resonate with Coppola's *real life* reveals more about the nature of *auteurism* in the mid-1980s, and of Coppola's

15. Coppola's biggest box office film of the 1980s: *Peggy Sue Got Married* (Tri-Star Pictures, 1986).

role within the ongoing redefinition of *auteurism* in the new Hollywood, than it does about Coppola's specific contributions to the film itself.[13] That *Peggy Sue Got Married* seemed somehow self-reflexive or autobiographical suggests that by 1986 it had become impossible to discuss a Coppola film without first considering the relationship between a kind of public discourse on Francis Coppola, the star-director, and the somewhat less important narrative of the film that bears his name above the title.

As Timothy Corrigan convincingly argued, it is Coppola's very much self-promoted image of himself as an *auteur* that has resulted in the widely held perception that virtually all of his work of late is autobiographical: "Attempting to synthesize his relation to his movies, [Coppola] becomes the presiding genius of the film of himself."[14]

The Commerce of *Auteurism*

I've had bank executives quote stuff about me from magazines while turning down a loan application.—Francis Coppola, 1990[15]

As his career continued to founder during the 1980s and critics displayed increasing difficulty understanding and appreciating his movies, it became convenient to view Coppola as something of a tragic hero whose pride and past glory were all he had left to offer.[16] Such a point of view is continually supported by Coppola himself in interviews.

It is clear that Coppola rather likes his reputation as a risk taker and as an artiste whose refusal to compromise has cost him dearly in the industry. But neither tag is completely accurate. At the heart of the "Coppola problem" these days is the very image he has fostered of himself in the media; he is, in the biographical sense, the best *known* American filmmaker. As a result, he can't seem to avoid a kind of media celebrity few directors have ever "enjoyed" and thus continues to find himself unable to separate his public image from his work, even when it would be in the best interest of a particular film to do so.

For example, though his name appears above the title, *Peggy Sue Got Married* is only nominally a Coppola film, especially in light of the sort of control he enjoyed while directing *One from the Heart, The Outsiders,* and *Rumble Fish*—three films, it is important to note, that are clearly not autobiographical. Coppola understood from the moment he agreed to direct *Peggy Sue Got Married* that he was producer Paul Gurian's third choice, behind Penny Marshall and then Jonathan Demme. By the time Gurian approached Coppola to direct the picture, the film was already cast (with Kathleen Turner a last-minute replacement for Debra Winger, for whom the picture was originally packaged), and the Jerry Leichting–Arlene Sarner script had been revised to suit Gurian and the studio, not Coppola.

In accepting Gurian's offer to direct *Peggy Sue Got Married,* Coppola seemed to understand not only his own diminished position in the industry in general but also the nature of the project itself. As a result, during the course of the production Coppola stuck to the original concept for the film, appearing resigned to, perhaps even relieved by, his role as a hired hand.

Coppola's reason for accepting Gurian's offer to direct *Peggy Sue Got Married* was simple. He needed the money. "*Peggy Sue,* I must say, was not the kind of film I normally would want to do," Coppola reminisced in an interview on National Public Radio in August 1987. "The nature of my debts is that I have to make gigantic [annual] payments in March, millions of dollars. And so when the time starts getting closer to the payment and I'm looking around saying what should I do, the project that was ready to go that wanted me was *Peggy Sue.* And at first, I felt the script—although it was OK—was just like a television show. . . . I was very reluctant to do it and finally did it because Fred Roos, who has great taste, said it would be successful."[17]

Roos, as it turned out, was right, and *Peggy Sue Got Married* was a box office success, eventually becoming Coppola's highest-grossing effort in the 1980s. But much like the more modest success of the (far inferior) *Outsiders*, another project recommended to Coppola by Roos, the box office success of *Peggy Sue Got Married*, which despite its development and production history was viewed largely as a "Coppola picture," was a mixed blessing. Along with its good reviews—Rex Reed, for example, championed the picture, calling it "Francis Coppola's best film since *The Godfather*," and Siskel and Ebert gave it two thumbs-up and called it "a classic"[18]—the film's success only served to remind Coppola how little he understood the mass audience in the 1980s and how far his own taste had strayed from the mainstream.

Gardens of Stone, Coppola's next picture, seems in retrospect all too obviously autobiographical, but again, unintentionally so. The film is based on a novel by Nicholas Proffitt about the Old Guard, the ceremonial Washington, D.C.–based army unit which, during the Vietnam War, was charged with performing a seemingly endless series of state funerals.[19] Unlike *Peggy Sue Got Married*, the *Gardens of Stone* project originated with Coppola. But while he developed the project himself, he nevertheless remained faithful to the book and to a preproduction deal with the Old Guard, which agreed to become a "friend of the production" only after Coppola acceded to a list of forty "suggested" changes to the original shooting script.

As a result of Coppola's concessions to the army and to Proffitt's introspective and uncinematic book, *Gardens of Stone* seems to lack *direction* in the purest sense of the term. Once the picture came out, reviewers had little to say about it; there just wasn't much there to critique. Instead, the reviews called attention to the eerie parallel between the film's focus on servicemen grieving for the war dead and Coppola's own manner of mourning the death of his son, Gian-Carlo, who drowned in a boating accident during the production of the film.

Tucker: The Man and His Dream

No one else can balance the ups and downs of wistful sentiment and corny humor the way Capra can—but if anyone else should learn to, kill him.—Pauline Kael[20]

Gardens of Stone's poor performance at the box office went a long way toward helping the studios forget the box office success of *Peggy Sue Got Married*. Its failure with the mass audience and with the mass-media reviewers was particularly inconvenient because Coppola had just begun pitching a "new" project to the studios, a not particularly commercial-sounding movie about the ill-fated automobile entrepreneur Preston

16 and 17. The two Tuckers: Jeff Bridges in Coppola's *Tucker: The Man and His Dream* (still 16: photo by Ralph Nelson Jr., Lucasfilm, 1988) and Preston Thomas Tucker, automobile entrepreneur and American visionary (still 17: photo from the Tucker Family Archives, Lucasfilm, 1988).

Tucker, with whom, in 1987, at least, Coppola seemed to have a lot in common.

Though *Tucker: The Man and His Dream* seems on the surface his most autobiographical film to date, Coppola's work on the project began long before any parallels between his life and Tucker's had taken shape. Coppola had begun *developing* a picture about Tucker even before purchasing the rights to his life in 1976. In fact, Coppola's first thoughts on a Tucker biopic date back to his days as a student at UCLA in the 1960s. At the time, Coppola envisioned a picture much like *Citizen Kane*, a kind of larger-than-life American story in which, in Coppola's own words, "Preston Tucker dies and his car dies with him."[21]

In 1988, just before the release of *Tucker*, Coppola recounted his second, 1976 concept for the film: "[It was] a dark kind of piece . . . a sort of Brechtian musical in which Tucker would be the main story, but it would also involve Edison and Henry Ford and Firestone and Carnegie."[22] While redeveloping the picture along the same lines in the mid-1980s, Coppola signed Leonard Bernstein to write the music for the picture and began negotiating with Betty Comden and Adolph Green to supply the lyrics.

But after the failure of *Gardens of Stone*, Coppola discovered that he could no longer afford to envision the picture in such unconventional terms. "People [in the industry] no longer felt what I had to offer was of value," he told the *New York Times* after the release of *Gardens of Stone*, "They thought my projects were too grandiose. With the collapse of my studio everything fell into a black hole—*Tucker* plus a lot of other things I wanted to do."[23]

In 1987, when Coppola began to pitch *Tucker* in earnest, all of the major studios turned down the project. At the heart of the problem was not just Coppola's Brechtian musical concept (which sounded an awful lot like *One from the Heart*), but also the proposed budget: $24 million. The studios not only had no interest in *Tucker,* a film about a real person nobody had ever heard of, they had no interest in *any* Coppola film in that price range.

In desperation, Coppola turned to his friend George Lucas, who had just completed producing Coppola's $20 million three-dimensional theme-park short subject, *Captain EO,* for Walt Disney World. Operating under the assumption that their combined clout in the industry would eventually compel a studio to finance the picture, Lucas reached into his own pocket in order to get the project under way. At first, Lucas had no more success than Coppola in finding a studio to take over the financing of the picture. "They said it was too expensive," Lucas recalled. "They all wanted $15 million *Three Men and a Baby* movies or *Crocodile Dundee, Part 73* sequels."[24] But despite the rejections, Lucas remained confident that he would eventually convince at least one studio executive to back the film.

After several months of pitching the picture, Lucas's persistence finally paid off and Paramount CEO Frank Mancuso committed to a front-end deal to distribute the picture. With the financing from Paramount in place, Lucas not only got himself off the hook, he at the same time strengthened his position, however unintentionally, as co-*auteur* of the project. When the financing fell into place, it was clear to everyone involved that Lucas was the picture's one real asset.

Though it is highly unlikely that Lucas ever had to "pull rank," it *was* Lucas who finally convinced Coppola to abandon the musical-comedy approach and reconceive the picture as more of a Capraesque fable in which an indomitable little man has a dream of defying an indomitable big system. That such a scenario sounded a lot like the story of the demise of Zoetrope Studios was lost on no one at the time. That it also referred to Lucas's ongoing battle with the system was a notion no one seemed prepared to acknowledge. Nevertheless, for Lucas, *Tucker* seemed to speak to a discomfort he too felt as an artist, or at least as an *auteur,* in 1980s Hollywood.

Though he readily acknowledged the similarities between Tucker's story and his own (and Coppola's), Lucas nevertheless convinced Coppola to concentrate on keeping the film upbeat and thus potentially marketable. "I wanted an uplifting experience that showed some of the problems of corporate America," Lucas remarked regarding his input, "and Francis didn't resist."[25] At the time he couldn't. As to his role as a producer, Lucas added, "Francis can get so esoteric, it can be hard for an audience to relate to him. He needs someone to hold him back. With *The Godfather*, it was Mario Puzo. With *Tucker*, it was me."[26]

Despite a growing reputation for being egomaniacal and unreasonable—such was the legacy of *auteurism* in the 1980s—Coppola appreciated his situation and seemed to welcome Lucas's role in the production not only as a financial necessity but as a potential avenue back into the box office mainstream. "I'd lost some of my confidence," Coppola explained. "I knew George [had] a marketing sense of what people might want. He wanted me to candyapple it up a bit, make it like a Disney film. [Lucas] was at the height of his success, and I was at the height of my failure, and I was a little insecure. I'd made a lot of films, a lot of experiments, but the only one a lot of people seemed to like was *Peggy Sue Got Married*. I decided, if that's what they want from me, I'll give it to them. I'll do *Tucker* in the style of *Peggy Sue*. I think [*Tucker* is] a good movie—it's eccentric and a little wacky, like the Tucker car—but it's not the movie I would have made at the height of my power."[27]

Despite Lucas's input, *Tucker* did not do well at the box office. Lucas's belief that Capra's peculiar populism would play well in conservative 1980s America seems smart, and had he directed the picture himself, *Tucker: The Man and His Dream* may well have had a wider appeal. But Coppola's visual style—which featured an incessantly moving camera to match Tucker's dizzying rise and fall and a systematic use of low-angle, full-figure shots to depict Tucker as larger than life—was too sophisticated, or at least too showy, to remind anyone of Capra.

Coppola's priority on style seemed once again to reveal a self-consciousness about authorship. And once again, his descent into style seemed to support the widely held belief that he had become too esoteric for his own good. Even with the steadying hand of George Lucas, Coppola could not resist turning *Tucker* into an *hommage* to another *auteurist* fable about power and success and failure, Orson Welles' *Citizen Kane*.[28]

For popular reviewers and academic critics who recognized the similarities between *Citizen Kane* and *Tucker*, Coppola's continued priority on style seemed finally to make sense. What emerged from many of the positive reviews was not only a growing appreciation of Coppola's efforts as a cinema stylist but also a seeming affirmation of his newfound marginality from the industry mainstream.

But what these critics failed to understand was that while Coppola was flattered by the comparisons to Welles, he had no desire, even though he sometimes said he did, to become quite as marginal as Welles became after the late 1940s. Much like Welles, Coppola has periodically vented his annoyance at the studio establishment. But it is clear that he has never really been attracted to the distant margins of Hollywood.[29]

In the mid-1970s, for example, when he had the power and the money to independently finance and even distribute his own low-budget movies, Coppola instead opted to make a big-budget studio picture, *Apocalypse Now*. In the early 1980s, when the purchase of Hollywood General seemed to afford him the chance to make movies independent of studio financing, he chose instead to make *One from the Heart*, a film that cost so much it required the financial support of a major studio to produce and distribute.

When the box office failure and relative critical success of *Tucker* seemed to suggest that his own future might somehow resemble Welles's ill-fated Hollywood career, Coppola made the only move he could. He offered to finally make the deal he knew, despite the failure of *Tucker* and a decade of ill will, the studios could not afford to refuse.

The Only Wealth in the World Is Children

I showed [Francis Coppola's three young nephews] how the fingers of God and Adam [on the Sistine Chapel ceiling] don't quite touch. An ordinary artist would have had them touch. I said that's a great moment and that's what your uncle is creating. Like Michelangelo, he's on his back creating his third ceiling.—Talia Shire, actress (and Francis Coppola's sister)[30]

The *Godfather, Part III* was a project Coppola had steadfastly resisted from 1974 to 1989. The Hollywood rumor was that Paramount wanted to cast John Travolta as the third-generation don and Coppola would have no part of it. But the truth of the matter was that Coppola had nothing to gain in further sequelizing his signature product. The first two films won Best Picture Oscars and established Coppola as an *auteur*. A third *Godfather* film seemed an undue risk; if it wasn't any good, it might cheapen the first two. If it was successful, it might further typecast Coppola as a director of only a certain kind of picture.

Coppola made no secret of his reluctance to turn *The Godfather* into a series (like *Star Wars* or *Raiders of the Lost Ark*). If he were ever to make *The*

18. Coppola's evocative use of low-angle in *Tucker: The Man and His Dream*. Photo by Ralph Nelson Jr. (Lucasfilm, 1988).

Godfather, Part III, he told the press, it would be a farce, *Abbott and Costello Meet the Godfather.*[31]

But in 1989 Coppola was on the verge of bankruptcy. The failure of *Tucker,* his latest attempt to make a commercial film, seemed to suggest that he would never be able to shoot a box office success on his own again. Paramount, the studio that owned the rights to *The Godfather,* had clearly done its job with *Tucker.* Frank Mancuso picked up the picture even though he knew it would never make any money, and then, when the movie faltered at the box office, he supported it anyway in the press. Perhaps such support was the least he and the studio could do—and once all the ancillary monies were factored in, Paramount may well have been in the black on the film anyway—but Mancuso's and the studio's support was a lot more than Coppola had grown used to in the 1980s.

Mancuso's support of *Tucker* went a long way toward enabling Coppola to forgive and forget Paramount's undermining of the release of *One from the Heart.* Just seven years after Barry Diller effectively put an end to Coppola's studio dream/dream studio, Coppola was inclined to believe that he actually owed Paramount a favor. Once again, it paid for everyone concerned to have a short memory.

Whether or not Mancuso cynically used his investment in *Tucker* to eventually convince Coppola to direct *The Godfather, Part III* is anybody's guess.

But certainly he did exploit both the picture's failure and Coppola's goodwill to get *The Godfather, Part III* into production. What also helped make the deal happen was that Coppola's need was nearly matched by Paramount's. Even a conservative accounting revealed that by 1989 the first two *Godfather* pictures had earned Paramount in excess of $800 million in theatrical rentals alone. Though the films were almost twenty years old by that point, they continued to earn the studio money through various ancillary accounts (pay and network television, videocassette sales, and rentals and licensing fees). Paramount further benefited from the films' worldwide fame and critical reputation.

What troubled the executives at the studio was that the prestige Paramount continued to cull from the two *Godfather* pictures also seemed to highlight the studio's inability throughout the 1980s to find another prestige project as good and as popular as Coppola's two 1970s gangster pictures. Just as Coppola had struggled at the box office and with the critics throughout the 1980s, Paramount periodically floundered as well, especially after the death of Gulf and Western CEO Charles Bluhdorn in 1983.[32] After Bluhdorn died, the far more fiscally conservative Martin Davis took over, and his first move as chairman of Gulf and Western was to get rid of Paramount chief Barry Diller. Though Diller had been promised by Bluhdorn that his control over the studio would increase in time, Davis didn't trust Diller and instead named Mancuso, then the head of marketing at Paramount, to run the studio.[33] Diller responded by filing suit for breach of contract, then took a parallel position at Fox. Soon after Diller announced his decision to leave the studio, his second in command, Michael Eisner, resigned.[34]

A few weeks later, Eisner was named CEO at Disney. Then, in a dramatic show of distrust for the new Paramount leadership, Jeffrey Katzenberg, Bill Mechanic, Helene Hahn, Richard Frank, and Bob Jacquemin—top executives in the creative and legal departments at Paramount—all left to join Eisner at Disney. What made the mass resignations all the more embarrassing was that at the time Disney was not even a major studio; indeed, it had just survived a calamitous buyout attempt and seemed destined to face another unless Eisner could turn the company around quickly.

To Davis's chagrin, by the end of the decade, Disney, under Eisner's leadership, was the number one studio in the industry and the most successful and powerful entertainment conglomerate on the planet. In the meantime, Paramount under Mancuso and Davis seemed to lack direction. The studio's principal assets were its control over the *Indiana Jones* and *Star Trek* films and its contract with star Eddie Murphy, who seemed able to turn huge profits even when appearing in awful movies like *Coming to America* and *The Golden Child*. The studio also scored with *Top Gun*, a picture quite like the 1982 Paramount hit *An Officer and a Gentleman*.

Though the studio continued to release successful big pictures, Davis and Mancuso realized that with the exception of *Fatal Attraction*, the studio's surprise number two hit in 1987, virtually all of Paramount's success after 1984 could be attributed to films that were either sequels to or subtle variations on films made at the end of the 1970s or movies featuring a star whose contract and best days dated back to the Bluhdorn-Diller-Eisner era. More troubling still, it was clear that Paramount had earned its reputation of being a high-concept studio no longer interested in or capable of producing prestige films.

Of course, Coppola's *The Godfather, Part III* promised to be yet another recycle job. But it was clearly a prestige project, one that recalled the very *auteur* renaissance Paramount had first tried to exploit (with the Directors Company) and then, ultimately, discarded (by undermining the release of *One from the Heart*).

It is hard to know now whether, in 1989, Davis and Mancuso cynically believed that the only films that made any money were remakes—or flukes like *Fatal Attraction* or MGM-UA's *Rainman*—or if they had come to doubt their own instincts or ability to come up with anything new. Whatever their mindset at the time, Davis and Mancuso's desire to produce a third *Godfather* film seemed to suggest that they believed that they needed a *Godfather* sequel not only to make some money but to regain a little respect in the industry.

The decision in 1989 to move ahead with *The Godfather, Part III* and Mancuso's efforts to secure Coppola's participation in the project hardly took the industry by surprise. From the moment Davis and Mancuso had taken over, the studio had been shopping the project around. Rumor had it that Mancuso had at one time offered the picture to director Andrei Konchalovski, to Sylvester Stallone, even to Eddie Murphy.[35]

Once Coppola agreed to direct *The Godfather, Part III*, he was given a provisional budget of $44 million, which turned out to be about $10 million short of what he eventually needed to complete the film. At first Paramount made a concerted effort to keep the picture's cost under control. When Robert Duvall demanded the same star salary as Al Pacino, Mancuso insisted that Coppola do the film without him. Though Paramount eventually saved money on Duvall's replacement, George Hamilton, the last-minute change in casting forced Coppola to write Tom Hagen, the character Duvall played in the first two *Godfather* films, out of the script and then develop a new character for Hamilton.

Because the casting (and accompanying script) change came at the last minute, Coppola was forced to begin principal photography without a completed screenplay. Though he had done it before—*Apocalypse Now,* another picture that went well over budget, comes to mind here—it proved very costly to rework the various script problems on the set. Thus, exactly how much money the studio saved in refusing to hire Duvall is subject to debate.

That *The Godfather, Part III* cost more than it should have, and that it was less coherent than it might have been, ultimately resulted from circumstances well beyond Coppola's ability to control. Though he had the right to final cut, his concessions to the studio, to time, and to his own future marketability (as a cooperative director) systematically eroded his ability to take credit as the picture's sole *auteur.* Once again, the complex set of circumstances attending the development and production of the picture had a lot to do with what ended up on the screen.

As often happens in big-budget movies, once the shoot was under way, the studio became far more free with cash. Once the production was in full swing, Mancuso, who had refused to meet Duvall's salary demands, decided that money was no object so long as Coppola stayed on schedule. Mancuso's priority once the shoot was under way was to have the picture ready for a Christmas-week release. For example, when Winona Ryder, who was cast as Michael Corleone's daughter Mary, arrived on the set too ill to play the part, Coppola told Mancuso that he wanted to replace her with his own daughter, Sofia—who, of course, would work for far less in salary than Ryder. Mancuso countered by offering to hire any actress in Hollywood, at any price—even Madonna!—but Coppola maintained that his daughter was perfect for the part and eventually prevailed.

Later, when the shoot fell behind schedule, Mancuso authorized considerable postproduction overtime in order to get the film out in time for Christmas. To Mancuso's credit, even when the film did not hit as big as he had hoped, he never publicly blamed Coppola for failing to keep to the budget. He understood that *his* rush to get the film out in time for the holidays was the "real" reason for the budget overage, and he no doubt realized that the film's initial domestic box office was just a very small part of its larger significance to the studio.

In its initial domestic release, *The Godfather, Part III* grossed almost $70 million; taken on its own, that is a disappointingly low figure. Adjusting for the change in the value of 1972, 1974, and 1990 dollars, for example, *The*

Godfather, Part III was, by a significant margin, the least successful *Godfather* film. But in Hollywood these days, theatrical box office is a very small part of a film's worth to a studio.

Thus, even though the domestic grosses were not up to the standards set by the earlier *Godfather* films, Mancuso realized that there was no reason to panic. In addition to the domestic theatrical release of *The Godfather, Part III*, the studio controlled the picture's videocassette and pay television rights and also stood to benefit from the foreign distribution of the film. Paramount executives realized that they could count on a sequel to *The Godfather* to become a significant film event in Europe, where Coppola's reputation has never flagged as it has here.

Paramount further protected itself against the initial domestic box office disappointment by piggybacking the simultaneous re-release of the first two *Godfather* pictures in a special videocassette box set, featuring, as has become a common industry practice, "footage never before seen" edited back into a so-called director's cut.[36] The studio also coordinated a rescreening of the first two *Godfather* films on HBO, which not only produced revenue for the studio but helped to turn the release of *The Godfather, Part III* into a multimedia event.

Even more importantly, Paramount's stake in the picture had no time limit. The studio could take its time releasing *The Godfather, Part III* to cable and to video rental and sales outlets. Moreover, *The Godfather, Part III* not only supported the video sales for the first two *Godfather* films, it also enhanced Paramount's reputation in the business. Just two months after its nationwide release, *The Godfather, Part III* received Academy Award nominations for Best Picture, Best Director, and Best Actor.

Even to the most cynical in the business, it seemed quite beside the point that Paramount had regained some much-needed prestige by simply retreading an old product. And though it would be equally cynical to point out that *The Godfather, Part III* was a concession on Coppola's part to an industry that had grown overly fond of such sequels, the Oscar nominations and the larger picture of the film's inevitable financial success enhanced Coppola's reputation in the industry as a cooperative (perhaps former) genius.

Bram Stoker's Dracula

That critics who continue to equate the witless thuggery of Steven Seagal with old-fashioned movie matinee thrills, and take an inane ode to the joys of fly-fishing [*A River Runs Through It*] for a serious delving of the American soul, have been unsympathetic to Coppola's ideas is no surprise. What is surprising is that movie audiences, to whom Coppola's newfound erudition is utterly meaningless, have been lining up for *Bram Stoker's Dracula*. Has Coppola—as the curtain on Act III rises—somehow zapped the *zeitgeist*? Not really. These moviegoers, most of whose memories barely go back as far as *Star Wars*, couldn't care less about film directing. They've never heard of Bram Stoker. Dracula, however, is someone whose name the culture values enough to suitably impress upon their videogame-besotted brainpans. Besides, they know a good show when they see it.—David Ehrenstien, film critic, 1993[37]

The success of *Bram Stoker's Dracula* was *the* major box office surprise of 1992. When Columbia, the studio distributing the film, first screened the picture in previews, test audiences hated it. The response was so negative and so strong that studio executives at Columbia prevailed on Coppola to recut the picture. When the mass-market reviewers disliked the recut version as well, the studio, assuming that the film was no good, planned a fast and wide release. Market research indicated that a lot of people were interested in seeing the movie without knowing much about it besides the title and the director. The picture's best chance at the box office, then, was a quick opening weekend payoff in advance of negative word of mouth and reviews.

At the time, Thanksgiving weekend 1992, executives at Columbia were prepared for the possibility that *Bram Stoker's Dracula* was going to be a $50 million bomb. Lucky for them, it wasn't. Even luckier for Columbia, when the picture hit, the studio distribution team had, unintentionally, platformed the picture perfectly. Had they believed all along that the movie would be a blockbuster, the distribution team no doubt would have opened the picture fast and wide anyway in order to turn its release into an event. When the picture became an event on its own, the executives simply sat back, let the film do its thing at the box office, and then took credit for its success.

As the executives at Columbia discovered, market research is not infallible, and occasionally people go to see a picture despite poor reviews. To their surprise and benefit, *Bram Stoker's Dracula* continued to do good business well after its initial weekend. By the end of its first four months of release, the picture had grossed in excess of $200 million worldwide. By virtually every measure of a film's net worth to a studio, Coppola's *Dracula* was a major success.

It would be easy to write off the success of the film to the familiarity of the story or to the 1990s audience's seeming attraction to recycled entertainment. But *Bram Stoker's Dracula* hardly looks like any vampire film anybody

19. Gary Oldman in Coppola's surprise box office hit, *Bram Stoker's Dracula* (Columbia Pictures, 1992).

else ever made. Its emphasis on style over content seems far more consistent with Coppola's work at Zoetrope—*One from the Heart,* which features many of the same theatrical visual effects, comes immediately to mind—than with *The Godfather, Part III,* Coppola's previous 1990s retread, which at least *sets out* to tell a story.

The box office success of *Bram Stoker's Dracula* was not, as I see it, simply the result of Coppola's willing return to the generic Hollywood fold; the film is not, in point of fact, a generic product in any sense of the term. Instead, the picture's success—despite the critics, despite conventional wisdom, despite the 1980s—seems to suggest not only that Coppola is back as a bankable director, whose name above the title can be enough to get people into the theater to see *his* movies, but that the mass audience has finally caught up with him and has grown as impatient with boring generic narratives as he has.

Whether or not "Hollywood" has figured this out is anybody's guess. So long as Coppola's films continue to make money, no one in the industry cares what the films are supposed to mean.

Back to the Future

The industry needs guys who are willing to make pictures like *Rambo 7* or *Rambo 8.* I need to be a solo guy, like when I had polio. I don't say that with bitterness. I'm just not going to participate any more. I'm going to experiment with my own ideas—experiment without fear that failure will finish me off.—Francis Coppola, 1988[38]

At this writing, the Coppola produced *Mary Shelley's Frankenstein* is in its first theatrical run. The film, a much-hyped big studio package teaming Coppola, British stage actor Kenneth Branagh (who directed and stars in the picture), and Robert DeNiro (who plays the monster), is a major disappointment. Just how much damage Branagh's film will do to Coppola is uncertain. No doubt Coppola had hoped to use the film—the affiliation with Branagh, the reunion with ex-*Godfather, Part II* star Robert DeNiro—to strengthen his position in the industry. Though it is Branagh who is likely to be blamed for the picture's apparent failure with both the critics and the mass audience, it is safe to say that the film will be of little use when Coppola negotiates his next deal, when he tries once again to establish some sort of control over the way his work will be produced, distributed and exhibited.

What Coppola still wants and likely will never have is the sort of control that can come only through ownership of a production studio and distribution apparatus. Even if it is impossible—even if Coppola knows that it is impossible—that he will ever be in a position powerful enough to take on the studio establishment again, it remains part of the legend Coppola himself seems to be writing that he simply has to talk as if, someday, he will.

Indeed, in an article published in *Business Week* in December 1992—at the very moment *Bram Stoker's Dracula* was in the process of becoming a surprise box office hit—we find Coppola once again talking about owning and running his own studio. "The first time around," Coppola reflected, "I didn't think I needed businessmen, that I knew all there was to know about my business. What I didn't realize was that you need a cushion of some money when you go through the lean times. And there are always some lean times."[39]

How serious Coppola is about yet another studio project is anybody's guess. Given the increased conglomeratization of the industry since 1980, and the ways the major players are now jockeying for position to gain access to the distribution-exhibition apparatus(es) for the near-future information-entertainment superhighway, the capitalization requirements for entrance into the new new Hollywood seem well beyond even Coppola's wildest dreams. That he nevertheless still dreams of autonomy seems heroic if nothing else.

As to his aspirations as a film director, Coppola has similarly refused to scale down his ambition. After the success of *Bram Stoker's Dracula,* he resumed talking about making *Megalopolis,* a picture he had once planned to shoot at Zoetrope. "[*Megalopolis* is] based in part on Roman history," Coppola told *Film Comment* back in 1983, "because it takes a period in Rome just before Caesar, in which the conditions of Rome were almost identical [to New York City in the present]. . . . I researched this period, taking the incident of the revolt of Catiline, and I wanted to tell a story in a kind of Plutarch vision of New York as the Roman city, although it's not going to look Roman, it's going to look like New York."

Though the film's allegory of greed and cultural decline sounds timely enough, Coppola's proposed plot structure seems hardly commercial. "The way I'm going to do it," Coppola pitched, "is in a kind of elaborate, novelistic structure which has an intermission and a very bizarre second half going later and later into the night until the section that deals with three in the morning is really a wild section which ultimately puts forth the basis for the concept of utopia in the course of this mad hallucination that goes on."[40]

One can only imagine a thirty-year-old studio executive (who was all of seven when *The Godfather* premiered) listening to this pitch, imagining how to cast such a picture, imagining how to develop it into a movie he might someday have to try to release. One can only imagine how powerful, how successful, Coppola will have to become in order to get such an ambitious and bizarre project financed. At this writing, he is just the seventeenth most powerful director in the industry. For the time being, at least, he will have to continue to learn to live with Hollywood; otherwise he will have to learn to live without it.

Coppola has always been a far more important and far better filmmaker than businessman. And he would, in a perfect world, a perfect industry, be better off just to make movies and not worry about where or how to finance his work. Of course, Hollywood is hardly perfect. But Coppola, despite so much evidence to the contrary, still seems anxious to believe that someday, for him, it will be. He is, if nothing else, an optimist; he had to be in order to survive the 1980s in Hollywood.

Notes

Introduction

1   Mark Singer, "The Joel Silver Show," *New Yorker,* March 21, 1994, p. 126.
2   "Nasser Bros., Coppola Reach Agreement on General Studios Deal," *Variety,* March 12, 1980, p. 6.
3   "General Studios Finally Coppola's; but He Stays with Frisco Base," *Variety,* March 26, 1980, pp. 3, 40; and Lane Maloney, "Coppola: Inflation Propelling Film to Electronics, Satellites," *Variety,* March 26, 1980, p. 40.
4   Peter Boyer, "Jeffrey Katzenberg's Seven Year Itch," *Vanity Fair,* November 1991, p. 162.
5   The term *new Hollywood* refers here to Hollywood after 1980, Hollywood after *Apocalypse Now* and *Heaven's Gate* symbolically put an end to the *auteur* 1970s and short-term interest rates and rising production costs forced the major studios to diversify and/or sell out. There have been, I know, a lot of new Hollywoods, dating back at least to the late 1940s and the seeming collapse of the old studio system, the late 1960s and the implementation of the ratings code, and the early 1970s when films like *The Godfather* and *Jaws* dramatically raised studio expectations regarding the potential profits of a single picture and at the same time signaled the emergence of a new breed of university film school–educated directors. By the end of this book, I find myself talking about the new new Hollywood of the 1990s and looking forward to yet another new Hollywood that may someday take shape in concert with the forthcoming information-entertainment superhighway. For a particularly good discussion of the concept of the new Hollywood, see Thomas Schatz, "The New Hollywood," in *Film Theory Goes to the Movies,* ed. Jim Collins, Hilary Radner, and Ava Preacher Collins (New York: Routledge, 1993), pp. 8–36.
6   Gay Talese, "The Conversation," *Esquire,* July 1981, p. 87.

One. Hollywood General

1   Susan Braudy, "Francis Ford Coppola: A Profile," *Atlantic* 238.2 (1976), p. 69.
2   Julia Phillips, *You'll Never Eat Lunch in This Town Again* (New York: Signet, 1992), p. xxvii.

3   "Coppola Expects to Have an L.A. Studio," *Variety,* May 16, 1979, p. 3.

4   "Coppola Interim Fees on Nasser Mortgage Generates Some Fog," *Variety,* July 18, 1979, p. 7.

5   Though Speidel did not have the money to pay Nasser in full, he nevertheless claimed that he did in order to counter Nasser's claim that Coppola's interim payments amounted to an assumption of his mortgage. The *Variety* headline was indeed apt: "Coppola Interim Fees on Nasser Mortgage Generates Some Fog," p. 7.

6   American Zoetrope was Coppola's production company based in San Francisco.

7   "Coppola Interim Fees on Nasser Mortgage Generates Some Fog," p. 7; also "Coppola Plea Mixed on General Studios," *Variety,* February 13, 1980, p. 7.

8   "General Studios Finally Coppola's; but He Stays with Frisco Base," *Variety,* March 26, 1980, p. 3.

9   James B. Stewart, "The Tipster," *New Yorker,* January 17, 1994, p. 71.

10 Gay Talese, "The Conversation," *Esquire,* July 1981, p. 79.

11 Lynda Myles, "The Zoetrope Saga," *Sight and Sound,* Spring 1982, p. 92.

12 Jack Kroll, "Coppola's Apocalypse Again," *Newsweek,* February 16, 1981, p. 79.

13 The studio distributing the picture, the production company that produced it, and perhaps independent investors, stars, directors, and producers with "points" on (percentages of) the profits earned by a film are arranged much like lien holders on any other sort of property. The studio, because it distributes the film into the marketplace, routinely is in line to receive a return on its investment first. The studio also controls how a film is distributed—how many prints are made and how many theaters are contracted to screen it—and thus also controls the box office potential of the film. The other interested parties, all further down the line as lien holders and profit participants on the property, have little or no power to protect their investment once the film is handed over to the studio.

14 Lane Maloney, "Coppola: Inflation Propelling Film to Electronics, Satellites," *Variety,* March 26, 1980, p. 40.

15 Kroll, "Coppola's Apocalypse Again," p. 79.

16 Coppola's electronic cinema process is discussed at length in chapters 3, 4, and 5. As to Sony's role as an industry nemesis, I am referring here to the company's retail launch of Betamax, which, at the end of the 1970s, met with significant opposition from Universal and Disney. Sony has, of course, since joined the studio establishment by purchasing Columbia Pictures Industries. For more information on the Universal-Disney-Sony case, see chapter 2.

17 Talese, "The Conversation," p. 79.

18 Talese, "The Conversation," p. 84.

19 Jean-Paul Chaillet and Elizabeth Vincent, *Francis Ford Coppola* (New York: St. Martins, 1984), p. 75.

20 William Murray, "*Playboy* Interview: Francis Ford Coppola," *Playboy* 22 (1975), p. 68.

21 Michael Pye and Lynda Myles, *The Movie Brats* (New York: Holt, 1979), p. 81.

22 Murray, "*Playboy* Interview: Francis Ford Coppola," p. 68.

23 When Coppola signed the American Zoetrope deal with Warners, his oeuvre included the "axploitation" picture *Dementia 13*, for Samuel Arkoff, Roger Corman, and American International Pictures (AIP); *You're a Big Boy Now*, a teen movie; the Broadway musical *Finian's Rainbow* (with Fred Astaire and Petula Clark); and the hippie-era road picture *The Rain People* (starring Robert Duvall and James Caan, both of whom were, of course, cast in starring roles in *The Godfather*). None of the films—three of which were produced for Warner Brothers—made money or got much attention from the mainstream critics.

24 Here Coppola was wisely accommodating Walter Murch, a sound engineer who would go on to work on both *The Godfather* and *The Conversation* and would become, though largely unheralded, a major influence on the new American cinema. Certainly Coppola's emphasis on sound in his 1970s films owes a lot to Murch.

25 Louise Sweeney, "The Movie Business Is Alive and Well and Living in San Francisco," *Show*, April 1970, p. 82.

26 Sweeney, "The Movie Business Is Alive and Well," p. 34.

27 *THX-1138* was an expanded version of Lucas's USC thesis film.

28 Francis Coppola, "On the Director," in *The Movie People*, ed. Fred Baker (New York: Douglas, 1972), p. 67.

29 Pye and Myles, *The Movie Brats*, p. 83.

30 Coppola, "On the Director," p. 67.

31 Coppola, "On the Director," p. 53.

32 Coppola, "On the Director," p. 64.

33 Pye and Myles, *The Movie Brats*, p. 97.

34 Pye and Myles, *The Movie Brats*, p. 97.

35 Pauline Kael, "The Current Cinema" (review of *The Godfather, Part II*), *New Yorker*, December 23, 1974, pp. 63–68.

36 Murray, "*Playboy* Interview: Francis Ford Coppola," p. 76.

37 Axel Madsen, *The New Hollywood* (New York: Crowell, 1975), p. 116.

Two. The New Hollywood

1 Kate Bales, "A Coupla Producers Sittin' Around Talkin'," *American Film*, May 1987, p. 50.

2 Michael Pye and Lynda Myles, *The Movie Brats* (New York: Holt, 1979), p. 81.

3 Davic Picker, "On the Distributor," in *The Movie People*, ed. Fred Baker (New York: Douglas, 1972), p. 25.

4 Chris Hugo, "The Economic Background, Part II," *Movie* 31–32 (1986), p. 84.

5 James Monaco, *American Film Now: The People, the Power, the Money, the Movies* (New York: Oxford University Press, 1979), pp. 36–37.

6 *Film starts* is an industry term referring to the number of projects in development that are actually produced. Through the first quarter of 1982, a period
coinciding with the release of Zoetrope's first feature, *One from the Heart,* 53
percent fewer projects reached the production phase than in the same quarter in
1981. *Announced film starts,* which refers to projects given the green light by the
studios, were down 66 percent through the same period. See "Major Starts
down by 53% This Year," *Variety,* April 7, 1982, p. 3.

7 For a particularly good discussion of high-concept films, see Justin Wyatt,
"High Concept, Product Differentiation and the Contemporary U.S. Film In-
dustry," in *Current Research in Film: Audiences, Economics and Law,* ed. Bruce A.
Austin (Norwood, N.J.: Ablex Publishing, 1990), pp. 86–105, and Wyatt, *High
Concept: Movies and Marketing in Hollywood* (Austin: University of Texas Press,
1994).

8 Monaco, *American Film Now,* p. 393.

9 Ken Auletta, "Back in Play," *New Yorker,* July 18, 1994, p. 29.

10 "Needed Cash for Bank Balances, Kerkorian Sold 2% of His MGM," *Variety,*
April 25, 1979, p. 4.

11 By the end of the 1980s, after a series of failed attempts to unload MGM,
Kerkorian bought United Artists, in effect reacquiring the very domestic distribution rights he had previously sold.

12 James Harwood, "Trial Begins on Col. Stock Buy," *Variety,* August 8, 1979, p. 5.

13 "Economics Professors Unalarmed if Distribs. Shrink or Combine," *Variety,*
August 15, 1979, p. 7.

14 James Harwood, "Dept. of Justice Draws a Defeat," *Variety,* August 22, 1979,
p. 53.

15 "Vincent Memo Defends Price as Pivotal Studio Power; Hits KK's Claims of
Stark Control," *Variety,* October 8, 1980, p. 36. A convertible debenture is an
unsecured corporate bond that is convertible into common shares at the option
of its owner. In this case, the convertible debenture allowed CPI to issue additional shares in order to get them into the "friendly" hands of in-house producer Ray Stark.

16 "Columbia, Kerkorian Agree to End Legal Strife; CPI to Buy KK's 25% Stake; 10-
Yr. Truce," *Variety,* February 18, 1981, pp. 3, 22.

17 See Jon Lewis, "Disney after Disney: From Family Business to the Business of
Family," in *Disney Discourse,* ed. Eric Smoodin (New York: Routledge, 1994),
pp. 87–105.

18 In the argot peculiar to the corporate takeover, *greenmail* refers to a cash payoff
made to a corporate raider in exchange for the raider's stock and promise to
back off.

19 Bales, "A Coupla Producers Sittin' Around Talkin'," p. 52.

20 Joseph McBride, "Columbia's Record Fiscal Yr.; Gross Up 27%, Net Climbs 15%;
Reduce Gain from Arista Sale," *Variety,* September 10, 1980, pp. 3, 50.

21 "Universal All Projects," *Variety,* September 10, 1980, p. 3.

22 "Actors at SAG's Benefit Sound off for Solidarity," *Variety,* September 24, 1980, p. 3.

23 A. D. Murphy, "Actors Walkout Hurts TV, Helps BO Boom," *Variety,* October 1, 1980, pp. 1, 126.

24 Jeanie Kasindorf, "Mickey Mouse Time," *New York,* October 7, 1991, p. 40.

25 "Betamax Testimony Ends; Judge Ducks 'Signal' Jam Thicket," *Variety,* March 13, 1979, pp. 3, 100.

26 "Betamax Suit in Final Phase; See Major Impact on Copyright," *Variety,* June 20, 1979, pp. 1, 84.

27 Pat Jordan, "Wayne Huizenga," *New York Times Magazine,* December 5, 1993, p. 55.

28 Linda May Strawn, "Samuel Z. Arkoff" (interview), in *Kings of the B's: Working Within the Hollywood System,* ed. Todd McCarthy and Charles Flynn (New York: Dutton, 1975), p. 266.

29 Theaters are encouraged to hold over big-studio films for weeks, even months because their percentage of the gate increases incrementally over time. In the first week, the theater's take might only be 10 percent after expenses. Several weeks later, it might be up to 30 percent or 40 percent. As exhibitors routinely opted to hold over the big studio films in the 1980s, B movies and independent prestige pictures became harder and harder to distribute.

30 Roger Watkins, "Arkoff Warns of 1969 Repeat," *Variety,* May 21, 1980, p. 34.

31 Arkoff tells a significantly different story in his recent memoir, *Flying through Hollywood by the Seat of My Pants* (New York: Birch Lane, 1992), pp. 226–36. Whoever we believe, the result of the disclosure was Arkoff's exit.

32 Stephen Klain, "Arkoff as Producer of Which Few Remain in Age Dominated by Deal Makers," *Variety,* May 27, 1981, p. 37.

33 David Barton, "Filmways '81 Loss Concentrated in Qtr.," *Variety,* June 3, 1981, p. 44.

34 "Filmways Banner Retired as 'New' Orion Pictures Raises Own Flag; Shareholders Double Stock Base," *Variety,* August 4, 1982, p. 26.

35 Julie Salamon, *The Devil's Candy* (Boston: Houghton Mifflin, 1991), p. 312.

36 I discuss the relationship between Lucas and Coppola at greater length in Jon Lewis, "The Independent Filmmaker as Tragic Hero: Francis Coppola and the New Hollywood," *Persistence of Vision* 6 (1988), pp. 29–32. The quotation is from Gay Talese, "The Conversation," *Esquire,* July 1981, p. 80.

37 Louise Sweeney, "The Movie Business Is Alive and Well and Living in San Francisco," *Show,* April 1970, p. 82.

38 David Thomson, *Overexposures* (New York: Morrow, 1981), p. 40.

39 Mitch Tuchman and Anne Thompson, "I'm the Boss," *Film Comment* 17.4 (1981), pp. 50–51.

40 Audie Bock, "George Lucas: An Interview," *Take One,* August 1976, p. 6.

Three. *One from the Heart*

1   Eleanor Coppola, *Notes* (New York: Simon and Schuster, 1979), p. 177. Eleanor Coppola was and is Francis Coppola's wife.

2   Steven Bach, *Final Cut* (New York: New American Library, 1987), p. 127.

3   For a more complete account of the production of *Apocalypse Now,* see both Eleanor Coppola's *Notes* and the feature documentary *Hearts of Darkness,* by Fax Bahr and George Hickenlooper, 1991.

4   Bach, *Final Cut,* p. 128.

5   Pauline Kael, "The Current Cinema: Why Are Movies So Bad? or, the Numbers," *New Yorker,* June 23, 1980, p. 92.

6   This "insider's view" of the relationship between *Heaven's Gate* and *Apocalypse Now* (more so as deals than as films) is taken largely from Steven Bach's *Final Cut,* pp. 127–30, 282–83. In the late 1970s, Bach was senior vice president and head of worldwide marketing at United Artists. When *Heaven's Gate* bombed at the box office, Bach was fired, along with virtually every other UA executive who "worked on" the film.

7   Gay Talese, "The Conversation," *Esquire,* July 1981, p. 80.

8   Joy Gould Boyum, as cited by Stephen Bach in *Final Cut,* p. 410.

9   Vincent Canby, "The Screen: *Heaven's Gate,*" *New York Times,* December 22, 1980, p. 100.

10 Roland Bogue, "The Heartless Darkness of *Apocalypse Now,*" *Georgia Review* 35.3 (1981), p. 626.

11 Charles Schreger, "Speaking Up on *Apocalypse Now,*" *Los Angeles Times,* May 14, 1979, part 4, p. 7.

12 Charles Michener, "Finally, *Apocalypse Now,*" *Newsweek,* May 28, 1979, p. 101.

13 Michael Dempsey, "*Apocalypse Now*" (review), *Sight and Sound,* Winter 1979–80, p. 8.

14 Dempsey, "*Apocalypse Now*" (review), p. 8.

15 Jack Kroll, "Coppola's War Epic," *Newsweek,* August 20, 1979, p. 56.

16 Robert Hatch, "Films" (review of *Apocalypse Now*), *Nation,* August 25–September 1, 1979, p. 152.

17 Stanley Kauffmann, "Coppola's War," *New Republic,* September 15, 1979, p. 24.

18 Coppola's indecision about how to end *Apocalypse Now* was so extreme that he decided to hand out questionnaires at one of the press screenings asking those in attendance to help him end the picture. Instead of responding positively to Coppola's offer to let them in on the creative process, the critics excoriated him for pandering to their vanity. What this incident seems to reveal is that by the fall of 1979 Coppola had clearly lost a good deal of his popularity with the press.

19 In her gossipy tour de force on the new Hollywood, *You'll Never Eat Lunch in This Town Again* (New York: Signet, 1991), Julia Phillips recounts a conversation she had with producer Nick Wechsler, who, when asked by Phillips about Oliver

Stone's Vietnam picture, *Platoon*, quipped: "If *Apocalypse Now* was a supernova, *Platoon* is . . . a light bulb" (p. 527). At least according to Phillips and Wechsler, *Apocalypse Now* is still the ultimate Vietnam picture.

20   Peter McInerney, "Apocalypse Then: Hollywood Looks Back on Vietnam," *Film Quarterly* 33.2 (1979–80), p. 30; David Thomson, *Overexposures* (New York: Morrow, 1981), p. 312.

21   Richard Thompson, "Stoked" (interview with Milius), *Film Comment* 12.4 (1976), p. 15.

22   Thomson, *Overexposures*, p. 307.

23   Francis Coppola, "Memorandum," *Esquire*, November 1977, pp. 190–96.

24   David Breskin, *Innerviews: Filmmakers in Conversation* (London: Faber and Faber, 1992), p. 47.

25   Coppola, "Memorandum," p. 190.

26   Coppola, "Memorandum," p. 195.

27   Coppola, "Memorandum," p. 192.

28   Coppola, "Memorandum," p. 194.

29   Coppola, "Memorandum," p. 196. Here Coppola is conveniently misquoting, though both the transposed version (in the memorandum) and the original are apropos. For the record, the original reads: "Those whom God wishes to destroy, he first makes mad."

30   Talese, "The Conversation," p. 80.

31   Peter Cowie, *Coppola* (New York: Scribner's, 1990), p. 145.

32   Talese, "The Conversation," p. 78.

33   It is worth noting that much of what Coppola was talking about in the early 1980s has begun to take shape today, in the early 1990s, with the full support of the major studios. At the time of this writing, discussions of extended-channel cable television and the broadcast of pay-per-view movies directly into homes across the country, supported by technologies developed for the audio-video, telephone, and computer industries, dominate press stories on the impending information-entertainment superhighway. For more on this, see chapter 7.

34   Generally, a completion guarantee is an arrangement between a major studio, the bank with which the studio has arranged financing, and the company or individuals responsible for a film production that literally guarantees that "reasonable funds" will be made available in order to meet the various expenses of producing the film, in effect guaranteeing that the picture will be completed. Very few studio films are made without such a guarantee—virtually none in the budget range of *One from the Heart*.

35   On January 18, 1982, *Time* reported that executives at MGM were unhappy with Coppola's deal with Paramount. The executives at MGM claimed that Coppola had sold the distribution rights to *One from the Heart* to Paramount without first buying those rights back from MGM. Within a little over a month, though, the dispute concerning who owned the rights to the property was moot because

by then it was clear that the picture was not going to make anyone any money. See Richard Corliss, "Presenting Fearless Francis!" *Time*, January 18, 1982, p. 76.

36   As late as August 1986, United Artists and Coppola could not agree about whether or not Coppola's debt to the studio—the loan that financed *Apocalypse Now*—had been paid in full. Given how much money the film had made by then, UA's position seems outrageous; apropos here is the old industry joke: "The Mafia tried to move in on the film business but they couldn't figure out how to do the books." See "Coppola, Zoetrope Say They're Relieved of '*Apocalypse*' Debt," *Variety*, August 6, 1986, p. 7.

37   Paramount's behavior is discussed at length later in this chapter under the heading "What's One Studio More or Less in the New Hollywood?" Talese, "The Conversation," p. 80.

38   The loan made by Diller and Eisner was separate from the back-end financing deal between Coppola and Paramount. At the time, no doubt, it seemed a supportive gesture on the part of the two studio executives. But Diller's and Eisner's roles in the various problems attending the release of *One from the Heart* seem to reveal the gesture to be an empty, cynical public relations ploy.

39   Todd McCarthy, "Coppola Rescue Spotlights Calgary's Megabuck Clan," *Variety*, March 4, 1981, p. 34.

40   Sid Adilman, "Singer's a Swinger on Can. Pic Scene, Coppola's Bankroll," *Variety*, November 25, 1981, p. 51.

41   Robert Venturi, Denise Scott Brown, and Steve Izenour, *Learning from Las Vegas* (Cambridge: MIT Press, 1972).

42   When Coppola failed to meet the payroll on *One from the Heart*, studio workers voted not to shut down the production.

43   While it is uncertain whether or not United Artists would have ever gone so far as to foreclose on his private property when Coppola secured a production loan from the studio to finance *Apocalypse Now*, it was clear that this time, Chase Manhattan would not hesitate to seize the property if Coppola defaulted on the loan.

44   Lillian Ross, "Onward and Upward with the Arts: Some Figures on a Fantasy," *New Yorker*, November 8, 1982, p. 80. Much of what I have to say about the release of *One from the Heart* is indebted to Ross's fine essay.

45   Complicating matters further is the fact that it is now difficult to ascertain exactly how much money charged to the *One from the Heart* production budget account actually went into research and development of the electronic cinema method.

46   Mike Bygrave and Joan Goodman, "Meet Me in Las Vegas," *American Film*, October 1981, p. 43.

47   Jonathan Cott, "*Rolling Stone* Interview: Francis Coppola," *Rolling Stone*, March 18, 1982, p. 25. This piece came out at an inopportune time; the interview took place before the film's release but was not published until after the film had

already bombed at the box office and with so many of the mainstream mass-media reviewers. Coppola's lofty claims about the picture seemed at the time (at best) ironical.

48 Breskin, *Innerviews*, p. 21.

49 Cowie, *Coppola*, p. 159.

50 Stephen Klain, "Paramount—Coppola Break 'Heart' Strings Before Gotham Previews; Zoetrope Seeks New Distrib. Tie," *Variety*, January 20, 1982, pp. 3, 35.

51 Corliss, "Presenting Fearless Francis," p. 76.

52 Ross, "Onward and Upward with the Arts," p. 90.

53 Ross, "Onward and Upward with the Arts," p. 100.

54 Ross, "Onward and Upward with the Arts," p. 101.

55 "Col. Firms Domestic Distrib. Tie to Coppola's 'Heart'; Theatrical Only," *Variety*, February 3, 1982, p. 32.

56 Vincent Canby, "Screen: *One from the Heart*," *New York Times*, February 11, 1982, p. C25.

57 Ross, "Onward and Upward with the Arts," p. 110.

58 Ross, "Onward and Upward with the Arts," p. 115.

59 *One from the Heart:* Dazzling Body, Empty Heart" (review), *Variety*, January 20, 1982, p. 20.

60 "New York Critics Scorecard," *Variety*, February 17, 1982, p. 8.

61 Pauline Kael, "The Current Cinema: Melted Ice Cream" (review of *One from the Heart*), *New Yorker*, February 1, 1982, p. 118.

62 Thomson, *Overexposures*, p. 35.

63 Kael, "The Current Cinema: Melted Ice Cream," p. 120.

64 To a great extent the film *was* directed from a trailer, Coppola's high-tech Airstream mobile home, *Silverfish*, from which he viewed much of the shoot on video monitors and interacted with his cast via two-way audio.

65 Kael, "The Current Cinema: Melted Ice Cream," p. 119.

66 See David Denby, "Empty Calories," *New York*, February 1, 1982, p. 54. Denby called *One from the Heart* "a bizarre and pointless movie."

67 Sheila Benson, "*One from the Heart*" (review), *Los Angeles Times*, January 22, 1982, section 6, p. 1.

68 Richard Corliss, "Surrendering to the Big Dream" (review of *One from the Heart*), *Time*, January 25, 1982, p. 71; David Ansen, "Coppola's Fairy Tale World" (review of *One from the Heart*), *Newsweek*, January 25, 1982, p. 74; Janet Maslin, "Screen: Preview of *One from the Heart*," *New York Times*, January 17, 1982, section 3, p. 56.

Four. The Zoetrope Legacy

1 Thomas Pryor, "Cost Aside, Coppola's 'Heart' Reflects Top Technical Research," *Variety*, January 27, 1982, p. 35.

2   A negative pickup is a film that is already complete—a film that has already been cut and is ready for processing into positive prints—that is "picked up" at the last moment by a studio for distribution.

3   The list of lien holders ahead of Singer included, in order, James Nasser, $2.8 million; Ellison Miles, $350,000; Glen Speidel, $1.3 million; and Security Pacific Bank, $8.8 million. The sum owed in each case dates to May 26, 1982. By the time the studio was sold, the liens were, given accrued interest, all significantly larger.

4   Nasser was the first lien holder because he ostensibly owned the studio when Coppola bought it. Though Speidel lost control over the sale of the property to Nasser in court, his equity in the studio was nevertheless significant.

5   The other remaining creditors in line behind Chase Manhattan included a roofer, a carpet company, and an electrical contractor.

6   Eventually Chase Manhattan sold the note to sometime Zoetrope producer Fred Roos, who, predictably, has proven to be a very patient creditor.

7   "Zoetrope vs. Bank: Delay Auction for Prospective Buyers," *Variety*, February 16, 1983, p. 7.

8   "Zoetrope Escapes Again; Nova Bid?" *Variety*, March 16, 1983, p. 34.

9   David Robb, "Jack Singer Forces Zoetrope Studios into Chapter 11 as Bank Finally Moves for an Auction," *Variety*, August 3, 1983, p. 28.

10 This is, of course, untrue. The bank(s) seemed anxious to give Coppola as much time as he needed to sell the property himself.

11 Robb, "Jack Singer Forces Zoetrope Studios into Chapter 11," p. 28.

12 "Zoetrope Studios Sale," *Variety*, September 7, 1983, p. 3.

13 "Report Buyers for Zoetrope Studio Lot," *Variety*, September 21, 1983, p. 5.

14 On January 2, 1985, Security Pacific placed a lien against Coppola's interest in the Sentinel Building in San Francisco.

15 David Robb, "Zoetrope Studio Saga at an End as Singer's $12-Mil Takes It All," *Variety*, February 15, 1984, p. 34.

16 David Robb, "Coppola's General Now Singer Studio after Wrap of Sale," *Variety*, March 7, 1984, p. 410.

17 Kirk Kerkorian's fire sale of MGM props and memorabilia after his leveraged acquisition of the studio in 1971 comes immediately to mind.

18 Lee Lourdeaux, *Italian and Irish Filmmakers in America: Ford, Capra, Coppola and Scorsese* (Philadelphia: Temple University Press, 1990), p. 175.

19 Sean French, "The *Napoleon* Phenomenon," *Sight and Sound*, Spring 1982, p. 96. Much of what I have to say about Coppola's dispute with the BFI is based on this essay. It is important to note here, then, that *Sight and Sound* is a British journal with ties to the institute.

20 French, "The *Napoleon* Phenomenon," p. 96.

21 Richard Kozarski, "The Youth of Francis Coppola," *Films in Review* 19.9 (1968), p. 530.

22 The telecast of the Wisconsin rally went so badly that it became fashionable in the industry to refer to it sarcastically as "Apocalypse 1980."

23   Stephen Klain, "Coppola Invests $250,000 into Tube-to-Screen 'Too Far to Go,'" *Variety,* April 4, 1982, p. 29.

24   Stephen Klain, "Coppola Invests $250,000," p. 29; the italics are mine.

25   Tim Hunter, "The Making of *Hammett:* How Two Directors, Three and a Half Writers, Several Studio Executives and Francis Ford Coppola Took Five Years to Make 90 Percent of What May Be a Very Good Movie," *New West,* September 22, 1980, p. 32. Much of what I have to say about the development of *Hammett* is culled from this essay.

26   Hunter, "The Making of *Hammett,*" pp. 33–34.

27   Hunter, "The Making of *Hammett,*" p. 34.

28   In 1980, Frederic Forrest was finally cast as Dashiell Hammett (with studio approval) even though DeNiro never officially turned down the part.

29   *Turnaround* is an industry term that refers to a project in development that is literally turned around by the studio; in other words, a green-lighted project that is subsequently shelved (usually forever).

30   Peter J. Schuyten, "United Artists Script Calls for Divorce," *Fortune,* January 16, 1978, pp. 130–38.

31   Steven Bach, *Final Cut* (New York: New American Library, 1985), p. 47. Bach's account of the breakup of United Artists is the primary source for my discussion here.

32   An advertisement run in *Variety,* January 25, 1978, pp. 26–27. The letter, signed by sixty-three prominent producers and directors, read as follows: "Dear Mr. Beckett: We the undersigned, have made films in association with Arthur Krim, Eric Pleskow, Bob Benjamin, Bill Bernstein and Mike Medavoy. The success of United Artists throughout the years has been based upon the personal relationships of these executive officers of United Artists with us, the filmmakers. We seriously question the wisdom of the Transamerica Corporation in losing the talents of these men who have proven their creative and financial leadership in the film industry for many years. The loss of this leadership will not only be felt by United Artists but by all of us."

33   Hunter, "The Making of *Hammett,*" p. 35.

34   The sets that no longer fit the revised *Hammett* scripts did not go to waste. They eventually were used in the Zoetrope production of Caleb Deschanel's much underrated children's picture, *The Escape Artist.*

35   Hunter, "The Making of *Hammett,*" p. 42.

36   Hunter, "The Making of *Hammett,*" p. 45.

37   Wenders would eventually get his revenge (sort of) in *State of Things,* his bitter but largely unseen picture about filmmaking in America.

38   "*Hammett*" (review), *Variety,* June 2, 1982, p. 15.

39   Carol Rutter, "Coppola in His Own Words," *Image,* May 17, 1987, p. 27.

40   Lillian Ross, "Onward and Upward with the Arts: Some Figures on a Fantasy." *New Yorker,* November 8, 1982, pp. 112–13.

41   Rutter, "Coppola in His Own Words," p. 27.
42   Karen Jaehne, "Schrader's *Mishima:* An Interview," *Film Quarterly,* Spring 1986, p. 16.
43   David Robb, "Zoetrope Presents 'Grey Fox,' 'Passion,' for UA Classics Release," *Variety,* March 23, 1983, p. 36.
44   Jaehne, "Schrader's *Mishima:* An Interview," p. 12.

Five. Exile in Oklahoma: *The Outsiders* and *Rumble Fish*

1   As told to producer Scott Rudin and cited by Philip Weiss, "Hollywood at a Fever Pitch," *New York Times Magazine,* December 26, 1993, p. 40.
2   Carol Rutter, "Coppola in His Own Words," *Image,* May 17, 1987, p. 27.
3   The piggybacked productions of *The Outsiders* and *Rumble Fish* on location in Tulsa in the early 1980s no doubt reminded Coppola of the circumstances surrounding *Dementia 13,* his debut film for Roger Corman and AIP in 1963. Twenty years before the release of *The Outsiders,* Coppola convinced Corman that he could shoot a film using the same sets, locations, insert photography, and cast and crew of another AIP picture that was about to wrap in Ireland. Corman gave *Dementia 13* the green light, and Coppola got his first semi–big break. Certainly, it must have been a sobering realization for Coppola that, some ten years after *The Godfather* had made him a major player in Hollywood, there were such obvious similarities between his position in the industry in 1963 and 1983.
4   Todd McCarthy, "WB Gets Coppola's 'Outsiders'; Teenage Pic Eyes Fall Bow," *Variety,* March 17, 1982, p. 172.
5   At that time, Warner Brothers distributed motion pictures for Orion.
6   Aljean Harmetz, "Making *The Outsiders:* A Librarian's Dream," *New York Times,* March 23, 1983, p. C19.
7   McCarthy, "WB Gets Coppola's 'Outsiders,' " p. 172.
8   Jean-Paul Chaillet and Elizabeth Vincent, *Francis Ford Coppola* (New York: St. Martins, 1984), p. 93.
9   Rutter, "Coppola in His Own Words," p. 27.
10   Even with the memory of the production delays and budget overages Coppola suffered while making *Apocalypse Now* and *One from the Heart* fresh in their minds, Warner Brothers's executives supported Coppola's desire to reshoot several scenes in *The Outsiders* when the performances by the teen cast seemed particularly weak. Because Coppola's reputation had already been hurt by his seeming *auteurist* excesses at the end of the 1970s and early 1980s, it was unnecessary for the studio to turn to the trades or the popular press to chastise him for once again failing to keep to a production timetable. Warner Brothers instead protected Coppola and the film from such criticism, and *The Outsiders* did well at the box office as a result.

11   "New York Critics Scorecard," *Variety,* March 30, 1983, pp. 4, 134.

12   Carol Rutter, "Coppola in His Own Words," p. 27.

13   Vincent Canby, "The Outsiders: Teen-Age Violence," *New York Times,* March 25, 1983, p. C3.

14   David Denby, "Romance for Boys," *New York,* April 4, 1983, p. 73; Gary Arnold, "Greasy Kids Stuff," *Washington Post,* March 25, 1983, p. C1.

15   David Thomson and Lucy Gray, "Idols of the King," *Film Comment* 19.5 (1983), p. 61. For additional discussions of *Rumble Fish,* see Jon Lewis, "The Road to Romance and Ruin: The Crisis of Authority in Francis Coppola's *Rumble Fish,*" in *Crisis Cinema,* ed. Christopher Sharrett (Washington, D.C.: Maisonneuve Press, 1993), pp. 129–46; and Lewis, *The Road to Romance and Ruin: Teen Films and Youth Culture* (New York: Routledge, 1992), pp. 144–50.

16   Michael Daly, "The Making of *The Cotton Club:* A True Tale of Hollywood," *New York,* May 7, 1984, pp. 50–51.

17   Chaillet and Vincent, *Francis Ford Coppola,* p. 103.

18   Michael Covino, "The Coppola Conundrum," *Image,* May 17, 1987, p. 38.

19   Stanley Kauffmann, "*Rumble Fish*" (review), *New Republic,* November 7, 1983, p. 31.

20   Kauffmann, "*Rumble Fish*" (review), p. 32.

21   "New York Critics Scorecard," *Variety,* October 19, 1983, p. 4.

22   Chris Hugo, "The Economic Background," *Movie* 27–28 (1986), p. 47.

23   Richard Corliss, "Time Bomb" (review of *Rumble Fish*), *Time,* October 24, 1983, p. B12.

24   Only Julien Temple's *Absolute Beginners,* which features a similar use of expressive sets and choreographed, stylized violence, and Michael Lehmann's *Heathers,* which shares *Rumble Fish*'s critical distance from the generic teen-pic narrative, approximate Coppola's radical departure from the popular genre. *Absolute Beginners* rather deliberately alludes to the entirety of Coppola's Zoetrope Studio work; its visual style and narrative music track seem indebted not only to *Rumble Fish,* but to *One from the Heart* as well.

25   In her review of *One from the Heart* ("The Current Cinema: Melted Ice Cream," *New Yorker,* February 1, 1982), Pauline Kael wrote that "[*One from the Heart*] feels like something directed from a trailer. It's cold and mechanized; it's at a remove from its own action" (p. 118).

26   Andre Bazin, "La politique des *auteurs,*" in *The New Wave: Critical Landmarks,* ed. John Peter Graham (Garden City, New York: Doubleday, 1968), p. 144.

27   Richard Thompson, "Stoked" (John Milius interview), *Film Comment* 12.4 (1976), p. 11.

28   Chaillet and Vincent, *Francis Ford Coppola,* p. 169.

29   Jack Kroll, "Coppola's Teen-Age Inferno," *Newsweek,* November 7, 1983, p. 128.

30   Lawrence O'Toole, "Strange Young Men in a Strange Land," *Macleans,* October 24, 1983, p. 60.

Six. *The Cotton Club*

1   Art Linson, "This Boy's Art," *Premiere*, May 1983, p. 47.

2   William Murray, "*Playboy* Interview: Francis Ford Coppola," *Playboy* 22 (1975), p. 59.

3   David Thomson and Lucy Gray, "Idols of the King," *Film Comment*, September–October 1983, pp. 72–73.

4   Julie Salamon, "Budget Busters: *The Cotton Club*'s Battle of the Bulge," *Wall Street Journal*, December 13, 1984, p. 22. In his foreword to Evans's 1994 memoir, *The Kid Stays in the Picture* (New York: Hyperion), Peter Bart, Evans's former right-hand man at Paramount and at present editor-in-chief of *Variety*, supports the contention that Evans significantly re-edited Coppola's film. "*The Godfather* was a seminal experience," Bart writes, "in that Evans was dissatisfied with Francis Ford Coppola's cut and spent months working round the clock with him on the film, even postponing its release date. . . . the gossip in town was that Evans was intruding on the prerogatives of young filmmakers. The reality was quite the opposite. I watched as a superbly shot but ineptly put together film was transformed into a masterpiece" (p. iv).

5   Michael Daly, "The Making of *The Cotton Club*: A True Tale of Hollywood," *New York*, May 7, 1984, p. 43. Daly's article is the primary source in my discussion of the production of *The Cotton Club*.

6   The reason the book was so expensive to option was that Evans had to buy the rights away from Charles Childs and Jim Hinton, two African-American producers who were themselves developing a television miniseries based on Haskins's account of the Cotton Club.

7   Pat Jordan, "Wayne Huizenga," *New York Times Magazine*, December 5, 1993, p. 56.

8   Evans was trying to convince Khashoggi to provide *production* financing. If Khashoggi agreed, then at best he would be in second position behind whichever studio ended up releasing the picture.

9   In *The Kid Stays in the Picture*, Evans tells a somewhat different story. According to Evans's account, he first met Adnan Khashoggi en route to a meeting with another potential *Cotton Club* investor, Menachem Ricklis. While in Las Vegas, he and Khashoggi played craps for high stakes, Evans won and Khashoggi agreed to fund the production. According to Evans, the deal was set until Essam Khashoggi entered the scene and objected to his brother's "caprice." Ultimately, Essam demanded that Evans put up his house as collateral against budget overages and when Evans refused the deal fell through. (pp. 329–32)

10 Daly, "The Making of *The Cotton Club*," p. 44.

11 Evans's deal with the Producers Sales Organization was announced in a two-page advertisement for the project in *Variety*, March 2, 1983, pp. 60–61. In *The Kid Stays in the Picture*, Evans claims that he made the deal in Cannes a year earlier. (p. 328).

12   The Orion-Evans deal was announced in a major feature piece in *Variety* by staff writer Jim Robbins with the ominous title, "Evans 'Club' Kicks Off 'Experiment,'" *Variety*, February 23, 1983, pp. 3, 22. The "experiment" mentioned in the title refers explicitly to Evans's unique deal with the New York Teamsters governing overtime compensation (discussed briefly later on in this chapter) and implicitly to Evans's dual role as producer and director of the film.

13   Robbins, "Evans 'Club' Kicks Off 'Experiment,'" p. 22.

14   "Evans Vows Lotsa Minority Jobs on His 'Cotton Club,'" *Variety*, March 2, 1983, p. 5.

15   Daly, "The Making of *The Cotton Club*," p. 46.

16   Coppola's reason for agreeing to help Evans was simple: Evans offered him $500,000 up front to fix the script and Coppola needed the money.

17   Julia Phillips, *You'll Never Eat Lunch in This Town Again* (New York: Signet, 1992), p. 248.

18   Daly, "The Making of *The Cotton Club*," p. 46.

19   Jean-Paul Chaillet and Elizabeth Vincent, *Francis Ford Coppola* (New York: St. Martins, 1984), p. 115.

20   Throughout 1992, Hollywood insiders spent a lot of time speculating about which Hollywood executive was the real-life model for Griffin Mill, the smarmy studio climber in Robert Altman's *The Player*. The scenes early on in the film when Mill is interviewed by the police in his office on the studio lot, and then later when he is terrorized in the Pasadena police station, bear an eerie resemblance to Evans's bout with the authorities in 1983. The Jacobs-Radin story is laid out in detail in Daly, "The Making of *The Cotton Club*," pp. 46–48, and in Evans, *The Kid Stays in the Picture*, pp. 364–77, 385, 389, and 395.

21   Evans, *The Kid Stays in the Picture*, p. 366.

22   Evans, *The Kid Stays in the Picture*, p. 370.

23   Evans, *The Kid Stays in the Picture*, p. 377.

24   Evans, *The Kid Stays in the Picture*, p. 376.

25   By the time Coppola and William Kennedy completed the shooting script, there was little left of Puzo's work. As a result, on the release print, Puzo, as something of a concession to his early drafts, receives a story credit.

26   Daly, "The Making of *The Cotton Club*," p. 49. Evans has a significantly different story to tell about his battle with Coppola for control of the picture. See "Intrigue, Anger, Blackmail, Deceit . . . ," later on in this chapter, and *The Kid Stays in the Picture*, pp. 327–51.

27   Peter Cowie, *Coppola* (New York: Scribner, 1990), pp. 182–83.

28   Daly, "The Making of *The Cotton Club*," p. 49.

29   Cowie, *Coppola*, p. 183. Music producer Jerry Wexler was also fired and paid off. For not working on the movie, Wexler received $87,500.

30   Daly, "The Making of *The Cotton Club*," p. 51.

31   Daly, "The Making of *The Cotton Club*," p. 52.

32   Daly, "The Making of *The Cotton Club*," p. 42.

33   Daly, "The Making of *The Cotton Club*," p. 53.

34   Daly, "The Making of *The Cotton Club*," p. 53.

35   "Set Hearing on Alleged 'CC' Title Steal," *Variety,* August 24, 1983, p. 3.

36   "Coppola Stays Home from 'Cotton' Shoot: No Pact or Checks," *Variety,* October 5, 1983, p. 3.

37   "Coppola Stays Home from 'Cotton' Shoot," p. 32.

38   "Overbudget Clause Cued 'Cotton' Flap," *Variety,* October 19, 1983, pp. 3, 33.

39   Though ancillary revenues significantly complicate calculations regarding a film's net profit or loss, studio executives tend to perpetuate the myth that in order to turn a profit a film has to gross (in domestic box office revenues) approximately three times its production cost.

40   " 'Cotton' Returning for Gotham Shoot," *Variety,* February 29, 1983, p. 3.

41   "Overbudget Clause Cued 'Cotton' Flap," p. 33.

42   Daly, "The Making of *The Cotton Club*," p. 59.

43   Daly, "The Making of *The Cotton Club*," p. 59.

44   Daly, "The Making of *The Cotton Club*," p. 60.

45   Evans's dealings with Diller and his plot to extricate himself from the Orion distribution deal are never mentioned in *The Kid Stays in the Picture.*

46   Jim Robbins, "Despite Complex Editing Chores, 'Club' on Sched. for Dec. 14 Bow," *Variety,* September 12, 1984, p. 24.

47   Ray Loynd, "Evans Regains Some Control of 'CC' in Court Showdown," *Variety,* June 20, 1984, pp. 4, 33.

48   In "The Making of *The Cotton Club*," Michael Daly notes that Joey Cusumano was "considered by the FBI" to be "close to Anthony Spilotro, who is considered to be the Mafia boss of Las Vegas" (p. 58). In the process of making the Cusumano-Spilotro connection, Daly seems also to be making a point about the Doumani brothers. At the very least, since *The Cotton Club* is partly a gangster picture, this seems a case of life imitating art.

49   Lloynd, "Evans Regains Some Control of 'CC' in Court Showdown," pp. 4, 33.

50   Cowie, *Coppola,* p. 186.

51   That the Doumanis ended up "holding the paper" on Evans's house suggests that when Evans told *Variety* that he'd have to stick to the film's $20 million budget, it wasn't just Hollywood hype. In the February 24, 1983, issue of *Variety,* Evans told staff writer Jim Robbins: "I have $20,000,000 to make [*The Cotton Club*]. Anything more than that and they're going to take my house away" (p. 22). Of course, from the very start Evans knew that $20 million was not going to be enough to make the picture. That he went ahead anyway, fully aware that he was dealing with the Doumanis, who were reputed to have connections to the Las Vegas Mafia, seems particularly foolhardy.

52   "Complaint to Enjoin Release of 'Cotton Club' to Be Heard 12/13," *Variety,* December 5, 1984, pp. 6, 31.

53   Ray Loynd, "Evans Relinquishes Remainder of 'CC' Power to Doumanis," *Variety,* January 2, 1985, p. 26.

54   Ray Loynd, "In Only One 'CC' Scene, Actress, with Points, Gets 100G," *Variety*, January 9, 1985, pp. 4, 194.

55   Loynd, "In Only One 'CC' Scene, Actress, with Points, Gets 100G," p. 194.

56   At the time, Mechsner's claims sounded pretty crazy. But recent allegations regarding Evans and some far more notorious "party girls" suggest that Mechsner may well have been telling the truth. For example, in the February 1994 issue of *Vanity Fair*, Lynn Hirschberg contends that in the sixty hours of phone tapes made by alleged Hollywood madam Heidi Fleiss, Evans is implicated in a procurement-blackmail scam involving Paramount CEO Stanley Jaffe, Jaffe's son Bob, and one of Heidi's "girls." According to Hirschberg, Fleiss and Evans set Bob Jaffe up with a Fleiss prostitute in London. Evans, again according to Hirschberg, planned to use photographs taken of Bob Jaffe and the prostitute to coerce Stanley Jaffe into extending Evans's production contract with Paramount. Though Hirschberg presents the allegations of Evans's and Fleiss's plot in some detail, to date the tapes are not a matter of public record, and Evans has steadfastly refused to comment to the press about his alleged relationship with Fleiss. Perhaps it is again a matter of perception being more important than reality, but Evans's relationship with Fleiss—as a client, confidant, etc.—seems widely acknowledged in Hollywood. See Lynn Hirschberg, "Heidi Does Hollywood," *Vanity Fair*, February 1994, p. 122. Certainly, if Evans's involvement with Fleiss is as deep as Hirschberg says it is, then it does not require a significant leap of the imagination to believe Mechsner's story regarding "parties" she participated in to convince the Doumanis to finance *The Cotton Club*. Also see Loynd, "In Only One 'CC' Scene, Actress, with Points, Gets 100G," p. 194.

57   Ray Loynd, "Doumanis Buyout of Evans Near 9 Mil; Plan More Joint Pictures," *Variety*, August 22, 1984, p. 3.

58   Loynd, "Doumanis Buyout of Evans Near 9 Mil," p. 136.

59   Evans, *The Kid Stays in the Picture*, p. 347.

60   James Traub, "More Than Friends," *New Yorker*, November 28, 1994, p. 51.

61   Evans, *The Kid Stays in the Picture*, p. 343.

62   Evans, *The Kid Stays in the Picture*, p. 344.

63   Evans, *The Kid Stays in the Picture*, p. 338.

64   Evans, *The Kid Stays in the Picture*, p. 350.

65   Paul Tough, "The New *Auteurs*," *Harpers*, June 1993, p. 42.

66   "New York Critics Scorecard," *Variety*, December 19, 1984, p. 4.

67   Pauline Kael, "The Current Cinema" (review of *The Cotton Club*), *New Yorker*, January 7, 1985, p. 67.

68   Kael, "The Current Cinema" (review of *The Cotton Club*), p. 70.

69   "*The Cotton Club*" (review), *Variety*, December 12, 1984, p. 16.

70   Jay Stuart, "Coppola in Rome for 'Club' Bow, Blasts Uniformity of Yank Pics," *Variety*, December 26, 1984, p. 21.

71   Loynd, "In Only One 'CC' Scene, Actress, with Points, Gets 100G," p. 194.

72   "Though Not 'Throwing in the Towel,' Orion Hints Bottom of 3 Mil in Losses With 'Cotton Club,' " *Variety,* January 23, 1985, pp. 3, 38.

Seven. Francis Coppola and the New New Hollywood

1   James B. Stewart, "Annals of Law: The Tipster," *New Yorker,* January 17, 1994, p. 71.

2   "The Power List," *Premiere,* May 1993, p. 75.

3   Jack Kroll, "The Corleones' Return," *Newsweek,* December 24, 1992, p. 58; Ronald Grover, "Francis Coppola May Be Sweating Blood No More," *Business Week,* December 7, 1992, p. 98.

4   Denby, as cited by David Ehrenstein in "One from the Art," *Film Comment,* January 1993, p. 27.

5   The thumbs-up on *Sneak Previews*–like shows on television has become essential to box office success. These days, Siskel and Ebert clearly belong someplace in *Premiere's* Top 100.

6   "The Power List," p. 85.

7   Terrence Rafferty, "The Current Cinema" (review of *New York Stories*), *New Yorker,* August 22, 1988, p. 62.

8   Pauline Kael, "The Current Cinema: Nannies and Noncoms," *New Yorker,* May 18, 1987, p. 84.

9   Kael, "The Current Cinema: Nannies and Noncoms," p. 85.

10   Stanley Kauffmann, "Books and the Arts: Manhattan Moods," *New Republic,* March 27, 1989, pp. 25–26.

11   Stewart Klawans, "Films" (review of *New York Stories*), *Nation,* March 27, 1989, p. 427.

12   Ron Rosenbaum, "All-American Dream Girl," *Mademoiselle,* December 9, 1986, pp. 93, 232.

13   "The commerce of *auteurism*" is a phrase coined by Timothy Corrigan in *A Cinema Without Walls* (New Brunswick, N.J.: Rutgers University Press, 1991). For Corrigan, the emergence of star *auteurs* significantly redefined the role of the film director in the industry and at the same time seemed to redirect the popular reception of certain *auteurist* films (e.g., *Heaven's Gate, Tucker: The Man and His Dream*). As I have discussed at length here, by the mid-1980s it had become impossible to talk about a Coppola film independent of all the press attending its production and release.

14   Ibid., p. 113.

15   Jack Kroll, "The Offer He Didn't Refuse," *Newsweek,* May 28, 1990, p. 69.

16   For a more extensive discussion in this vein, see Jon Lewis, "The Independent Filmmaker as Tragic Hero: Francis Coppola and the New American Cinema," *Persistence of Vision* 6 (1988), pp. 26–40.

17 Jeffrey Chown, *Hollywood Auteur: Francis Coppola* (New York: Praeger, 1988), p. 199.

18 While the vast majority of the mainstream reviewers liked the film, *Peggy Sue Got Married* was received far less enthusiastically in progressive magazines and academic journals. For the most part, the progressive and academic reviewers objected to the film's seeming naïveté regarding gender relations and sexual politics. See Susan Dworkin, "Back to the Future for Grown-Ups," *Ms,* November 1986, p. 17; Roberta Pearson, "*Peggy Sue Got Married*" (review), *Cineaste* 15.3 (1987), p. 47; and Bob Bartosch, "And Invited Charlie to Dinner," *Jump Cut* 32 (1987), p. 4.

19 Nicholas Proffitt, *Gardens of Stone* (New York: Carroll and Graf, 1983).

20 Hal Espen, "Interview: Kael Talks," *New Yorker,* March 21, 1994, p. 140.

21 Jill Kearney, "The Road Warrior," *American Film,* June 1988, p. 23.

22 Robert Lindsey, "Francis Coppola: Promises to Keep," *New York Times Magazine,* July 24, 1988, p. 26.

23 Lindsey, "Francis Coppola: Promises to Keep," p. 26.

24 Lindsey, "Francis Coppola: Promises to Keep," p. 26

25 Lindsey, "Francis Coppola: Promises to Keep," p. 27.

26 Lindsey, "Francis Coppola: Promises to Keep," p. 26.

27 Lindsey, "Francis Coppola: Promises to Keep," p. 27.

28 For more on the Welles-Coppola connection, see Corrigan, *A Cinema Without Walls,* pp. 108–15; and Richard Macksey, "The Glitter of the Infernal Stream: The Splendors and Miseries of Francis Coppola," *Bennington Review* 15 (1983), pp. 2–16.

29 See Jon Lewis, "The Independent Filmmaker as Tragic Hero," pp. 26–40.

30 Kroll, "The Offer He Didn't Refuse," p. 68. "The only wealth in the world is children" is the opening line of *The Godfather, Part III.*

31 Kroll, "The Corleones' Return," p. 58.

32 At the time, Gulf and Western owned Paramount.

33 Barry Diller reemerged ten years later in a failed attempt to take over Paramount Communications. Symbolically, at least, Diller's attempt to buy the studio seemed to suggest that he was after some sort of revenge. But when Viacom and Sumner Redstone carried the day, Diller likely regretted his move on the company. In the final accounting, all Diller accomplished was to drive up the sale price, in effect making more money for his longtime enemy Martin Davis.

34 When Diller opted to quit Paramount and take the position at Fox, he didn't bother to tell his second in command, Michael Eisner. By the time Eisner found out about Diller's move, he had been left "twisting in the wind," as both Davis and Mancuso had plans for Paramount's future that clearly did not include him. Eventually, Eisner ended up at Disney (and the rest is history), but at the time he had good reason to be angry at Diller for failing to keep him informed. Rumor has it that Eisner and Diller are no longer on speaking terms. They clashed again

in 1984 over Eisner's decision to build a Disney Studio motion picture theme park in Orlando to compete with a similar facility built by Diller's friend Sidney Sheinberg for MCA-Universal. These days, again according to industry rumor, the two CEOS refuse to occupy the same room or even contribute to the same charity. See Jon Lewis, "Disney after Disney: Family Business and the Business of Family," in *Disney Discourse*, ed. Eric Smoodin (New York: Routledge, 1994), pp. 87–105.

35   Kroll, "The Offer He Didn't Refuse," p. 69; and Kroll, "The Corleones' Return," p. 58.

36   Well before the release of *The Godfather, Part III*, Paramount released a video box set titled *The Godfather Saga*. Reedited by Barry Malkin, *The Godfather Saga* chronologizes (and thus more or less combines) the two films and supposedly includes footage "never before seen" in the release versions of *The Godfather* and *The Godfather, Part II*.

37   David Ehrenstein (taking back all those smarmy things he said about Coppola), "The Aesthetics of Failure," *Film Comment*, June 1983, p. 28.

38   Lindsey, "Francis Coppola: Promises to Keep," p. 27.

39   Grover, "Francis Coppola May Be Sweating Blood No More," p. 99.

40   David Thomson and Lucy Gray, "Idols of the King," *Film Comment*, September–October 1983, p. 71.

Index

Jon Lewis is Associate Professor of English at Oregon
State University. He is the author of *The Road to
Romance and Ruin: Teen Films and Youth Culture.*

Library of Congress Cataloging-in-Publication Data
Lewis, Jon, 1955–
Whom God wishes to destroy : Francis Coppola and the
new Hollywood / Jon Lewis.
Includes bibliographical references and index.
ISBN 0-8223-1602-1
1. Coppola, Francis Ford, 1939– —Criticism and
interpretation.
I. Title.
PN1998.3.C69L48   1995
791.43′0233′092—dc20   94-44270CIP

$23.95

DATE			
MAY 6 1996			
APR 03 2005			

BAKER & TAYLOR